TRANSCRIBING FOR SOCIAL RESEARCH

Sara Miller McCune founded SAGE Publishing in 1965 to support the dissemination of usable knowledge and educate a global community. SAGE publishes more than 1000 journals and over 800 new books each year, spanning a wide range of subject areas. Our growing selection of library products includes archives, data, case studies and video. SAGE remains majority owned by our founder and after her lifetime will become owned by a charitable trust that secures the company's continued independence.

Los Angeles | London | New Delhi | Singapore | Washington DC | Melbourne

TRANSCRIBING FOR SOCIAL RESEARCH

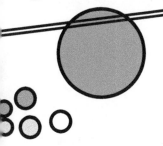
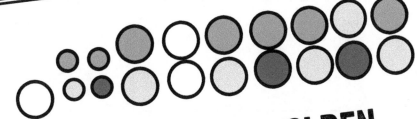

ALEXA HEPBURN • GALINA B. BOLDEN

Los Angeles | London | New Delhi
Singapore | Washington DC | Melbourne

Los Angeles | London | New Delhi
Singapore | Washington DC | Melbourne

SAGE Publications Ltd
1 Oliver's Yard
55 City Road
London EC1Y 1SP

SAGE Publications Inc.
2455 Teller Road
Thousand Oaks, California 91320

SAGE Publications India Pvt Ltd
B 1/I 1 Mohan Cooperative Industrial Area
Mathura Road
New Delhi 110 044

SAGE Publications Asia-Pacific Pte Ltd
3 Church Street
#10-04 Samsung Hub
Singapore 049483

Editor: Jai Seaman
Assistant editor: Alysha Owen
Production editor: Ian Antcliff
Copyeditor: Andy Baxter
Proofreader: Thea Watson
Indexer: Martin Hargreaves
Marketing manager: Susheel Gokarakonda
Cover design: Shaun Mercier
Typeset by: C&M Digitals (P) Ltd, Chennai, India
Printed by: CPI Group (UK) Ltd, Croydon, CR0 4YY

Library of Congress Control Number: 2016955840

British Library Cataloguing in Publication data

A catalogue record for this book is available from
the British Library

ISBN 978-1-4462-4703-7
ISBN 978-1-4462-4704-4 (pbk)

Contents

List of Contributors to Expert Boxes

To find out more about the concepts discussed in this chapter, see examples of real transcriptions, and test your knowledge through exercises and quizzes, visit the supporting website at **https://study.sagepub.com/hepburnandbolden**

Acknowledgments

We have both been fascinated by the musicality of speech and the nuance of prosody since our start as academics. We struggled with what to make of the sounds of upset and the complex challenges of translating intonation. It was not our goal to turn this into a statement about how transcription should be done and yet that is where we have ended up. Partly this is down to Tanya Stivers and Jack Sidnell and their invitation to write about transcription for the *Handbook of conversation analysis*. It turned out that we had much more to say than could fit into a single chapter! Hence we started work on what would turn into this book.

It is really important at the start to thank our wonderful colleagues. We have talked to many of them about these issues over the years and now they have donated their expertise on a range of transcription issues. We are enormously grateful to them, and have included their voices throughout this book – in order of appearance: Paul Drew, Jonathan Potter, Elizabeth Couper-Kuhlen, Irene Koshik, Mardi Kidwell, Ray Wilkinson, Elliott Hoey, Ignasi Clemente, Jenny Mandelbaum, Charles Goodwin, Lorenza Mondada, Kobin H. Kendrick, Maria Egbert, Saul Albert, Elizabeth Stokoe, Joanne Meredith, Jeffrey D. Robinson and John Heritage. We would also like to thank our anonymous referees for their helpful and thoughtful comments, and to successive editors at Sage Publications, most notably Jai Seaman and Alysha Owen for their enthusiasm, help and patience. Grateful thanks also to Anya Bolden, for lending her technical expertise, and to Jonathan Potter, for keeping us on track!

We would like to reserve special thanks to Manny Schegloff, for being a wonderful source of inspiration and guidance, and for always insisting on seeing transcription as an integral part of analysis. He gave his time to write the Foreword, and we are honored that we could start the book with his words. We are also indebted to Gail Jefferson for providing the motivation not simply to take transcription seriously, but to take delight in the production of an accurate transcript. We benefitted from talking to Gail – always the most exacting, and the most focused of transcription critics – and in many ways this book is dedicated to her and her brilliance and insight.

The Companion Website

Visit **https://study.sagepub.com/hepburnandbolden** to find a range of additional resources that aid in both study and practice.

On this website, you can:

- Watch **author-selected videos** to get deeper insight into select concepts, see first-hand how the transcription process works, and learn more about the practical skills needed to foster successful transcription approaches and habits.
- Explore **examples of transcriptions** to understand how transcription practices can be applied to the types of data you would encounter in your own research.
- Test your knowledge through **exercises and quizzes** and get the feedback you need to help you succeed in your assignments and research.

Foreword

Limitations of health require that I set aside most of what I might have otherwise contributed to this volume, including a more detailed appreciation of the materials collected herein. This limitation allows me, instead, to focus my energies on calling to readers' attention a very special resource cited in this volume: Gail Jefferson.

For Gail Jefferson, Los Angeles was the place where she grew up. UCLA was where she did her undergraduate work. A dance major in the 1960s, she had the so-called 'breadth' requirements to fulfill, and found herself in a sociology class taught by this young new faculty member named Harvey Sacks. She found in what he was saying, and how he was saying it, something penetrating, true, different, honest, brilliant.

She got involved. There was some money from a grant, and an interest in getting some tape-recordings of talk transcribed – some adolescent kids in group therapy sessions, and later telephone calls of various kinds (from Sacks); and, from a colleague in New York (me, in those days), tapes of disaster sites and radio talk shows, and various other sorts of material. She took the task of describing 'what you hear on the tape' very seriously indeed. Instead of dismissing it as a merely mechanical, stenographic chore, she in effect invented a technical research craft. A 'Jeffersonian-type transcript' became known as a distinctive research step and object, and for many uses it became the standard to aim for, across many disciplinary and sub-disciplinary boundaries. This while she was still a student (first undergraduate, then graduate), though she continued to develop and hone her craft after its initial development, and continued to do so in several American universities, then in the UK for several years, and in the Netherlands until her death in 2008.

For years, Gail was focused on honoring the materials she was addressing, instead of the methodological 'apparatus' that others used. She grounded her attention in the ways the participants do the talking and responding, insisting that the participants guide the ways in which the data are communicated. She focused on figuring out what the talk was doing.

As her body of work grew over the years, she took time to develop resources and/or be a resource for others who might be interested in using a similar approach in their own work. Such resources can be easily tracked down. Readers of this volume are most likely to benefit substantially from her work, and from the extensive attention and analysis it is given here.

There is no better way to become alert to the actual 'events' of which interaction is composed than by listening under the mandate of producing a detailed and accurate rendition of what the participants actually said and did. Before starting that, however, you should begin by engaging with the transcribing conventions described in this volume. May you all find useful resources in the reading, and have it trigger in you some insights of your own!!

Best wishes,
Emanuel A. Schegloff
Distinguished Professor Emeritus
University of California, Los Angeles

ONE
Introduction

Social scientists are increasingly recognizing the value of examining the social world as it unfolds. A key challenge is to find ways of representing the words, gestures and conduct of the people being studied. This book explores the issues involved in this representational process. How should social scientists transcribe what happens in social interaction in analytically useful ways? What might be the payoffs of systematic and detailed transcription practices? This book is both a practical guide to the process of transcribing as a research tool and an introduction to the social science behind it.

At first glance, it might appear that capturing what is said on paper is a straightforward task: isn't it easy to just write down what people say? Far from it! A simple illustration shows that transcripts, even fairly 'accurate' ones, can be misleading.

In 2010, *The New York Times* reported on a satellite interview conducted by Rachel Maddow, an MSNBC journalist, with Rand Paul, who was running for a Senate seat:

(1)

> Asked by Ms. Maddow if a private business had the right to refuse to serve black people, Mr. Paul replied, "Yes." (*The New York Times*, 20 May 2010)

The following day (21 May 2010), Chris Hayes, another MSNBC journalist, claimed that *The New York Times* relied on the following transcript of the interview and, as a result, misinterpreted what Paul said:

(2)

```
MADDOW:   Do you think that a private business has
          the right to say we don't serve black people?
PAUL:     Yes. I'm not in favor of any discrimination of any form.
```

Chris Hayes argues that when we watch the recording of the interview, it is clear that Paul's 'yes' was not a response to Maddow's question – in other words, that the transcript, while technically accurate, is misleading. Is it possible to capture what actually happened in the interview in a way that does not misrepresent the interaction that took place? Here is a detailed transcript of this interaction that uses some of the transcription conventions we will discuss in the book:

(3)

```
The Rachel Maddow Show 19 May 2010 8:05
1    MADDOW:    Do you think that a private
2               bu[siness has a right [to say we don't=
3    PAUL:        [I-I'm not in-      [I'm not in:
4    MADDOW:    =serve [Black people.]
5    PAUL:             [I'm   not  in]:
6               (1.8)
7    PAUL:      >↓Yheh<=I'm not in favor: of any
8               discrimina:tion of any fo:rm,
```

There are several obvious differences between the detailed transcript (Extract 3) and the journalistic one (Extract 2). First, Extract 3, lines 1–5 show that Paul and Maddow speak at the same time (the overlap is marked by square brackets, see Chapter 3), as Paul is attempting to formulate a response to Maddow's question (which she had asked prior). Second, in line 6, there is a 1.8 second silence before Paul begins his response (Chapter 3), which appears to be due to the transmission delay as Paul waits Maddow out before attempting to respond again. Third, what was transcribed as 'yes' in the simple transcript is actually 'yeah'. While we might think of 'yeah' as a non-standard or colloquial production of 'yes', it is a rather different kind of 'response token' – in other words, a different way to deal with the question. Fourth, the transcript provides some details on how 'yeah' was articulated: very quickly (marked via minimal spelling 'yeh' and > <; see Chapter 3), with slight breathiness (marked by addition of 'h' in 'yheh'; Chapter 5) and at a lower pitch than his usual delivery (marked by the down arrow; Chapter 4). Finally, we see that Paul immediately extends his turn with 'I'm not in favor': the quick start of this expansion is marked by the equal sign (=; Chapter 3). We can also observe that this is a repeat of the response he was attempting to produce in lines 3 and 5. What difference do these details make in our understanding of this interaction? They provide the specific evidence that allows us to see that Paul's 'yeah' is his acknowledgement of having heard the question rather than an affirmative response to it.

There is a widespread assumption across the social sciences that simple transcripts using standard orthography can stand in for the interaction itself. A casual leaf through any major qualitative methods handbook reveals that many qualitative social scientists often see data transcription as a straightforward job of reproducing what was said in a standard orthography. However, in the last 50 years, new ways of understanding the relationship between people, practices and institutions have been established. One outcome has been the development of a sophisticated and theoretically nuanced empiricism that focuses on talk as the central medium for action and understanding. This has begun to facilitate an understanding of human conduct in complex situations that is distinct from conceptions offered by methods such as experiments and surveys. As researchers in conversation analysis, discursive psychology and ethnomethodology have shown in increasingly sophisticated ways, talk is a medium of action; everyday social phenomena – ordering a pizza, sentencing someone in a court of law, answering interviewers' questions or breaking bad news in a medical interaction – are all realized through talk in interaction in orderly and reproducible ways.

The discipline that has done most to lay the groundwork for the systematic recording and analysis of human conduct has been conversation analysis (see Box 1.1). Rather than collecting data through experiments or surveys in order to test hypotheses generated by the social scientist's own pre-existing theories and assumptions, the aim has been to create corpora of naturalistic data and transcripts that can be used for analysis and for generating data-driven theory and understanding of the social world. Crucially, this allows researchers to base their analyses on close observations of the world as it happens, and to do so in a way that allows fellow researchers insights into the original data that produced the analysis. This development has been massively facilitated by technology – word processors, audio and video editing software, combined with increasingly high-quality recording equipment that is non-intrusive, portable and easy to operate, producing data that is simple to edit, anonymize and share. Alongside these technological developments there needs to be a paper system of representation that makes all of this portable, editable, shareable and therefore conventional; a standard system of transcription that captures the specifics of social action will allow researchers to share data and collaborate in analysis. This book provides the basic framework for that shared system of conventions.

-------- **BOX** *1.1* --

What is conversation analysis?

Conversation analysis (CA) is an interdisciplinary field of study that investigates the fundamental communication processes that make human interaction possible. Founded by Harvey Sacks in collaboration with Emanuel Schegloff and Gail Jefferson, CA is rooted in two key developments in sociology: Erving Goffman's micro-sociology of 'the interaction order' and Harold Garfinkel's ethnomethodology. CA aims to explicate how people accomplish and understand social actions when interacting with others. A distinctive feature of this empirical approach to the study of communication is its reliance on video- and audio-recordings of naturally occurring talk-in-interaction. In spite of its name, conversation analysis is not limited to the study of 'conversation' per se. CA research examines diverse forms of talk and visible conduct in numerous social settings: casual conversations between friends and family members, interactions in courtrooms, classrooms, medical offices, news interviews, workplace meetings, calls to emergency services and helplines, and many others. CA takes human interaction to be at the center of social life and offers social science researchers a unique set of tools for uncovering its workings.

In this chapter, we will set out the assumptions that underlie our approach to transcription, and argue for when and why we might need a transcript that captures not simply the words, but interaction in all its animated detail, as it is analyzed and responded to by participants themselves. We also outline the basics of how to get started with this form of transcription. We suggest some useful ways for laying out a transcript, and cover a number of basic (largely conversation analytic) findings about interaction that have shaped some of the central elements of transcription. This sets the scene for demonstrating *how* to transcribe in the remainder of the book.

REANIMATING TALK THROUGH TRANSCRIPTION

We're dealing with something real and powerful … little tiny things that God might have overlooked, perhaps. (Sacks, 1992: I: 238; cited in Jefferson, 2004a: 22)

In our everyday social interactions, we might notice delays, changes of emphasis, tiny laughter particles, words that are cut off and restarted. This is what grounds our very strong intuitions, for example that a speaker is conveying something complex or challenging, that they are unhappy or angry about something, or simply being ironic or flippant. Such attention to specifics allows us to animate our responses accordingly. Tuning in to the infinite variety of actions that are performed by adjusting the rhythm and musicality of interaction is the ambition that the transcription system we discuss in this book is designed to support.

The transcription system explored here was originally developed by Gail Jefferson (see Expert Box 1) as part of the nascent conversation analytic research enterprise and is now widely known as Jeffersonian transcription. A Jeffersonian transcript can initially appear complex and hard to read, mainly due to its unfamiliarity – it is a technical and rigorous practice for which training is needed. However, the system is intended to build intuitively on familiar ideas (underlining for emphasis, capital letters for elevated volume, etc.). The apparent increase in complexity reflects the fact that there just *are* more things that we need to attend to in interaction than are registered in orthographic or play-script transcript.

········ **EXPERT BOX** *1* ···

Gail Jefferson and the development of transcription

Paul Drew, Professor of Conversation Analysis, Loughborough University, UK

Gail Jefferson's extraordinary transcribing skills predate her career as a conversation analyst. Whilst an undergraduate at UCLA, majoring in dance, she had a part-time job transcribing recordings of race sensitivity training sessions held for prison guards. In her last publication, Jefferson gives an account of how, when she worked with Harvey Sacks at UC Irvine in the late 1960s, she was inspired by Sacks's first efforts to transcribe laughter. She began to go further in trying to capture and represent in her transcriptions some of the detail of the occurrence of laughter, such as precisely where laughter began, how it began and how the pulses of audible out-breath were configured and what other participants were doing (were they laughing, and if so, again precisely how?). All of which were relevant to an analytic understanding of what speakers were doing when they laughed. Jefferson persuaded Sacks of the importance of transcribing recordings in the kind of detail for which her system has become so renowned; she demonstrated to Sacks, then to others, that transcribing the details of talk was an essential part of the analytic process, of analyzing the moment-by-moment contingencies of interaction.

When she moved permanently to the Netherlands in the mid-1980s she learned Dutch, and with her exceptional ear for language, developed a facility for transcribing Dutch recordings and worked extensively with Dutch colleagues on Dutch data that she had transcribed.

It is sometimes supposed that Jefferson worked only on audio-recordings; this is not the case – she worked frequently with video data, especially in the earlier years of her career when of course video was

(Continued)

(Continued)

a much more clunky medium than now. She tried to adapt a system used to transcribe dance, the Laban system, to capture the details of non-vocal movement and conduct. But she acknowledged her experiments with the Laban system were not satisfactory; she was a great admirer of the approach that Chuck Goodwin was developing to transcribe the non-vocal details of embodied, face-to-face interactions.

REPRESENTING WORDS

One of the most striking features of a more precise Jeffersonian transcription is its representation of talk in non-standard orthography. This approach has been criticized from two sides: those who prefer using standard English language orthography (typically, social scientists) and those who prefer using a standard phonetic transcription system, such as the International Phonetic Alphabet (linguists). On the one hand, qualitative social scientists complain that Jeffersonian transcription is too difficult to read, transcriber-dependent, and presents speech in a caricature fashion of 'comic book' orthography which makes speakers look stupid (see Jefferson, 1983, for a response to these critics). On the other hand, linguists criticize Jeffersonian transcription for being too unsystematic in its representation of phonetic details and advocate the adoption of a standard phonetic transcription system, such as the International Phonetic Alphabet (IPA). We tackle some of these latter comparative issues and respond to various concerns and problems with Jeffersonian transcription in more detail in our final chapter.

In response to advocates of a standard orthographic or 'play-script' version of transcript, or even 'Jefferson Lite' (Potter, 2003), we would argue that such transcripts are not a more neutral or simple record; rather they are a highly consequential transformation of the original. For example, orthographic transcript imposes the conventions of written language, which are designed to be broadly independent of specific speakers and readers. Conversation analysts have repeatedly shown that such a transformation systematically wipes out evidence of the intricate coordination and recipient design that are so obviously oriented to features of talk.

TRANSCRIBING INTERVIEW TALK: DO WE STILL NEED THE INTERACTIONAL SPECIFICS?

The process of transforming spoken words into written form is taken as a prerequisite for conducting all kinds of qualitative research. But how do we decide when it will be necessary to transcribe the specific elements of how those words are delivered? For example, if one were interested in conducting interviews in order to identify discourses or repertoires, why would such detail be necessary? To help us address this question, let us consider an example of interview talk. The interviews were designed to explore the discursive construction of teacher–pupil conflict, and a major component of this was talk about teacher stress.

As Potter and Hepburn have noted (2012) the form of interaction favored by most researchers is interview talk, and overwhelmingly this involves standard 'verbatim' or orthographic transcription – transcribing word-for-word what is said. Sentences tend to appear as grammatical, false starts and 'ums' are typically omitted, and standard usage of punctuation is maintained. However, there are few discussions of the problems that this might lead to. Below is a typical example of how interview talk is reported – as a decontextualized quote providing evidence of this teacher's 'own views' about teacher stress[1].

(4)

```
BFH:5, 6:47
I think all teachers are stressed. Because they're stressed they may
react inappropriately in certain situations, because they are near
the edge themselves.
```

Such responses would be collected and used as evidence for themes or discourses related to teacher stress, or subject to interpretative phenomenological analysis, where it might provide evidence for overwhelming feelings, or simply evidence of this teacher's personal opinion about stress. So if your research questions involve a focus on these things, surely it's fine to simply represent interview talk in this way?

From a conversation analytic perspective, where we start to understand the way talk performs actions, various features of this stretch of talk become crucial. Some of the most obvious are: the question design of the interviewer, how interviewee turns are responded to, whether participants' final unit contours are closing or questioning, or whether the parties are speaking in overlap. While most researchers accept that the interview is an interactional occasion, they typically fail to provide this kind of information. For example in Extract 4 above, note the lack of interviewer question and uptake. Below is how the example would be more fully transcribed for a conversation analytic study:

(5)

```
BFH:5, 6:34
01  Int:   So d'you feel then that the constrai:nts on teachers'
02         ti::me and the resources that are available to you,
03         actually .hh (0.2) c- er constrain your ability to
04         do your job well.=To deal effectively with- (0.2)
05         °with kids: an° (0.2) (              )
06  Tch:                          [ U : : m :    ] (0.9)
07         ((swallows)) Ye:s, (0.7) I think all teachers are
08         stressed.
09         (0.2)
10  Int:   Mm:.
```

---

[1]Taken from Hepburn and Brown (2001) and discussed in Potter and Hepburn (2012).

```
11  Tch:    Er because they're stressed,  (.) they may react (0.5)
12          u::hm inappropriately.
13  Int:    Mhm.
14          (0.2)
15  Tch:    In certain situatio[ns.]
16  Int:                       [ M ]hm.
17          (0.4)
18  Tch:    Because they (.) are near (.) the edge themse:[lves.]
19  Int:                                                  [Yeah.]
20          (0.4)
21  Int:    °Yeah.
```

In setting out an accurate transcript, it is important to begin at the points where you can see something being started, such as a question being asked, a compliment being given, some news being delivered, rather than starting with a response. Here the teacher has been asked a rather challenging question, which calls into question her ability to 'do your job well'. This is immediately latched with an equally challenging elaboration, invoking her inability to 'deal effectively with kids' (lines 4–5). It's notable that in the design of this second unit the interviewer gradually trails off, becoming less audible, rather than coming to a final stop. Taken as a whole, the interviewer's turn might sound decidedly disaffiliative.

We can then turn to the evident trouble that the teacher has in producing a response. The gaps and pauses preceding and throughout the seven lines of her turn (and her transformation of 'your ability to do your job' into 'all teachers are stressed', Hepburn and Brown, 2001) show her careful handling of the question, crafting a response that isn't personally incriminating.

There is obviously more that can be said about this small extract, but the point is that this is what conversation analysts are referring to when they say that these specific features of delivery – the trailing off, the pauses, the stretched, emphasized and cut-off sounds – are not simply insignificant distractions from the main business of talk, rather they are highly consequential to understanding the actions that talk is performing. So even if our focus is on generating interview data in order to identify discourses or narratives, we should still be sensitive to what our interviewees are doing with their talk – how they are vigilantly crafting responses that deal with the ongoing business being done by the interviewer. It is not enough to simply note that this teacher's response is organized by an overarching 'stress' discourse, or that her 'opinion' is that 'all teachers are stressed', as this bypasses the nuanced design and rhetorical function of her utterance in its specific sequential location. The same arguments hold for the type of simulated interactional data created experimentally, as researchers typically work with standard orthography in order to code it for different communication processes. The practice of transcribing in more detail gives us a way of slowing down the talk and capturing these relevant interactional features on the page. An accurate transcript is an investment of time that supports much more robust analytic claims, and as such provides other researchers with a useful resource to interrogate those claims.

········· **EXPERT BOX** *2* ···

Representing interview talk

Jonathan Potter, Rutgers University, USA

Through much of the 1980s I had worked primarily on the analysis of interviews. Although I was very familiar with the Jeffersonian system overviewed and developed in this book it seemed too cumbersome and time consuming for working with large quantities of interview material. Margaret Wetherell and I (Potter and Wetherell, 1987) suggested a cut down system for use with interviews that I subsequently called Jefferson Lite – a transcription system with many of the significant features omitted (Potter, 1998). Round about 1990 I stopped working with interviews – they seemed like I was having a conversation with myself, and there was richer excitement to be had with ordinary phone calls, social workers talking to parents, and political disputes. Yet interviews were a central part of my scholarly world, as I would get asked to review interview studies – sometimes more than one a month.

Looking back over those reports I can see my frustration with transcripts that failed to capture the actions of the interviewer – he or she was being written out of the narrative by the very form of representation being used. I wrote pleas to editors to ask authors to be more precise in capturing the actions of the interviewers as I didn't feel I could assess the claims without that. Often, I thought the claims were only sustainable by greying out the actions of the interviewer. Later on I felt something similar with visitors to Loughborough Discourse and Rhetoric Group meetings. We asked them to bring the recording and it was often clear that crucial features of the interaction had been missed and the understanding of what was going on was thereby fatally handicapped.

I found something particularly striking where critical psychologists were simultaneously calling for more attention to emotion and to unconscious processes, and resisting the richer Jeffersonian capturing of interview material. For participants it is clear that features of delivery – intonation, breathiness, stress, pace – are fundamental for displaying and orienting to actions as angry, upset, cold and so on. This book illustrates the best available system for capturing these things, and, in my view, psychologists interested in feelings would find this a powerful and productive system for representation. Projecting forward, I believe that psychologists and other social scientists who are not interested in conversation would nevertheless find the careful capturing of delivery a powerful investigative resource.

I do not underestimate the time and effort required for achieving a precise transcript. However, my view is that all interview researchers would benefit from the focus on the interactional production of their 'raw' data and working with a video and high-quality transcript for at least one full interview will be productive, surprising and maybe salutary.

OUR APPROACH TO TRANSCRIPTION

Our starting point with transcription is that standard orthographic transcripts miss basic features of timing, overlap, intonation, emphasis, volume and many other features that interaction analysts now recognize as central to understanding ongoing activities in talk. Talk also emerges in real time such that it can be slowed down or speeded up, and speakers can closely coordinate changeovers, or speak over one another. These features of the delivery of talk are fundamental to the way speakers build and respond to specific actions. As this volume will repeatedly show, changes in these features can make a critical difference to the meaning and function of an utterance, and as such, the parties to the interaction treat them as relevant in one way or another.

If talk were a relatively transparent medium for the communication of one person's mind to another then more orthographic forms of representation would make sense; however, if talk is seen to be a live and enacted medium for action, then forms of representation that try to capture elements of action rather than 'just the words' are what is needed. In this volume we lay out the rationale for the latter perspective, and detail the specifics for how to transcribe. Where possible we aim to show the relevance of different transcription conventions with studies that have utilized them. Most of the studies that we will draw upon come from conversation analysis as the discipline that has done most to develop a science of human interaction.

To summarize, central motives for using the Jeffersonian transcription system include:

- It attempts to capture the talk as it is heard and responded to by speakers.
- It is necessary for performing an adequate analysis of what is happening in talk, both for analysts, and, more importantly, for the speakers themselves.
- It provides a window into the orderly practices that speakers are engaged in, in a way that 'slows down' the interaction to a level that is hard to discern just by listening.
- It allows other researchers to have direct access to the data that you are using to make your analytic claims.
- It avoids the limitations of researchers' and informants' memory about what happened, and minimizes the possible role of your preconceptions about what people are saying and doing in interactional data.

PREVIEW OF THE BOOK

In Chapter 2, we outline some of the basic features of transcripts. We suggest some useful ways for laying out a transcript and managing issues of ethics and anonymity.

In Chapter 3 we explore temporal and sequential relationships, which concern how different parts of talk are related in time. We also cover some of the basic conversation analytic findings about interaction that shape some of the relevant features of transcription.

Chapter 4 focuses on aspects of speech delivery, including changes in pitch, loudness, tempo, degrees of emphasis and voice quality. We also explore transcription issues and challenges related to proficiency and competence, including transcribing talk of young children, non-native speakers, and the talk of persons with speech disorders.

Chapters 5 and 6 explore ways of representing various other activities in interaction that don't necessarily involve speech. In Chapter 5 we focus on breathing and related interactional activities, such as sighing and laughing. In Chapter 6 we explore transcribing expressions of upset and pain. We also focus on the representation of non-speech sounds such as tutting and throat clearing.

Chapter 7 then moves on from transcribing audible behaviors to exploring different methods for capturing aspects of participants' visible conduct – including eye gaze and gestures – and discusses ways of working with and representing video data.

Since the transcription system was originally developed for the English language, researchers working with other languages face particular challenges. In Chapter 8 we discuss approaches to transcribing talk in other languages and presenting data to audiences unfamiliar with the language.

Chapter 9 outlines software and data management tools that aid transcription and considers some of the pros and cons of their use.

In Chapter 10 we explore some of the more conceptual issues and concerns surrounding transcription. We outline a number of the more well-known alternatives to Jeffersonian transcription and address epistemological concerns around the nature of the transcription system. We conclude with a discussion of future opportunities and challenges for transcription in social science research.

Web resources. The book is designed to be used together with web resources. The web resources will allow readers to practice and check up on their developing transcription skills. A series of short web-based exercises accompany each chapter.

Expert boxes. Each chapter includes boxes where experts in the field share their experiences and expertise on aspects of transcription.

CONCLUDING COMMENTS

A Jeffersonian transcript represents an attempt to capture actions in talk, and this separates it from disciplines such as linguistics or phonetics. Some fundamental features of an interactionally sensitive transcript are:

- Transcribing what we hear people say not what we think they *should* say. This may involve using non-standard orthography and capturing people's 'errors'.
- Capturing details of *how* people talk, not just what they say.
- Capturing precise timing of turns relative to each other.
- Representing relevant visible conduct.

Done sensitively, a Jeffersonian transcript represents a magical engagement with the lived moment-by-moment features of interaction. The richness and psychological complication, the irony and delicacy loaded into different features of delivery: an accurate transcript becomes something alive. The benefits of going the extra mile in producing our transcripts are much more than being able to say we've done it accurately; a detailed Jeffersonian transcript really starts to open up what's happening interactionally for participants, and that, of course, improves analysis. An added benefit of all this wonderfully engrossing effort is that you produce transcript that is genuinely useful both to your own future research and to the wider community of interaction researchers. Transcript will exist as a live resource for future researchers in a way that experimental protocols and even interview records rarely are.

RECOMMENDED READING

For arguments that are cautious about adding the specifics of delivery to transcription (particularly in research interviews) see:

Parker, I. (2005) *Qualitative psychology: Introducing radical research*. Maidenhead: Open University Press.

Poland, B.D. (2001) Transcription quality. In Gubrium, J.F. and Holstein, J.A. (Eds) *Handbook of interview research: Context and method*. London: Sage.

For a debate in which Potter and Hepburn encourage interview researchers to use more rigorous forms of transcription see:

Potter, J. and Hepburn, A. (2005) Qualitative interviews in psychology: Problems and possibilities. *Qualitative Research in Psychology, 2*, 281–307.

Smith, J. (2005) Advocating pluralism. *Qualitative Research in Psychology, 2*, 309–11.

Hollway, W. (2005) Commentary on 'Qualitative interviews in psychology'. *Qualitative Research in Psychology, 2*, 312–14.

Mischler, E. (2005) Commentary on 'Qualitative interviews in psychology'. *Qualitative Research in Psychology, 2*, 315–18.

Potter, J. and Hepburn, A. (2005) Action, interaction and interviews – Some responses to Hollway, Mischler and Smith. *Qualitative Research in Psychology, 2*, 319–25.

For another debate where the issue of transcription and representation is key (partly as a response to Potter and Hepburn, 2005) see:

Griffin, C. (2007) Being dead and being there: Research interviews, sharing hand cream and the preference for analysing 'naturally occurring data'. *Discourse Studies, 9*, 246–69.

Potter, J. and Hepburn, A. (2007) Life is out there: A comment on Griffin. *Discourse Studies, 9*, 276–87.

Henwood, K. (2007) Beyond hypercriticality: Taking forward methodological inquiry and debate in discursive and qualitative social psychology. *Discourse Studies, 9*, 270–75.

Griffin, C. (2007) Different visions: A rejoinder to Henwood, Potter and Hepburn. *Discourse Studies, 9*, 283–87.

To find out more about the concepts discussed in this chapter, see examples of real transcriptions, and test your knowledge through exercises and quizzes, visit the supporting website at

https://study.sagepub.com/hepburnandbolden

TWO
Getting Started with Transcription

Embarking on transcription for the first time can be a daunting task. This chapter will walk you through the things you need to attend to in setting out a transcript. Before you begin, it is important to consider (a) how much data you have, and (b) the time you have available for transcription. A simple rule of thumb for a standard orthographic transcript (just the words) is that for every hour of talk you have collected you will have four hours of transcribing to do. For more detailed transcription, unless you are an experienced transcriber, you can expect to spend at least ten times that! At this early stage, it is therefore important to think about your goals when you transcribe. It may be best to simply listen to your data first, and think through these issues. Listening to your data can also provide a way of tuning into your participants, especially those with unfamiliar accents and delivery styles.

PRODUCING A STANDARD ORTHOGRAPHIC (OR VERBATIM) TRANSCRIPT

There are different levels of how much to capture from the sound or video files that form your data. When setting out, a standard orthographic transcript may be enough to familiarize you with your data, and to provide you with a searchable and shareable record of what the speakers said. You can also add in timings and key words that you may find helpful later, such as when speakers laugh or sound angry or upset (we cover different software programs that can do this for you in Chapter 9). Don't be tempted to 'tidy up' the grammar, e.g., change words around and introduce words that aren't there. If you want a searchable verbatim record, spelling words correctly will be important, so *don't* change the spelling of words to reflect regional pronunciation at this early stage.

Having produced a verbatim transcript, you can then think about which sequences to pull out for more detailed examination. This can allow you a good sense of how many examples you might have altogether in your data, i.e. how prevalent your focus is.

How much data to transcribe?

How much to transcribe depends on why you are transcribing, and how much data (that is, audio- or video-recordings) you have. Many researchers at the outset of the project will collect large amounts of recordings, which would require significant resources of time/money to transcribe in detail. While standard orthographic transcripts are fairly cheap and easy to produce, Jeffersonian transcription is much more labor intensive, both to learn and to produce. A key focus here will be to work carefully with the data until you have identified which sequences to pull out for more detailed examination.

HOW TO LAY OUT A TRANSCRIPT

In this section, we will start to set out and discuss guidelines for producing clear and useful transcripts. As will be evident throughout this book, and in the literature more widely, the majority of examples presented in conversation analytic work use a standard layout for setting out transcripts. This layout illustrates three key features (illustrated in Extract 1) that are important to emphasize – speaker identification, speaker delivery, and the presentation of text, each of which are discussed below.

Speaker identification

After initial naming of speakers, either in the transcript (Extract 1, line 2), or in the prior text, normally a shortened three-letter form is used, followed by a colon. Often at the start of transcripts, the full name is spelled out, except where speaker identification is too long, for example 'child protection officer' is the full form of CPO.

Speakers are identified at each point where speaker transition is relevant (Sacks et al., 1974); so, for example at line 5, speaker designation of CPO is reinserted, even though the CPO was the last person to speak. This is because at line 4 there has been a transition relevant place, or TRP, in which the Caller might have elaborated on their turn. See Chapter 3 for more discussion of these issues.

(1)

```
NSPCC DG Daughter and Fleas, 1.59
01   CPO:      It's a bit acrimonious [is it,]
02   Cal:                             [Ye:s ] iddis.
03   CPO:      Ri:ght. Okay, .hh ER:m (0.3) tk (.) Ri:ght.
04              (0.5)
05   CPO:      .hh I MEAN THERE MAY BE (.) VARIous rea:sons,
```

If it is unclear who the speaker is, use empty parentheses in place of the speaker's identifier. If the speaker identifier is a guess, a question mark can be used after the first two letters, as in the following extract from an interaction involving four participants:

(2)

```
Chicken Dinner 1;30-32
01   NAN:   (Ah need two:,)
02           (0.2)
03   NA?:    °(t'nahh)°
```

Presentation of text

Talk is represented as it is produced, not as it might have been intended or as it 'should' have been produced. So for example at line 2 of Extract 1 above, the caller's delivery of 'it is' sounds like 'iddis'.

Student question: How do I decide when to use standard and non-standard spelling?

Answer: Jeffersonian transcription attempts to strike a balance between having a clearly readable transcript, and faithfully representing pronunciational particulars using non-standard orthographic representation. Jefferson (1983) defends this kind of representation, noting, across a number of examples, that different 'pronunciational particulars' can be detected in the same speaker. A particularly vivid example, reproduced in Jefferson (2004a: 20) is a speaker from the Bronx (a neighborhood of New York City), who produces several versions of 'there' (and 'they're') sounds (bolded), alternating between a 'd' and 'th' sound:

(3)

```
Frankel:USI:117:R
01 Vic:   We get in they:uh (0.5) en they're uh (0.2) the tu- (.) u
02        (.) t-two    ↓guys uh deyuh, 'n me 'n James ↑Wal↓kuh's dere
03        'n th'   broa:d is in th' bed.
```

As Jefferson (2004a) noted, and it is still the case, the interactional payoff for including most of these specifics is yet to be fully explored. Our advice to beginning transcribers would be to use caution in adopting non-standard orthography, apart from when a particular pronunciation is interactionally significant, for example, where speakers correct themselves or mishear one another due to non-standard pronunciation, and where speakers' talk is markedly different from their usual pronunciation.

Following a clear set of conventions for presenting text allows researchers to organize their accumulated transcripts. We cover here the method that Jefferson used in her transcripts, as it provides a template for including information that you will find useful, both for locating your transcript in the broader corpus of data, and for sharing transcripts and data across larger teams.

Transcript headers

In Extracts 1–3 above you may have noticed the numbering of examples and the inclusion of a header to identify the data. This header generally represents some version of the following:

- the transcriber's code for the data, e.g., Field:88U.2.4 – here the Field corpus, plus identifying features within that corpus;
- following a colon, you can add the page number (where appropriate[1]), e.g., Field:88U.2.4:24, which locates the fragment on page 24 of the complete Jefferson transcript;
- where no page number is needed, a comma would be used, followed by the location of the clip in the complete sound file in minutes, colon, seconds. For example: Field:88U.2.4:24, 12:11 – locating the clip as starting at 12 minutes and 11 seconds in; with no page number this would be Field:88U.2.4, 12:11.

---

[1] Jefferson employed the practice of having a master copy of a transcript with set page numbers, however this is typically no longer done, due to difficulties of transferring between different formats, e.g., UK A4 and US letter.

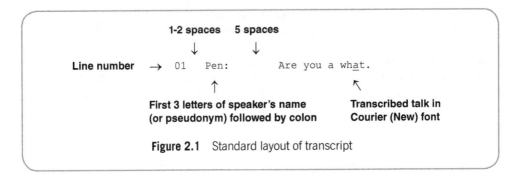

Figure 2.1 Standard layout of transcript

Other conventional features are highlighted in Figure 2.1:

- A 'fixed width' font such as 'Courier' or 'Courier New' is used to facilitate the clear alignment of overlapping talk and/or visible behavior.
- Sizing of font is 10–12 point.
- Numbered lines and numbered extracts. This facilitates clear reference to specific elements of analysis.
- Three letters for names or designation (conventionally followed by a colon) allows for greater clarity of speaker designation than simply labeling 'A' and 'B'. Clarity may be possible with fewer letters, e.g., 'Dr' or 'CT' for call taker.
- Include five spaces between the speaker designation and talk, to allow a two-character courier arrow (->) and, if needed, a number for the arrow if you need more than one.

Line numbers

Line numbering can be set to 'continuous' for formatting your master document. When cutting and pasting the numbering won't be retained, but can serve as a useful locator for pulling clips out of their wider context. Many researchers use manual numbering for smaller clips in written analyses, starting 01, 02, 03, etc., so that the width stays the same when you get to double digits.

Student question: I have seen some transcribers use separate line numbers for simultaneous spoken and visible behavior, but some only number spoken lines. Which is best?

Answer: Where visible behavior stands in place of a turn at talk, e.g., a responding shrug, head nod, etc., then there is a clear warrant for numbering the line – see line 3, Extract 4 below:

(4)

Rapper [GB Bodies10 MH_3girls_Part1 16:10]

01 BRI: You kno::w (.) uh:m: (0.2) that show >What I like

```
02              about you with Amenda Binds¿<=
03   ASH:      =(( nods while drinking))
```

Where interactionally relevant visible behavior, e.g., a gesture, accompanies a speaker's utterance, it may be sufficient to include that detail on the same line or in overlap with the talk, without necessarily assigning it a new line number. For further discussion on this issue see Chapter 7.

······· **BOX** *2.1* ··

Tips for the layout and presentation of your transcripts

- Make transcript lines short, as longer lines may not fit on a printed page.
- Use manual (rather than auto) numbering for numbering transcript lines if you want to avoid problems with cutting and pasting short extracts into new documents.
- When using transcripts in a publication or a presentation, the usual practice is to start with line 1 in each data segment. However, if it is important to show a temporal relationship between different extracts from the same interaction, line numbers from the original full transcript can be used.
- Sometimes, parts of a transcript need to be omitted in a publication or presentation (to save space or for clarity). Typically, the line numbers would not be consecutive then but rather indicate how many lines have been omitted.

Use of parentheses

Double parentheses are used to mark a transcriber's description of events, rather than representations of them. Thus ((cough)), ((telephone rings)) and the like. These can be done in overlap with gaps and pauses, as in Extract 4, lines 2–3, or with talk, further along in lines 2–3. See also Chapter 7 on the use of double parentheses to represent non-vocal conduct. Note Jefferson's use of dashes in line 3 of Extract 5 to visually represent the onset and offset of the one second gap from Dana, in overlap with Gordon's hearable out-breath and 'fidgeting and munching' noises on line 2. Dana then resumes her telling on line 3 as Gordon continues to fidget and munch.

(5)

```
Holt:88U:1:4:5.
01 Dan:     we went back there,
02 Gor:     [hhm-hhmhhhh ((fidget[ing munching noises))
03 Dan:     [--------(1.0)-------[hA::nd u- (0.3) we were there.
```

Double parentheses can also be used to allow a pre-characterization of the quality of voice delivery that might be difficult to transcribe, e.g., 'dumb voice' below:

(6)

```
Chicken dinner: 22:21-22
01  SHA:    En you sid ((dumb voice)) nuh they duh make'm
02          tihgether,
```

One reason for double parentheses is to mark a distinction between a comment by the transcriber, and a possible hearing by the transcriber, which is represented by **single parentheses**, e.g., Extract 7, line 1 below:

(7)

```
Wilson 02
01 Dad:        [  (That wz)  ]
02 Lisa:       [They wouldn't] remember each other.=
```

Empty parentheses are used when something has been said but the transcriber is unable to capture what was said. The length of the space between parentheses represents the duration of the talk, as in lines 1 and 3 of Extract 8:

(8)

```
Holt:X(C)1:1:6:6.
01    Mum:      (    [          )
02    Les:          [Becuz you c'n ↑go[by bu:s:[:
03    Mum:                         [(    )  [Hm::.
```

Additionally, empty parentheses are used when it is unclear who the speaker is.

In addition, the transcriber can indicate two possible hearings and mark them with a **forward slash** in parentheses:

(9)

```
Holt:88U:1:5:5
01 Dan:    Yhhou (can't oh/get on-) w'that's why you [get on
02         with im.=.hh
```

Parentheses may also appear in your transcript when you are transcribing laughter (see Chapter 5 on plosive particles of aspiration).

Anonymization and related ethical issues

In order to protect privacy of participants, data and transcripts are anonymized, except when the data involve public figures and are in the public domain – e.g., President Nixon. This involves giving participants pseudonyms and replacing other identifying information (such as addresses and telephone numbers). When choosing a pseudonym, it can be helpful to choose names that contain similar characteristics as the original. For example, if your participant's original name has three syllables (Annabel) replace with something similar (e.g., Emily). This allows you to capture important elements of speech production where participants are directly addressed by name. We cover the technical aspects of how to anonymize recordings and visual representations in Chapter 9.

CONCLUDING COMMENTS

In this chapter we have offered some guidelines on how to get started with transcription. Starting out with these conventionalized practices helps researchers locate their own and one another's data sources. They are therefore useful practices for both conducting and sharing our transcripts and analyses.

TRANSCRIPTION CONVENTIONS INTRODUCED IN THIS CHAPTER

((ring))	transcriber comments
(word)	uncertain hearing
( )	unrecoverable speech or speaker identifier
(word1/word2)	two possible hearings
NA?	uncertain speaker

RECOMMENDED READING

For a discussion of the interactional significance of non-standard spelling in transcription see: Jefferson, G. (1974) Error correction as an interactional resource. *Language in Society*, *3*(2), 181–99.

Jefferson, G. (1983) Issues in the transcription of naturally-occurring talk: Caricature versus capturing pronunciational particulars. *Tilburg Papers in Language and Literature*, 34.

To find out more about the concepts discussed in this chapter, see examples of real transcriptions, and test your knowledge through exercises and quizzes, visit the supporting website at
https://study.sagepub.com/hepburnandbolden

THREE

Timing and Sequencing in Transcription

One of the most consequential contributions of conversation analysis (CA) has been the introduction of timing and sequential position in interaction. Timing is a fundamental element in CA transcription conventions, precisely because it is central to interlocutors; we notice and often respond to delays that are in the order of microseconds. Accurate timings therefore give us an important tool for analysis. In this chapter we review the fundamentals of timing and sequencing that can be shown to be particularly important to participants' analysis of one another's actions – namely overlapping and latched talk, and silence between and within turns. In doing so, we will inevitably draw upon other elements of transcription and interactional phenomena that are explained further into the book. We begin with a discussion of the importance of accurately representing where there is a lack of talk.

SILENCE: GAPS AND PAUSES – WHAT'S THE DIFFERENCE?

Detailed transcription and analysis has shown that transitions between one person's turn and another's overwhelmingly occur with few gaps and simultaneous utterances. The timing of turn transitions also reveals that silence measuring more than two-tenths of a second between one speaker and the next can be heard as interactionally consequential. It is important at the outset to clarify some terms of reference for different kinds of silences in talk. Conversation analysts distinguish between **gaps**, which are silences that occur *between* turn constructional units (TCUs – see Box 3.1 for an explanation of how to identify TCUs), and **pauses**, silences within a TCU (Sacks et al., 1974). Silences are measured to the nearest tenth of a second and placed in single parentheses – importantly they are placed *between* lines of talk for gaps as in Extract 1, line 2 below:

(1)

```
Tiwa2 The Schedule
01 Hel:     So: >wu'time're we< waking up.
02          (1.0)
03 Syb:     I'm waking up at <seven thirdy.>
```

And on the same line as the preceding and subsequent talk for pauses, as in Extract 2, line 1 below:

(2)

```
Rapper [GB Bodies10 MH_3girls_Part1 16:10]
01  BRI:    You kno::w (.) uh:m: (0.2) that show >"What I like
02          about you" with Amenda Binds¿<=
03  LYD:    =↑↑Yeh
```

A period/full stop in parentheses indicates a *micropause*, a hearable silence that is less than two-tenths of a second – e.g., the first pause in Extract 2, line 1 above. Note that micropauses can also appear within words, to mark their broken delivery, as in the example of Nixon's expletive 'shi(.)t' on Extract 3, line 2 below:

(3)

```
4-13ne1: p22
01 Nixon:    With Liddy crackin:gk, .hahh If Liddy ↓cra:cks:
02           en: en ↑Hunt cracks ↑shi(.)t ↓uh:: Wuh no Hunt's
03           hear↓say though.↓
```

······· **BOX** *3.1* ·······

Relevant terminology I – turn constructional units

The turn-taking system (Sacks et al., 1974) describes how turns at talk are exchanged between speakers. It is a key resource for both participants and analysts, and therefore also transcribers. When transcribing, it is important to know what makes something a unit in a turn at talk.

Turns are built out of constituent turn constructional units (TCUs). These are words, phrases or sentences that constitute a complete action in a given context. In other words, turn construction has to do with three resources: grammar, pragmatics and prosody.

(4)

```
Watergate 4.13 NH:4
01 Nixon:    ↑↑No:.
02           (0.4)
03 Nix:      My: ↑Go:d.=Ada:ms wuuz ah- ei-Eisenhower'ss a:lter
04           ↑eg↓o.
```

In extract 4 above the first TCU by Nixon is *lexical*. Pragmatically, in action terms, 'No' here forms a turn by itself and has turn-final intonation (as well as very high pitch, see Chapter 4). Note the *gap* on line 2, a place where another speaker could have started up, and the return of same speaker designation on line 3, where Nixon continues speaking. His next TCU is *phrasal* – 'My God'. Notice the latching to the following TCU in his own turn, which is *sentential* – the latching marks the lack of the normal 'beat of silence' between TCUs, even when uttered by the same speaker (see the discussion below about timing gaps). Note that each new TCU gets a capital letter.

Student question: Why does the difference between gaps and pauses matter?

Answer: The distinction between gaps and pauses is crucially important when one considers their relevance in indicating a space where speaker change could (in the case of gaps or transition relevant places (TRPs, see Box 3.2) or should not (in the case of pauses where transition is not projectable) be occurring. In the first example (Extract 1), a speaker has finished a hearable action, and a next one is due, but doesn't happen immediately, so the gap is represented on its own line. This already tells us something analytically interesting about these two turns – is the responder having some kind of trouble with the question? In the second example (Extract 2), the speaker clearly has not finished her turn at the points where she pauses – she may simply be searching for the right word. Accurate timing of gaps and pauses is therefore an important part of transcription practice when our focus is on the production of units of action and their consequences. Another issue that illustrates the importance of marking gaps between speakers' talk is what conversation analysts have termed '*preference organization*' (Pomerantz, 1984; Pomerantz and Heritage, 2013). Here we are looking for clear actions, such as invitations, offers, assessments, announcements, etc., that carry a 'preferred' response – acceptance of an invitation, agreement with an assessment, etc. If responders can't comply with the expectations of the first turn, they will often delay the production of their response with an extended transition space, or gap. In addition it might involve other kinds of delay – engaging in other activities before responding directly. This might mean using turn-initial particles such as 'well' or 'uh', doing appreciation for the invitation, and accounts for why it can't be accepted and so on.

An accurate representation of gaps can therefore facilitate important insights into how people seek to maintain social solidarity (Heritage, 1984).

Timing gaps between turns

CA research has amply demonstrated the significance of the incredible precision with which interlocutors coordinate their talk (e.g., Jefferson, 1973, 1984a, 1986, 1989; Sacks et al., 1974; Schegloff, 2000b, and see Recommended Reading below). Timing is therefore taken very seriously in CA transcription conventions, nowhere more consequentially than in the gaps between turns at talk. An interesting thing to note at the outset is that a gap of silence can be analyzed as something that is avoided by interlocutors. Where they occur, they can belong to both the speaker and the recipient of a turn – both can either begin or extend their turns in this space.

········ **BOX *3.2*** ···

Relevant terminology II – transition relevant places

As Sacks et al. (1974) show, speakers have the right and obligation to produce one turn constructional unit (TCU). As that TCU comes to a place of *possible completion*, a transition to the next speaker may potentially occur; hence this becomes a *transition relevant place* (TRP). However, the current speaker may elect to continue – hence transition to the next speaker is only a possibility here. The speaker may elect to start a new TCU or they may add some kind of appendage, for example an increment, onto their just prior talk (Schegloff, 2000a). As we have seen in Box 3.1, Nixon continues, producing three different TCUs as part of his turn.

A key analytic skill here is being able to identify a TCU's possible *completion* – this requires examining what is happening pragmatically, intonationally and grammatically. For example, Robbie's turn on Extract 5, line 4 below projects more to come, and her continuation on line 6 is hearably a completion of her prior TCU rather than a new TCU in itself, despite its physical location on a new line after the next speaker's turn on line 5.

(5)

```
Holt: M88:1:5:12
01  Les:           [Eh: ↑WE:LL eh ↑WHAT I RANG up ↓about was ehm
02             di-↑did you have ↓anybody want a photogra:ph?
03                  (0.5)
04  Rob:       I'll be honest with ↑you
05  Les:       No.=
06  Rob:       =haven't a:sked ↓th'm.
```

Sometimes turns are built to be deliberately ambiguous about completion. Also speakers can neutralize normal requirements of turn-taking – for example, story-telling gives the speaker a right to more than one TCU. There are lots of places where there are possible completions, which would otherwise be TRPs, but the speaker is building a multi-unit turn, and co-participants can cooperate by producing continuers, etc.

The placement of 'continuers' (Schegloff, 1982) also demonstrates that participants orient to and project TRPs. By producing a continuer, the participant confirms the current speaker's entitlement to continue speaking by passing up the opportunity to take a turn. For instance, see Jenny's turns in lines 3 and 5 of Extract 6 below, where Vera is in the midst of story-telling:

(6)

```
Rahman:B:2:JV(14):10
01  Ver:                         ['e tea:sed'er en she went wuhr:shu
02          kno[w.
03  Jen:       [Mm:.
04  Ver:    Ahn' I s'd Jean I js cahn't stand it'n she said o[h well=
05  Jen:                                                     [(°Yes°)
06  Ver:    =this is wot we fi:nd when they come up,
07          youkno[:w,
08  Jen:          [°Oh::[:.°
09  Ver:              [Buut
10          she said oh ah'v 'ahd th'm u u-two days'n
11          ah'm prayin f'th'm tih go:,
```

The point is that actions of various kinds are needed to take up more than one TCU. It follows that by starting to transcribe well, we are starting to analyze.

....

Whether a turn transition space is *compressed* (e.g., when the next turn is latched as shown in Extract 2, line 3), *extended* (a timed gap, as in Extract 1, line 2), or *unmarked* (a normal transition with a 'beat of silence' between turns, as in lines 4 and 5 of Extract 5 in Box 3.2) has interactional consequences for interlocutors (Jefferson, 1984a).

Where a timed gap appears after speaker transition has been made relevant, it marks trouble for a recipient in starting up their turn in a place where there was a right and obligation to do so (Sacks et al., 1974). A gap where a response is due strongly projects an upcoming disagreement – a *dispreferred response* (Pomerantz, 1984; Schegloff, 2007). For example, in Extract 7 below, the gap at line 2 alerts A to trouble – an upcoming rejection of her suggestion to have partners at a bridge game they are organizing. That A hears it this way is evident by her backing off and giving L an out at line 3:

(7)

```
SBL3-3
1    A:    Why wd'n it be nice tih play pa::rtners.
2          (0.7)
3    A:    Or w'tchu li:ke tha:t.
4          (2.8)
5    L:    tch We:ll, (0.2) I don't know how wud we get partners.
```

Speakers also show an orientation to the length of silence. For example, Jefferson (1989) noted that a silence of approximately one second might be a 'standard maximum' allowance for silence, at which point interlocutors begin some activity designed to resolve the problem (e.g., lines 2–3 of Extract 7). Moreover, precise measures of silence have been used as evidence for a cyclical application of the turn-allocation rules (M. Wilson and Wilson, 2005; T. P. Wilson and Zimmerman, 1986), as well as to investigate possible cross-cultural variability in turn-taking (Stivers et al., 2009).

The transcription conventions were developed measuring silence relative to speech rhythm so that silence is understood relative to the tempo of the talk. To time silences following this method, one acclimates to the pacing of the talk and then, when the silence is reached, begins counting by saying a counting phrase at the pace of the preceding talk (Auer et al., 1999; T. P. Wilson and Zimmerman, 1986). For example, some people use 'none one thousand, one one thousand … ', etc., to time the silence as following: if the silence is broken immediately following 'none', a 0.2 second silence is indicated; if the silence is broken at 'none one,' a 0.5 second silence is marked; if the silence is broken at 'none one thou-', a 0.7 second silence is indicated; if the silence is broken at 'none one thousand', the silence is a full second in length, and so on. If there is a noticeable silence but it is shorter than 'none', it is a micropause. If it occurs between TCUs, then it is most likely a 'beat of silence' – the normal amount of time left between TCUs – and therefore will remain an *unmarked transition*.

Some CA studies (Couper-Kuhlen, 2012; Stivers et al., 2009) rely on absolute measures of silences, often obtained through computer-aided methods. Crucial here is listening for the beat of silence between TCUs and leaving it unmarked.

Timing pauses within turns

Timing pauses is far more straightforward, and can be done with either the counting method or absolute timings. If the latter method is used, minor adjustments such as rounding up or down to the nearest 0.1 of a second, can be made according to the relative speed of the talk.

OVERLAPPING TALK

Simultaneous talk by two or more interlocutors is represented by lining the overlapping talk up and marking it with *square brackets*. Overlap onset is marked with the left square bracket ([):

```
[wonderful.
[En then uh,
```

And overlap offset is indicated with the right square bracket (]) as shown at the end of lines 1–2 below:

```
01   Edn:    OH.w'l that's [ wonderful.]
02   Mar:                  [En then uh,]
```

Note the precise alignment of square brackets across lines 1–2 in the text, visually displaying the precise location of the overlapping talk. In older transcripts this was represented with a double forward slash (//).

(8)

```
Field: M88:1:5:3-4
01 Rob:      Well it's quite a relief to hear you say that.=c[uz
02 Les:                                                      [Yes I
03           found they got ↑very high last term an' I kept saying to
04           Miss ↑↑Pelch:: that I .hhhh e-were hers hi::gh? a:n:'she
05           wz saying no everything wz going along steadi↑ly'n .hh[hh
06 Rob:                                                          [W' l
07           I[(won-)    ]
08 Les:       [mine were] ↑terribly ex↑cited.=f: f'↓some[reason.
09 Rob:                                              [Ye::h.
10              (0.3)
11 Rob:      .h Well I wonder you know I don't always know what to..
```

This extract illustrates that marking overlap is important for a number of reasons. On lines 2, 6 and 9, both speakers project where to start their talk – i.e. they project a 'transition relevant place' (TRP, see Box 3.2) by scanning for possibly complete 'turn constructional units' (TCUs, see Box 3.1). They do this (we all do this!) by listening for whether a TCU sounds finished, using resources of grammar, action and prosody. In this way, the careful transcription of overlaps and gaps facilitated the discovery that turn-taking is not a result of speakers simply waiting for one another to finish talking. Rather, they are *projecting turn completion* ahead of time, using the rules of turn-taking – most notably 'one speaker at a time'. Importantly, this shows that they are not competing with one another in overlap (see discussion below), or 'interrupting' each other; rather the first speaker is continuing past a TRP, there is some ambiguity about the matter (as in Lesley's contracted 'steadi↑ly'n .hh[hh' on line 5), or the second speaker is misprojecting the end of a TCU or enthusiastically beginning their turn (as with Jenny's exoneration of Vera's apology in Extract 9, line 2 below).

Student question: When do I have to mark the offset of overlapping talk?

Answer: It is always better to mark the offset of the overlapping talk, just as you mark its onset. However, some transcribers do not mark offset consistently, especially when the overlap is very short, such as a single syllable. When the offset is not marked, it is ordinarily assumed that the placement of words on the transcript more or less accurately shows when the overlap is over. For instance, in Extract 8, lines 1–2, a reader may assume that only Lesley's 'yes' is produced in overlap and 'I' is in the clear. As a rule of thumb, however, it is always better to be more precise and mark the offset.

As we saw with Robbie's turns on lines 1 and 6–7 of Extract 8, when speakers find themselves speaking at the same time, they tend to drop out of overlap very quickly (Schegloff, 2000b). Careful transcription allows us to notice that on line 5 Lesley quickly adds a further continuing element "'n' (a contraction of 'and') to her possibly complete utterance 'going along steadi↑ly'n .hh[hh' before taking a breath, and she also fails to deliver it with any kind of prosodically final contour. However, Robbie exploits the in-breath and the proximity to a possibly complete TCU to begin her own turn, which she quickly abandons when it becomes clear that Lesley is continuing her turn on line 8 (and note the lack of capital letter at the start of line 8, visually indicating a continuation of a prior turn).

In marking overlap we may want to parse out elements of overlapping utterances, e.g., in lines 1 and 2 of Extract 9 below:

(9)

```
Rahman:B:2:JV(14)
01 Ver:  I'm sorry yih hahd th'm all o[n you [J e n n y] like that]
02 Jen:                                 [.hhh  [↑Oh don't] be    sill]y=
```

This can allow an understanding of how much of the ongoing talk one speaker could hear before they continued with their own turn, i.e. how far they could be said to be competing in overlap. So in Extract 9 above, the square brackets mark that 'Jenny' is overlapped by 'oh don't' and 'like that' by 'be silly'.

Student question: How should I break up lines when I transcribe overlapping talk?

Answer: There is no need to start a new line every time there is overlap. For example, in the example below, the visual placement of the overlap makes it transparent that Edna continues with her turn:

```
01 Edn:  OH.w'l that's [ wonderful.]
02 Mar:                [En then uh,]
```

Similarly, in Extract 9 above, the transcript gives a clear sense of the continuation of both speakers' turns. However, sometimes the overlap is long and the entire turn cannot be fitted into a single transcript line. Then it makes sense to start a new line just before the overlap starts, so as to fit the entirety of the simultaneous talk on one line:

```
Rahman:B:2:JV(14)
01 Ver:     I'm sorry yih hahd th'm all
02          o[n you [J e n n y] like that]
03 Jen:      [.hhh  [↑Oh don't] be    sill]y=
```

Sometimes the overlapping talk needs to be broken into separate lines. In that case, equal signs have to be used (see the section on 'latching' below).

Competing in overlap

Where speakers persist in overlap, it may be that they have competing, but not necessarily misaligning projects that they wish to prosecute. For example in Extract 9 above, in exonerating Vera's apology, Jenny jumps in at the first possible transition point (see Box 3.2) after 'on you', having geared up with a hearable in-breath (see Chapter 5). But also note that, unlike many speakers who find themselves in overlap, Jenny doesn't stop exonerating, nor does Vera stop apologizing. The affiliative nature of this type of adjacency pair entails that it doesn't sound competitive.

Conversely, sometimes speakers' persistence in overlap can indicate interactional trouble. For example in Extract 10 below, Joyce and Stan are engaged in competing courses of action – Stan is outlining his sandal requirements while Joyce is focused on his hat. Note that in line 4, Joyce starts her turn interruptively, i.e. not at a possible completion of Stan's in-progress TCU (see Box 3.1):

(10)

```
Joyce and Stan 2.30
01 Stan:   The ↑pair of sandles I don't want anything
02         fa:ncy:_=er: yihknow (all that) jus' something
03         [that's comfta-]
04 Joy:    [Whaddayou need] a ha:t for.
05 Stan:   that's something' ↑wait lemme finish something-
06         su- som- something that's comfortable:_
```

Here Stan attempts to hold the floor by emphasizing his delivery (which increases its volume and slightly elevates its pitch) in line 3. Having dropped out, he explicitly orients to the overlap by not attending to the action of Joyce's turn, instead inserting a somewhat censorious element 'wait lemme finish' (line 5) into his continued description of the sandals. Aspects of overlapping talk can thereby convey speakers' stances towards each other, such as impatience or disagreement, or enact eagerness to hold on to one's own turn.

As we have seen, speakers competing in overlap may increase their volume and elevate their pitch. They may also change the speed at which they talk and repeat just prior elements. As Schegloff (2000b; 2002) suggests, attention to the beat-by-beat production of elements of overlap, and to careful transcription of its onset and offset is therefore necessary for a grounded analysis of the interactional consequences of simultaneous talk. As with many of the other features of talk that we cover in this volume, this illustrates the crucial role of detailed and accurate transcription in producing new analytic insight.

Overlap can impair a turn beginning and thus, potentially, make the understanding of the turn problematic. To avoid this, speakers may deploy a 'pre-placed appositional', such as 'well', 'but', 'so', 'you know' and so on (Schegloff, 1987b: 74). These don't necessarily project a plan for the turn's construction, and so aren't crucial to recycle for the other speakers. Other practices such as elevated volume, sound stretches and identical repeats of turn beginnings occur regularly following an overlap, as in Extract 11 below:

(11)

```
TG, 18:36-43
01 Bee:    t! We:ll, uhd-yihknow I-I don' wanna make any-
02         thing definite because I-yihknow I jis:: I jis::t
03         thinkin:g tihday all day riding on th'trai:ns
04         hhuh-uh hh[h!
05 Ava:              [Well there's nothing else t'do.<↑I wz
```

```
06 Ava:     thinkin[g  of  taking  the  car anyway.] .hh  ]
07 Bee:           [that I would go into the    s: ]=I wou]ld
08          go into the city but I don't know,
```

Here Bee builds her turn on line 7 as a continuation of her prior turn finishing on line 4. Schegloff (2000b) notes that Bee's sound stretch (s:) at the end of Ava's turn is so positioned to allow her to absorb the hearable end of Ava's turn before reaching a possible completion of her own TCU (I would go into the (city)) and emerge in the clear. She then recycles her turn free of overlapping talk. This also provides an example of how speakers can track one another's talk even when they are speaking in overlap.

Overlap therefore provides evidence for the rules of turn-taking (see Sacks et al., 1974). Where participants are co-present it can also be useful to show overlap boundaries where speakers are doing interactionally important non-vocal actions, such as nodding or addressing recipients through gaze (see Chapter 7 for further examples):

(12)

```
Tiwa: The schedule 0sec
01 Glen:    ((gaze [to Sybil, [back to tablet))
02 Glen:           [What's     [this:_
```

See also the following example for how the placement of the overlapping transcriber's description ((door slam)) can be included and parsed out across lines when there is further overlapping talk with the next speaker:

(13)

```
Field May88.2.04:1
Dee:      [Yes alright dea[r thank y[ou.
          [((door slam))   [         [
Les:                       [gn-      [Goo:d heh heh[.hhhh
Dee:                                              [Lovely to speak
          to you an[y↓wa[y::. ]
Les:               [.t  [.hhhh]And you ↑here's uh::↑ (.) Skip.
```

See also below for the precise placement of a timed gap of 0.7 seconds between first and second speakers, during which there is an in-breath from the first speaker. As with other gaps such timing represents the silence (plus beat of silence) between the end of the utterance in the first line (line 2) to the beginning of the utterance in the last line (line 5).

(14)

```
Holt:2:15:4
01 Joy:     She's not only clever MENtally she's clever with her
02      ___ fingers as we:ll
03       |  (0.5)
04 Joy: (0.7).hh[hh
05 Les:_|_      [Oh::[w:well I]don't kno::w?=
```

A further convention usually reserved for extended overlap relates to spacing out letters – note that Vic's turn on lines 3 and 5 below does not represent anything about the tempo of his turn – e.g., it doesn't show stretching of the talk. It is rather a way to ensure proper alignment of the overlapping talk.

(15)

```
US, 43 (from Schegloff, 2000b:33)
1 Jam:     [Hu[h?
2 Mik:        [Th-
3 Vic:        [You know I cut [ m y s e l f    o n ]=
4 Mik:                       [Th' least they c'd do-]=
5 Vic:     =[yo' f r e a k I n'   gla:ss,]
6 Mik:     =[Th' least they coulda do:ne,]
```

LATCHING

Latched production or what Jefferson (1986) has called 'absolute adjacency' is represented by equals signs, and it marks the absence of any discernible silence between two turns or between parts of one turn. Latching indicates that an ordinary 'beat of silence', which represents a normal transition space (or an unmarked next position) between one turn and another, is not there (Jefferson, 1984a; Schegloff, 2000b). Latching can therefore occur between different speakers' turns:

(16)

```
NB:II:3:R:2:1.11
01  Emm:   'mA::gine a hunnerd'n fiftee:n.
02  Lot:   Oh: Go::d.=
03  Emm:   =En ar air conditioner went out. Comin ba:ck so: Go#:d.=
04  Lot:   =O[h:: G#o:d.
```

Here the stretching at the turn endings creates an environment conducive to the next speaker's early turn start.

Latching can also occur within the same speaker's turn, as when a speaker 'rushes through' to extend his/her turn at a TRP (see Box 3.2):

(17)

```
01 Rob:    Well it's quite a relief to hear you say that.=c[uz
```

Or between TCUs:

(18)

```
GB Bodies10 MH 3girls Part1 16:10
01  ASH:    ↑I [↑↑KNOW:!]
```

```
02  BRI:      [ I ↑DIH]dn't KNO:w.=Lh[Isten.=Okay] wait hold on.
03  ASH:                         [ Ahhh  hheh]
```

Here Briana's turn on line 2 has latched elements as she rushes between her TCUs, in her attempt to hold the floor.

In older transcripts, latching was marked by running together TCUs with no space between them, as in lines 19, 20 and 23 below:

(19)

```
NB:VII Power Tools.3:1.55
19 Mar:   [ngY e : : s.] Oh: yes.She luiv-u-She's up et uh: Larry's
20        mo:m's no:w, she wen'up (.) Sundee.hhh-.hh-.hh They came down
21        f'r dinner: [en then] uh: shil I'll go get her tuhmorrow.
22 Edn:                [Mm:-hm:]
23 Edn:   OH.w'l that's [°wonderful.]
24 Mar:                 [En then uh,]
```

The equals sign offers a more conspicuous way of marking these.

Latched production can be critical for understanding what is being accomplished inter-actionally. For instance, Local (2004) shows how the latched together unit 'and=uh(m)' can mark any subsequent talk as not related to immediately prior talk, but rather resuming an earlier topic.

Equals signs can also show that a speaker's talk, broken up into separate lines on the transcript to accommodate the placement of overlapping talk, is nevertheless 'through produced', as in Extract 20 (lines 1 and 4 and 2 and 5):

(20)

```
AH Location, Location, Location
01  Phil:   [I don't    [think you're gonna give 'im]=
02  Hazel:              [a h H A H   H A ↑HA ↑HAH ]=
03  Kir:    =[hih  ha  hah hah ha .h]  [i.h] h h]=
04  Phil:   =[a MO:MENT'S CHOI:CE:! ]  [Hh ]
05  Haz:    =[ahah  hah  ha hah  .hh] [h h h  ]=
```

TEMPO

Speeded up talk

The combination of 'greater than' and 'less than' symbols (> <) indicates that a stretch of talk is compressed or rushed (line 3 of Extract 21 below).

(21)

```
Wilson 10 3:09
01  Lisa:   Remember (1.0) my pyjamas.
```

```
02              (0.4)
03   Mum:       Oh pyjamas. >We mustn't forget °that.<=
04              =Which ones a'ye gunna wear.
```

Speeding up talk can display that it may be parenthetical or slightly superfluous – at line
3 Mum's second TCU is hearably doing a 'note to self'.

Slowed down talk

Used in the reverse order (< >), the signs indicate that the talk between them is slower
or more drawn out than the surrounding talk (lines 1 and 3, Extract 22). This can add
emphasis to talk – here it surrounds reported speech:

(22)

```
Wilson 13 11:59
01 Ell:        Angela s[ai:d:, .hhh <follow>       ]=
02 Mum:                [(°°ooh (                    )]=
03 Ell:        =<your nose.>=
```

Stretched sounds

While the greater/less than signs are reserved for stretched delivery of more than one
word, colons (:) indicate the prolongation or stretching of the sound just preceding them
(see, for example, Extract 22 above). Note that the placement is important – is it next to
a vowel sound or a consonant? Stivers and Heritage (2001) noted important differences
in what was conveyed by 'No', 'No::' and 'N::o' in patients' responses to history taking
questions in medical encounters.

(23)

```
Tiwa the schedule
Glen:    What's this:
(0.8)
Sybil: ((gaze on schedule))//My:: pretend schedu:le,
```

It follows that the more colons we add, the longer the stretching. Note also the use of the
double forward slash as one way to mark the overlap of a speaker's gaze and utterance
(see Chapter 7 for further information about transcribing non-vocal elements).

Stretching talk can be implicated in overlap, e.g., when a speaker's stretch on the last
syllable and the next speaker's start on the current TCU's projected completion lead to
terminal overlap (Jefferson, 2004b).

Student question: I have talk with stretching of various lengths – how many colons should I use?

Answer: A rule of thumb in deciding how many colons to add would be to include one for every beat of talk, which you can track using a counting method, or by objectively measuring the stretch – a beat being somewhere around 0.1–0.2 seconds. Note however that if your speaker has a very fast pace of delivery, then your digital timing will be at the low end. The key, as with all different aspects of transcription, is to practice using different examples of sound stretch, ideally with transcripts done by Jefferson. If we test this with an example, we can compare the stretch in the following identical utterances of 'my husband asked at work' done by Gail Jefferson:

(24)

```
Field: 88U:2:1:1
01 Les: -> .hhhh No:w (0.3) u-we-e m-my hus↑band asked et wo::rk,
02            an' some peh- u-we've never been there .hhhh I, our
03            ↑two local places've gone down hill ↓rather,hhh h-uhm
04       -> .p.hhh but u-my ↑husband asked et work 'n: people said
05            th't the Smithy et Charlton: Mus↓grove was quite good.↓hh
```

We can hear that Lesley's production of 'work' takes roughly a beat of silence to complete, whereas the first stretched production takes 3 beats altogether. If we time them objectively one is 0.2 seconds, the other is 0.6.

Cut-off sounds

A hyphen (-) after a word or part of a word indicates a *cut-off* (phonetically, a 'glottal stop'):

(25)

```
Wilson 03 8:07
01    Mum:     ...I al:ways thought that people from Jamaica
02             [were always bla- very dark skinned.]
```

Cut-offs can be used to initiate self-repair (see Schegloff et al., 1977) as in Extract 25, where Mum starts to produce 'black' but then cuts this word off and replaces it with 'very dark skinned' (line 2).

Jump-start

The 'less than' symbol by itself (<), or pre-positioned left carat, indicates that the immediately following talk is *'jump-started'*: 'a practice by which speakers bring off a start to the following talk that sounds earlier than it is, and seems to be produced by an over-loud first syllable' (for a phonetic account of this as an 'abrupt join', see Local and Walker, 2004; also known as a 'left push'; Schegloff, 2005: 473). The jump-start/left push is one way of holding on to the turn that has come to a possible completion (a 'rush through' discussed above is another practice) so may often be done by speakers to hold the floor at TRPs:

(26)

```
Wilson 03 7:47
01  Mum:  Ah think John enjoyed it didn'e.<He's ↑ni:ce
02         isn'e.=John:,
```

Here Mum is disagreeing with a prior turn in her first TCU, and quickly jump-starts into a change of topic with her second.

Clipped delivery is represented by a post-positioned left carat and is rarely seen in transcripts but can be a useful way of marking a sudden stop or clipped sound where there is no change in the formation of the word. So although the word appears fully complete, it seems to come to an abrupt halt. Jefferson (2004a) gives the following example visible on the word 'cramp':

(27)

```
Meier: Uh well I fel' like my lef ' side of my (·) chest I c'd (·)
        mah had a k- cramp<
```

And here's another example, showing the abrupt completion of a laughter particle on line 5:

(28)

```
Holt:M88:1:2:7.
01  Joy:  Oh::h
02  Les:  hhu[h huh-huh].hhe:ohhh
03  Joy:     [ uh uh, u]h uh
04  Les:  [.hhnh]
05  Joy:  [hhn< ]Oh: dear.
```

CONCLUDING COMMENTS

In this chapter we have reviewed key elements of the transcript that represent timing within, between and across different units of talk. We have tried to demonstrate the importance of accurately tracking silence between and within turns and overlapping and latched talk, as well as representing talk that is speeded up and slowed down. Analysts represent these elements not simply for the fun of it, but because these are key interactional resources that participants themselves are using. Marking timing and sequencing is crucial for understanding how participants negotiate turn-taking to achieve smooth speaker transition and carry out courses of action. Such precision timing and orderly turn-taking is a characteristic feature of all human interaction, and for analysts it provides an important 'key' to unlock what participants are accomplishing in their talk.

TRANSCRIPTION CONVENTIONS INTRODUCED IN THIS CHAPTER

(0.8)	Silence measured in seconds
(.)	Micropause
[	overlap onset
]	overlap offset
=	latching

Conventions for speed/tempo adjustments

Speeded up talk – 'greater than' and 'less than' symbols: >We mustn't forget ∘that.<=

Slowed down talk: <seven thirdy.>

Stretched sounds – colons – of the whole word: No::, or a specific sound in the word: N::o

Cut-off sounds – a hyphen after a word or part of a word: bla-

Jump-start or pre-positioned left carat – the 'less than' symbol by itself: <He's

Post-positioned left carat – sudden stop or clipped sound: cramp<

RECOMMENDED READING

There are many studies that show the relevance of timing both gaps and pauses in talk. For contemporary discussion on the role of timing in *dispreferred* responses see:

Kendrick, K.H. and Torreira, F. (2015) The timing and construction of preference: A quantitative study. *Discourse Processes, 52*(4), 255–89.

Pomerantz, A. and Heritage, J. (2013) Preference. In J. Sidnell and T. Stivers (Eds) *The handbook of conversation analysis* (pp. 210–28). Oxford: Blackwell.

Much of our section on overlapping talk has been drawn from:

Schegloff, E.A. (2000) Overlapping talk and the organization of turn-taking for conversation. *Language in Society, 29*(1), 1–63.

(Continued)

(Continued)

A discussion of latching can be found in:

Jefferson, G. (1984) Notes on some orderlinesses of overlap onset. In V. D'Urso and P. Leonardi (Eds) *Discourse analysis and natural rhetoric* (pp. 11–38). Padua, Italy: Cleup Editore.

Jefferson, G. (1986) Notes on 'latency' in overlap onset. *Human Studies, 9*(2/3), 153–83.

To find out more about the concepts discussed in this chapter, see examples of real transcriptions, and test your knowledge through exercises and quizzes, visit the supporting website at
https://study.sagepub.com/hepburnandbolden

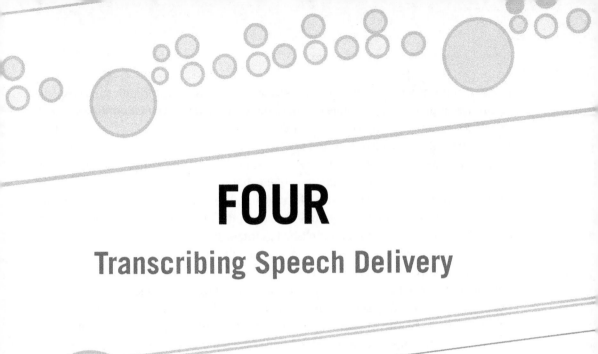

FOUR
Transcribing Speech Delivery

In most forms of written talk, conventional substitutions for communicative elements of talk are employed, for example commas, question marks, exclamation marks, italics, capital letters and underlined text. However, as we will see, this only captures a fraction of the communicative features that are present. In this chapter we explicate how to transcribe details of speech delivery and demonstrate their central role for communicating not just emotional or ironic content, but also for conveying what action an utterance is accomplishing (for example, statement, command, accusation or question). Our argument throughout this volume is that wiping out these elements impoverishes our understanding of what is accomplished in interaction.

Speech delivery includes changes in pitch, loudness, tempo, and degrees of emphasis and voice quality. Conversation analysts represent these using various symbols and punctuation marks. In Chapter 3 on time and sequencing we covered the symbols associated with tempo and speed of delivery, such as stretches of words and phrases, cut-offs and jump-starts. In this chapter we will cover turn endings, emphasis, volume, pitch change and other important elements of delivery and pronunciation. We reserve sounds of breathing – inspiration/aspiration – for Chapter 5. Throughout, we focus on the interactional relevance of attending to these features of talk; where we can, we will provide evidence for their interactional role in forming actions in talk.

------- **BOX** *4.1* --

Tips for transcription beginners

As with all of the different areas of transcription, it is crucial to practice hearing and representing these until you are confident that you can transcribe what you hear accurately. While you are learning to transcribe, it is often better to use fewer symbols rather than misapply them; although both can result in a misleading analysis, at least a transcript with less detail would *raise* questions about delivery rather than incorrectly answer them.

INTONATION AT TURN OR TURN CONSTRUCTIONAL UNIT ENDINGS

In Chapter 3, we learned about the importance of clearly representing the incredible precision timing associated with how people go about taking turns at talk. *Prosody* is one important element that indicates a complete turn constructional unit (or TCU, see Chapter 3), which in turn allows smooth speaker transitions to occur (e.g., Couper-Kuhlen and Selting, 1996). It follows that we need a clear representation of what happens when people approach the end of their TCUs, as intonation at turn endings indicates essential information about the action underway – it is something speakers attend to closely when designing their next actions. To mark different ways that speakers can end their turns we use mostly punctuation marks, such as periods, commas and question marks. These punctuation marks are not being used grammatically, as in writing, but to indicate the final *pitch contour* of a turn. They may also be used in the course of a turn, for example to mark boundaries between turn constructional units within multi-unit turns.

The *period* or *full stop* indicates a falling intonation contour, usually coming at the end of a turn constructional unit and marking its possible completion, as in the following example:

(1)

```
Wilson 10 3:09
01   Lisa:    Remember (1.0) my pyjamas.
02            (0.4)
03   Mum:     Oh pyjamas.=>We mustn't forget °that.<
04            =Which ones a'ye gunna wear.
```

Note the unit-final contour indicating turn boundaries on 'pyjamas' on line 1 and 'wear' on line 4. Also note the unit-final contours on line 3, after the second 'pyjamas' and 'that'. Here Mum marks each of her three separate turn constructional units with a falling, unit-final contour. Note also the marking of each new unit with a capital letter, and the latching of the unit boundaries to mark the compressed transition throughout.

Question marks indicate strongly rising intonation, not necessarily following an interrogative grammatical form. For example, see the unit-final rising contour after 'it' on line 1 in the Extract below:

(2)

```
01 Ehrl:    No question about it?=uh hHerb thet I would (.)
02          never knowingly hev put chu in any kine of a ↑spot.
```

Question marks should not be equated with interrogatives. Many interrogative forms get falling or only slightly rising intonation. For example, lines 1 and 2 below show falling and slightly rising intonation respectively:

(3)

```
01 Colson:  hhh How'r we do↓in'.=ehheh
02 Hunt:    Well: uh: 'bout iz well ez c'n be expected How er you:,
```

Commas indicate slightly rising intonation. They do not necessarily mark a clause boundary or that the speaker is 'continuing'. Some TCUs may end on a slight rise as line 2 above 'How er you:,' shows. Commas can mark the continuation of a story, in which many TCUs are projected, or as with line 2 above, following an interrogative form.

Inverted question marks (¿) represent a stronger rising contour than a comma but weaker than a question mark. (To produce an inverted question mark on a US Mac keyboard, press Shift+Option+?.) This final contour can also be represented by a question mark in *italics*, as in line 2 below:

(4)

```
01 Nixon:        Where was it- (.) where'd they hold it.=
02 Colson:       =Et the Statler?h
```

Note that line 1 shows another example of an interrogative produced with a falling contour.

Underscores (_) at turn ending represent continuation with the same intonation – designed to sound monotone throughout the word. On line 3 of Extract 5 below, Ellie responds using a single toned 'Me::_', and on line 5 she repeats and upgrades this by raising the pitch, again continuing with the higher pitch throughout:

(5)

```
Wilson 03 0.52
01 Mum:        So who's excited about hollyda:ys.=
02 Lisa        =(( raises hand))
03 Ellie:      ((raises hand))//Me:[:_
04 Lis:        ((with mouthful))     [Mughm=
05 Ell:        =↑Me::_
```

Student question: These small differences in pitch at the end of a turn are really hard to distinguish – why do they matter?

Answer: Unit-final intonation conveys important information about actions accomplished by the turn constructional unit, for example, in terms of the speaker's epistemic stance relative to that of the recipient (Heritage, 2013a, 2013b). Similarly to interrogative morpho-syntax, unit-final rising intonation may indicate the speaker's low epistemic access or entitlement to what is being said (as in an intonational question), while falling intonation may convey a higher degree of access/entitlement (e.g., Bolden, 2010; Raymond, 2010). Additionally, unit-final intonation plays a central role in turn-taking and specifically in projecting and indicating a TCU's possible completion point (e.g., Couper-Kuhlen and Ford, 2004; Fox, 2001). In fact, due to the importance of prosody in talk-in-interaction, and the difficulty some transcribers have in transcribing it accurately, some (interactional linguists) advocate more sophisticated methods than the symbols outlined above (e.g., Couper-Kuhlen and Selting, 1996).

------- **BOX 4.2** --

Tips for transcribing unit-final intonation

- The best way to develop your ability to hear different intonation is to practice hearing the difference between different unit-final contours using our exercises, as well as transcripts done by

Jefferson. This will give you a clearer sense of what symbol goes with what sound. In one sense you are already an expert – you do these yourself the whole time!

- It is often useful to slow down the sound to hear the prosodic changes better. Sometimes it is also useful to stop the recording just at the unit boundary to better hear if something sounds complete or not.
- Some projects may benefit from speech analysis software that can create graphical representations of prosodic contours (see Chapter 9). Note, however, that a contour that appears to rise or fall on a graph may, in conjunction with other phonetic cues, be perceived by the human ear differently (see Walker, 2012).

Note that all of the markings in this section are for turn and TCU boundaries. Pitch adjustments and contours in the midst of turn production are discussed in the remainder of this chapter.

VOLUME

When something is produced noticeably louder or softer than the rest of the talk, it should be marked on a transcript. Since volume is gradable, the transcript should indicate the extent to which something is loud or soft, and different ways to mark volume differences are used, such as underlining and capital letters. This raises a problem for transcribers: What is the difference between these symbols? Additionally, emphatic production often involves a change both in volume and in pitch, making transcribing yet more complex. In this section we provide guidelines for making these transcription decisions. The included examples – along with exercises to develop your skills – should help clarify these issues.

Increased volume

Especially loud talk may be indicated by *capitals* or *upper case*; the louder the talk, the more letters are in upper case. Competing in overlap is a common place to find elevated volume (Schegloff, 2000b):

(6)

```
Wilson 02 4:24
27 Mum:     When you get a c[(   )
28 Ell:     ((to Lisa))       [↑NO ↑MAYBE next we could do
29          dogs.
```

Note that new TCUs, as well as things that would normally be started with a capital letter, retain this convention, so they do not mark elevated volume.

Reduced volume

Degree signs (°) mark delivery of talk with a reduced volume. This symbol can mark that the single word that follows is noticeably quieter than the speaker's normal talk (e.g., °Yeh.), or degree signs can enclose the string of talk that was markedly quieter or softer. For example 'here I've godda gid' on line 1 below is delivered with slightly reduced volume, giving the impression of information being conveyed 'in confidence':

(7)

```
4-17nd.31-39
01 Nixon:    I said now look °here I've godda gid° out here, ·hehhhhhh
```

When there are two degree signs (°°), the talk between them can be barely audible or whispered. (To transcribe, you may want to use a software program to boost the sound; see Chapter 9.) In the following example this marking indicates speaking sotto voce, as in lines 1, 5 and 7 below. Mum and Dad are discussing their co-present three-year-old daughter:

(8)

```
Extract 13 Crouch 13 9.05
01 Mum:     °°Nick (.) She's not eatin anythin.°°
02          (2.0)
03 Dad:     [((puts food in mouth, chewing))]
04          [              (1.6)           ]
05 Dad:     ((through mouthful))// °°W'ye ↑speak to 'er.°°
06          (1.6)
07 Mum:     °°↑I ↑↑hhave°°
```

Double degree signs have also been useful to mark whispering or 'mouthing', e.g., due to extreme upset (Hepburn, 2004, and see Chapter 6).

Adding emphasis

Underlining is used to indicate some form of stress or emphasis, but what does that mean? In practice it can be either a moderate increase in volume or a raised pitch – often it is both. The more underlining within a word, the greater the emphasis. Therefore underlining can sometimes be placed under the first one or two letters of a word that has a pitch/volume elevation.

In the following example, Nixon emphasizes the whole words 'Oh' and 'I'. The emphasis mid word on 'Linda', and on vowel sounds of 'to', 'night' and 'got' shows that the sound was 'punched up' (Jefferson, 2004a: 26) on the vowel sounds only (or the 'i' and 'n' sounds for 'Linda'), so the pitch contour dropped following this:

(9)

```
4.17 1.35
01 Nixon:  Oh I ↓see yah. Yah.↓ I got l:Linda: gʰot something
02         to me las' night.=
```

······· **BOX 4.3** ·······

Tips for transcribing volume changes

- When marking emphasis, think about the natural emphasis that words carry with them. For example, words like 'information' or 'interruption' are typically pronounced with a mild emphasis (on the 'may' and 'rup' sounds respectively), so there is no need to mark this unless the speaker adds further emphasis.
- Use capital letters sparingly to indicate very loud talk or shouting.
- Sometimes one side of a telephone call recording is significantly quieter than the other. If a speaker speaks quietly throughout the recording, do not mark the decreased volume.

PITCH

Within-unit changes in pitch are marked via up and down arrows and a combination of underlining and colons.

The up and down arrows (↑↓) mark sharp changes in pitch – that is, resetting of the pitch register at which the talk is being produced[1]. It is important to note that these need to be sharper rises or falls in pitch than regular up and down contours through words (indicated by combinations of colons and underlining, as discussed below).

As with other markings, they can precede either the word, as with Dad's '↑speak' in Extract 8, line 5 above, or enclose a string of words (surrounding the string with arrows) as the two examples below indicate:

(10)

```
Wilson 02 15:25
01  Ellie:   Can ↑we pl'se bring↑ the matt:↓ress:.
```

(11)

```
4.17 1.35
01 Nixon:  Oh I ↓see yah. Yah.↓ I got l:Linda: gʰot something
02         to me las' night.=
```

Here everything within the arrows is markedly higher (in Extract 10) and lower (in 11) than the surrounding talk. Pitch shifts can also be marked mid word: in Extract 10 above

---

[1]Sometimes, circumflex symbols (^ and ˘ or pipes l) are used to indicate a rise/fall in pitch.

there is a pitch shift midway through 'mattress', where the pitch drops more than might be expected with a unit-final contour.

Most of the time you will probably use a single arrow for a single word's delivery. Note that the arrow always *precedes* the sound that it marks. Double arrows can also be used for particularly sharp pitch resets, as in Mum's delivery of 'have' below (see Chapter 6 for more examples):

07 Mum: °°↑I ↑↑hhave°°

Triple arrowed talk is rarely marked but might be heard where big downward shifts occur in already high-pitched talk, or vice versa, or where delivery becomes squeaky.

········ **EXPERT BOX** *3* ··

Why transcribing prosody matters

Elizabeth Couper-Kuhlen, University of Helsinki, Finland

For most languages it is an accepted fact that prosody matters. In English, for instance, an utterance such as 'The buses are not running today' delivered with final rising pitch is likely to be heard as asking, rather than telling the recipient something. And that means a confirmation is more appropriate as a response than a news receipt. Similarly, if the utterance 'Chocolate is toxic' is produced, e.g., with a sudden shift to creaky voice, it is likely to be heard as a quotation of what someone else has said rather than a proclamation of the speaker's own belief. In the former case, a mocking response might be appropriate; in the latter, it would be an insult. Prosody is thus relevant not only for what action a turn is heard as implementing but also for what stance and/or footing a speaker is displaying in delivering it and for how a recipient is expected to respond in next turn.

But if prosody matters, does it follow that *transcribing* prosody matters? After all, describing the way something is said is no easy matter, since auditory impressions are fleeting and sound categories must be learned. Moreover, beyond underlining for emphasis, we learn very few conventions at school for systematically relaying the prosodic dimensions of talk when writing.

Yet if we wish our transcripts to capture those details of talk that lead to participants making the interpretations they do, then we must, of needs, transcribe prosody – or at least those aspects of it that are of interpretive relevance. (Which aspects these are can vary from language to language and must be ascertained through careful conversation analytic work.)

Transcribing interpretively relevant prosody has at least three major advantages. First, it draws our attention as analysts to dimensions of talk that transcend the word, forcing us to attend to the same level of detail that enters into participants' interpretation of talk. Second, it allows us as analysts to reconstruct how participants arrive at their inferences and in doing so, makes the trajectories of talk they produce more comprehensible. And third, it allows readers of our transcripts to reconstruct, albeit imperfectly, the way the talk sounded. This can go a good way towards making our analyses verifiable by others.

As Jefferson's work has shown, 'order at all points' holds for the finest of details in the timing of turns at talk. Similarly, other prosodic dimensions of talk (pitch, loudness, speech rate, creak, etc.)

can be shown to make orderly contributions to the work participants are accomplishing in interaction. This means that both the lexico-syntactic content of turns and the prosodic details of their delivery are relevant when addressing the omnipresent question of 'Why that now?'.

Using underlining and colons to mark pitch movement

Underlining can indicate a gentle rise in *both* (or either) volume and pitch. The following example shows that, even where the volume of the word is decreased, there is a moderately raised pitch on the 'he' of Nixon's production of 'here':

```
01 Nixon:    I said now look °here
```

Up to down and down to up contours

Speakers can often be heard moving up and down intonation contours in the course of word production. These contours are marked with underlining in combination with colon signs (which alone indicate sound stretching – see Chapter 3). An underlined element followed by a non-underlined colon indicates a gentle up-down contour through the word. For example, in Extract 12, pitch moves from up to down through the production of the word 'pa:ssing' (line 1).

(12)

```
Holt:SO88:2:11:2.
01 Gle:     Yes I will[do. when I'm: (.) when I'm next pa:ssing.
02 Les:             [.hhh
03 Les:     .hhh Right. .h Now the other thing is, as part of his
04          Christmas presen:' I would like t'give Gordon a few
05          les'n:s=
```

A colon underlined indicates opposite gentle pitch movement – sliding from down to up through the word – e.g., 'les'n:s' in line 5 above.

> **Student question:** Why can't we simply use the arrows for all pitch adjustments? I find it hard to hear the difference anyway.
>
> **Answer:** There are important interactional distinctions between pitch shifts and contour modulations. Pitch plays an important role in accomplishing a wide range of actions in conversation (see Couper-Kuhlen's Expert Box 3). For instance, elevated pitch is often associated with heightened emotion. Hepburn (2004) noted its frequency, along with a range of other features, where speakers are talking through upset (see Chapter 6). Elevated pitch can also accompany laughter (Hepburn and Varney, 2013; see Chapter 5) and contribute to an enactment of 'surprise' (Selting, 1996; Wilkinson and Kitzinger, 2006). Pitch, together with other aspects of prosody, has been found to play a role in delivering and receiving news as 'good' or 'bad' (Freese and Maynard, 1998), in

providing reasons for calling (Couper-Kuhlen, 2001) and in conveying something about people's relationship to one another in greetings (Pillet-Shore, 2012).

On the other hand, indicating places where speakers' intonation gently slides up and down throughout a word is also important. For example, starting up, sliding down and then back up (as in 'No:::,') allows speakers to inflect their talk with 'warning' intonation (Hepburn and Potter, 2011). Here due to the action of the turn as a warning rather than an admonishment, the speaker may want to hold off inflecting their talk with too much emotional content.

Even relatively slight variations in pitch (and volume) may be interactionally significant. For example, Jefferson (1993) noted the importance of tracking these contours in terms of managing recipiency. She discussed three separate 'Yah' tokens, two of which were 'flat' – 'Yah.' – and the third of which had an up-down contour 'Ya:h'. Jefferson made a case for the two 'flat' tokens being recycled prefaces to topic shifts, while the up-down contour Ya:h displaying the recipient as 'topically engaged and responsive' (p. 6). Further, Schegloff (1998b) shows that 'a speaker can regularly project by a pitch-peak ... the *next* possible completion at which the turn-unit or the turn has been designed to end' (p. 238).

Overall, there is no doubt that speakers make incredible use of fine-grained adjustments in pitch, and it is therefore important to practice hearing and representing them as best we can.

········ BOX 4.4 ········

Tips for transcribing pitch

- It's common for beginners to overuse up and down arrows. As you start tuning into the delivery of talk, you notice how important pitch shifts and contours seem to be for the design of different actions. It's useful to try to distinguish between different ways of representing pitch shifts, by listening to, for example, recordings transcribed by Gail Jefferson.
- To hear subtle pitch movements, you may want to try to produce the phrase in a monotone or robot voice. This will highlight how different the talk you hear on the recording is and may help you notice the pitch movements.

MISCELLANEOUS ELEMENTS OF SPEECH DELIVERY

Here we discuss some of the common, and some not so common, elements of speech delivery. We begin with the more commonly used symbols and later cover more subtle sounds, typically only used in Jeffersonian transcriptions.

Smiley voice

Speech that is marked or enclosed by the 'pound' sign (£) indicates that the speaker sounds like they are smiling or suppressing laughter, as with Lesley's 'cook them' below:

(13)

```
Holt:J86:1:4:2.
Les:  I haf to buy my own stea:ks 'n £cook th'm£ ehh ↑hehh
```

Where speakers are co-present and video is available, there may be more precise ways of representing smiling while talking (see Chapter 5 for more detail on transcribing laughter).

Creaky delivery

Creaky voice (or laryngealization) is also known as 'vocal fry' or 'glottal fry'. In early transcripts Jefferson used the asterisk to represent 'creaky voice'. However, given the use of asterisks for other phenomena, more recent developments have used the hash sign (#). (We cover some examples of this in Chapter 6, as it is a common feature of both speech delivery through upset and pain cries.) Here's an example from some crying transcription showing the creaky delivery across a string of words 'ma best' in line 30 and preceding a single word 'do' on line 31. Interestingly both examples come at the end of TCUs:

(14)

```
Pop Idol
30  Cont:  ~THAt wasn' #ma best.#~  That wus the one
31          thing ah ~wanted to #do,~ (.)
```

Clipped delivery

We covered the use of jump-starting, cut-offs and abrupt stops in Chapter 3. Here we extend the coverage of clipped delivery in the course of speech production. It has been most commonly tracked in response tokens, such as 'yes' and 'no'. These can be delivered with mouth either opened (e.g., yeah, yeh, nuh) or snapped shut (e.g., yep, yup, yip, nope, nup) at the end of the utterance. The clipped, close-mouthed production is indicated via alternative spellings, typically ending with the 'p'. (Open-mouthed versions of these response tokens are transcribed with 'eh' or longer 'eah' endings, and are quite common, as in line 4 in Extract 15 below.)

'No's and 'yes's done with the mouth snapped shut at the end – e.g., 'yep's and 'nope's – convey a resistant stance toward the initiating turn (Raymond, 2013). As Hepburn and Potter (2011) noted about the caller's 'yep's in lines 3 and 6 of Extract 15 below (an example where there has been sustained resistance to the call taker's advice), clipping a 'yes' into a 'yep' (even when the delivery is stretched, as below) seems to display the redundancy or 'already known' nature of the prior turn, and as such is another feature of how resisting a proposed course of action is achieved.

(15)

```
NSJX Neighbour and Son 15.29
01 CPO                ##Mm:. BUT IT does sound as though you need
02                    to sort it ou:t don't you really.
03 Caller:            Ye:p
04 CPO:               Yeah.
05                    (0.8)
06 Caller:            Ye:[:p.]
```

A similar display of the resistance to the interactional project of the prior turn can be seen in Extract 16. Here, in line 7, Rick pursues an elaboration from Linny, and in line 8, Linny resists with a close mouthed 'Nope' (taken from Heritage and Raymond, 2016):

(16)

```
[M:CB(b):16:2-3]
04  Rick:      Didjeh git mad,
05  Linny:     No?
06             (0.7)
07  Rick:      Yih didn't,
08  Linny:     Nope,
```

Animated delivery

Exclamation marks can be useful for marking talk that is particularly animated, for example, see Lesley's turn-initial 'great' in Extract 17:

(17)

```
Holt:88U:2:4(1):37.
Les:      ↑G[r:ea ]:t! sh:e hhheh[((chuckling----------))
```

> **Student question:** How do I distinguish between 'animated' and simply loud or high-pitched delivery?
>
> **Answer:** The use of exclamation marks can send transcribers down a slippery interpretative slope that is typically best avoided! As usual, the key is that when in doubt, avoid using a convention, rather than over-using and risking distortion. In terms of how it sounds, what you should hear is a turn or TCU ending that is more occupied with maintaining an animated (often elevated) pitch and/or volume contour, than with indicating closure, questioning or continuation (although you may also hear these elements of closure). You can also look to the context of the utterance for what kind of action it accomplishes. For example, the turn on line 2 below sounds surprised and appropriately pleased:
>
> (18)
>
> ```
> 01   BRI:   So- congratu↑lations Maya,
> 02   MAY:   U-O::h th↑a::nks!
> ```

Here we can see it marking Gordon's attempt to diffuse Dana's complaint-relevant opening:

(19)

```
Holt:88U:1:4:1
1       Dana     Hello where've you been all morning.=
2       Gor      =.hh HELLO!
```

Exclamation marks may also be useful when transcribing surprise (see also Wilkinson and Kitzinger, 2006), for example Lesley's response below:

(20)

```
Holt:X(C)1:1:3:6
1       Phi:     Uh:: ehYes they came yesterda:y.
2       Les:     Oh!
```

More subtle specifics of sound articulation

There are a number of markings that signify more subtle changes in word delivery, some of which represent a level of transcription mostly only seen in Jefferson's transcripts, or in IPA transcription (see Chapter 10). However, Jefferson evidently saw these as potentially interactionally significant, but little is known about their function.

Hardened consonant sounds

Jefferson (2004a) illustrates a range of ways that consonants can be given an unusually crisp or dentalized sound. Early transcripts are marked with an asterisk, e.g., 't*', 'd*', however later transcripts are given a boldface consonant, e.g., the 't' endings on 'that' and 'it' on lines 2 and 6 below:

(21)

```
Nixon
01 Kalm:     .hh.hh Then uh- (0.5) that w'z a:ll, thet I needid
02           (.) tuh be assu:red thet I wasn' putt'n my family
03           in jeopardy.
04 Ehrl:     Su:re.
05 Kalm:     hhh And .h I would °uh° I w' jist (.) understa:nd
06           thet uh: you en I are deh- abs'ooly dihgether
07           on tha:t,
```

Shortened and fully formed vowel sounds

By shortened, Jefferson means that whereas sounds such as a standalone 'i' or 'e' might be heard as their 'long' vowel sound ('eye' or 'ee'), marking them with two dots over the vowel – 'ï' and 'ë' – shortens the vowel sound to 'ih' and 'eh'. Of course sometimes it will be okay to simply represent this as 'ih' or 'eh', but where sounds are more fleeting, the shortened vowel symbol can be used.

Another useful time to employ this marking is where the routine pronunciation can typically omit sounds. Jefferson gives the example of 'c'nditioner' which typically doesn't get a 'con' and 'for' which gets a 'fer' sound. Where a speaker gives it a fully formed vowel sound it becomes 'cönditioner' and 'för' in order to show that the normal spelling wasn't a lapse of transcriber attention. In older transcripts Jefferson marked this sound with a dot beneath the vowel.

Incipient sounds

A parenthesized italicized letter indicates an incipient sound. Jefferson (2004a) gives the example of the following, where it's possible to hear Ehrlichman gearing up for the word 'point' by closing his lips, without actually forming the 'p' sound, then stopping to replace a shortened 'theh' sound with the standard 'thuh' sound:[2]

(22)

```
4-19ekalm:2.53:5
01 Ehrl:    [But they- (.) thë(p)    the point is thet rather then
02          Mitchell calling you direct Mitchell knew dar:n we:ll,
03          (0.2) thet chu were no longer availa↓ble.
04          (0.2)
05 Kalm:    Yeuhp?
```

Unvoiced production is represented by an italicized letter and can be useful in in-breath or quiet laughter particles where there's an open-mouthed sound of the vowel present, but no hearable production of the vowel. We can see this below (Extract 23) in the in-breath '.hɑhh' on line 1. Another example is the 'p' sound in Kalm's 'Yeuhp' in Extract 22, line 5, above.

(23)

```
4-13ne1:12.35:22
01 Nixon:   With Liddy crackin:gk, .hɑhh If Liddy ↓cra:cks:
02          en: en ↑Hunt cracks ↑shi(.)t ↓uh:: Wuh no Hunt's
03          hear↓say though.↓
```

Guttural delivery

A 'gh' added into a word indicates gutturalness. Jefferson (2004a) notes that the 'gh' may be italicized in some transcripts. She used this example to illustrate the sound of

---

2While 'thuh' is standard prior to a consonant, 'thee' is more common prior to a vowel.

the speaker having phlegm in their throat through their production of 'ground': 'The: ghghroun' flo". Jefferson also noted the presence of guttural delivery in conveying 'laughter relevance' (Jefferson, 2010: 1478; see also Chapter 5).

CONCLUSIONS ON SPEECH PRODUCTION ELEMENTS

Many of the speech production elements covered here are fairly subtle, and require a practiced ear to form a collection and distinguish their relevance to the ongoing production of actions in talk. Much of this research is still to be done, and in this regard, as Sidnell noted, 'a conversation analyst is as much a detective as an explorer' (2013: 98).

TRANSCRIBING ATYPICAL SPEECH

Transcribing atypical speech – such as talk by adult and children language learners and speakers with speech production difficulties – can be particularly difficult. Here we discuss some of the issues involved and offer guidelines on how one might proceed with these sorts of materials.

Transcribing 'non-native' pronunciation

Transcribing talk by 'non-native' or 'second/foreign language' speakers[3] presents unique challenges. One common issue has to do with capturing aspects of pronunciation that sound 'non-native'. Should the speaker's 'accent' be transcribed, and if so, when and how? The answer to these questions will be shaped by the researcher's goals.

On the one hand, the transcriber may attempt to consistently capture the accented speech (e.g., by using modified orthography). This approach is perhaps most useful when participants' pronunciations are the focus of the analysis. However, one significant downside is reduced readability of such transcripts – a problem that may become particularly acute when the talk exhibits other aspects of 'non-native' speech, such as, syntactic, morphological and lexical errors. For this reason, many researchers working on language learner data transcribe non-native speech broadly, for the most part only slightly modifying the standard orthography (e.g., Koshik, 2005; Olsher, 2003). The problem of

---

[3]We have to be careful about what terms we use here as there is some controversy in applied linguistic literature about the notions of 'nativeness' and 'non-nativeness' and the distinction between 'native' and 'non-native' speakers (e.g., Firth and Wagner, 1997). Some people use 'language learners' or 'second/foreign language speakers' or 'language novices' instead. Note that 'language learners' and 'language novices' will include children acquiring their first language, however.

readability can, however, be ameliorated by providing 'translations' of unreadable segments in standard orthography, as is done with children's speech sometimes (see below).

Another approach to transcribing accented speech is to be selective about representing the speaker's non-native accent. This involves capturing it only when aspects of the
speaker's pronunciation become an oriented to feature of interaction – in other words,
when participants themselves demonstrably treat 'non-nativeness' or inadequateness of
the pronunciation as relevant. For example, mispronunciations become 'relevant' and
'procedurally consequential' (Schegloff, 1987a) when pronunciation errors are corrected
by others (e.g., Gaskill, 1980; Kurhila, 2001).[4] This can be seen in Extract 24, taken from
a conversation between Russian American immigrants, who are non-native speakers of
English. In this segment, Seva's mispronunciation of the English word 'filing' (as 'feeling'
in line 3) is corrected by another interlocutor (line 6). Seva subsequently accepts the
correction (lines 8 and 10). (Curly brackets indicate borrowing of English words into
Russian. For transcription of foreign languages, see Chapter 8.)

(24)

```
Filing separately (I14; 23:05)

((about tax regulations))

01    S:      Eta ligal'na/
              this legal
              This is legal

02            Ty mozhesh (0.3) eta byt' {marrie:d,} (.)
              you can            PRT be
              You can be eh married

03            i {fee:lin' separetly¿}
              and

04            (0.2)

05    K:      [(yeah)

06    M:      [Filing.

08            (.)

09    S:      Fi[ling.

00    K:         [(filing)

10    S:      Feeling=>that's right<=Filing separately¿
```

<hr>

[4]This is of course not limited to 'non-native' language speakers. Anybody can be treated as a 'novice' of a
particular language, dialect, professional jargon, etc. (cf. Kitzinger and Mandelbaum, 2013).

In transcribing this segment, the mispronounced word can be represented either via modified orthography (as in line 3) or phonetically by, for example, using the International Phonetics Alphabet (IPA) symbols: roughly, [filin] for 'feelin' (see Chapter 10 for a discussion of IPA). Notice that this stretch of talk would be incomprehensible without a transcript that captures this aspect of Seva's pronunciation. On the other hand, Seva also pronounces the English word 'married' (in line 2) in a non-standard way: for example, the stressed vowel in 'married' is pronounced as [ɛ] rather than [æ], as is the norm in American English. However, the participants do not treat this pronunciation as problematic, and the transcriber may choose not to represent its particularity on the transcript.

········ **EXPERT BOX 4** ···

Transcribing talk by non-native speakers

Irene Koshik, University of Illinois at Urbana-Champaign, USA

Some special issues come up when transcribing talk by speakers who are not yet fully competent in a language. The most obvious is what to do about talk that is incomprehensible to co-participants, the audience, or even to the transcriber. The speaker's interlanguage (the language spoken by a learner) is, after all, no one's native language, though a transcriber who is familiar with the speaker or the speaker's first language may have learned to understand this interlanguage to some extent.

Grammatical or lexical problems do not at first seem to be transcription issues, but if the transcript is used to enable an audience to test the claims of the author, then glosses in double parentheses may need to be provided if the meaning is not clear from the context, for example: 'my memorize ((i.e. memory)) not so good.', just as glosses are provided for languages other than English.

Pronunciation issues are more complex. Should we attempt to transcribe accents? What about isolated mispronunciations, for example, placing the stress on the wrong syllable so that 'committee' sounds like 'comedy'? I generally don't attempt to transcribe a speaker's accent. It makes the transcript very difficult to read, and it's also ethnocentric, as if the transcriber's variety is the only one without an accent. However, both accents and isolated mispronunciations need to be transcribed when they prove consequential for subsequent talk, for example, when a recipient initiates repair that indicates lack of understanding, as in this example from Seo and Koshik (2010: 2235) (modified):

```
01   SW:     my::: uh: friend is studying in
02           the .h uhvan flanning,
((lines deleted))
11   TN:     what- what is he::
12   SW:     uhvan (f/p) lanning.
13   TN:     oh::: yeah. urban planning
```

Mispronunciations may also need to be glossed if the meaning doesn't become clear from the context. If an utterance is unintelligible to the transcriber, and the context doesn't make it clear, there are transcription conventions to indicate unclear or unintelligible talk. However, if much of the talk is unintelligible, it's questionable whether it's worthwhile transcribing. An analysis will be difficult to do and to warrant.

(Continued)

(Continued)

Another issue concerns the speed of the talk. Speakers not yet fully competent in a language may have much slower speech than co-participants, and their pauses may consequently be much longer. Silences can be measured relative to the speed of the talk or by using an 'absolute' measurement (Hepburn and Bolden, 2013: 60–1). A machine-measured half-second pause by a slow speaker who lacks fluency may not carry the same interactional significance as a similar pause by a competent speaker of the language. So when transcribing talk by limited language speakers, I think it's better to measure the silence relative to the speaker's speed. When co-participants talk in different speeds, there may also be a temptation to use 'greater than' and 'less than' symbols for one or both of the participants' talk. I would use these symbols only if the talk is faster or slower relative to the rest of that speaker's talk.

Transcribing young children

Similar issues sometimes arise when talk of young children is transcribed. There are different ways of dealing with these issues, depending on the analytic goals of the project. One way to represent the speech of a young child is to capture the sounds phonetically (using modified orthography) and then provide 'translations' or candidate hearings for the readers of the transcript. An alternative approach might be to represent speech by young children using the IPA with 'translations'; these may also be supplemented with a visual representation of prosodic contours (for one example, see Wells, 2010).

Extract 25 illustrates the use of modified orthographic representations with 'translations' of child speech via footnotes. Here candidate hearings of lines 1, 6 and 12 are given in single quotes in footnotes. Anna is a three year old and Katherine is a five year old:

(25)

```
Crouch 04 9.39
01 Kath:    Don't want #ahee m:(uh)ore.#⁵
02          [                 (0.5)                    ]
03 Mum:     [((Leans over to look in Katherine's bowl))]
04 Anna:    ((holding up some food)) (Doee [ dab cor,)          ]
05 Mum:                                    [Mm j's a bit more,]
06 Anna:    nm Ah duhnt lah:k [        ( a dhat bit)⁶      ]
07 Mum:                       [>If you juss< leave it in ] the
08          bowl love.
09          (1.9)
10 Kath:    I don't ~want (°iht °°an my tuhmmy's hhurtin°°)
11          (6.2)
12 Anna:    Ay dahnt ~warnt⁷ #annhy more,#~
13          (0.3)
14 Mum:     No Anna you 'aven't 'ad enough yet.
```

⁵'any more' delivered with creaky voice and a sob particle.

⁶'I don't like' and candidate hearing of 'that bit' in overlap.

⁷'I don't want'.

Note that Mum doesn't display any trouble in understanding and responding to either of her daughters' utterances (lines 3, 5, 7 and 14). Sometimes the transcriber may not understand what is being said by a child, even when other participants appear to have no trouble. The best approach then is to transcribe the sound without providing a candidate hearing, as is done on line 4. This approach – simply transcribing the sounds that are there – can be useful when analyzing talk by individuals having a variety of speech production difficulties.

Candidate hearings of the child's speech may also be provided on the transcript itself (rather than in footnotes), either in double parentheses, or as a second line. For both examples, see line 1:

(26)

```
Crouch 04 9.39
01 Kath:      Don't want #ahee m:(uh)ore.#   (('any more'))
                            any    more
02            [                   (0.5)                      ]
03 Mum:       [((Leans over to look in Katherine's bowl))]
```

········ **EXPERT BOX 5** ···

'Narrative description' and transcribing very young children's interaction

Mardi Kidwell, Associate Professor of Communication,
University of New Hampshire, USA

How do you represent the movement and positioning of bodies in interaction when there is little or no talk? How do you represent faces, feet, hands and eyes that are constantly on the move? This is the challenge of 'transcribing' the interactions of very young children, children who are between the ages of 1 and 2½ years. One form for representing very young children's interaction that is useful is 'narrative description' in conjunction with video stills. A narrative description is used to provide empirical evidence of an analytic claim just like a traditional transcript is. One challenge with this form is to use descriptive terms that are different from the analytic terms, although some amount of analytic referencing is necessary in the narrative description for the sake of clarity.

Let's consider the example of object tease sequences. Children's object tease sequences (in which one child offers another child an object and then retracts it just before the other can take hold of it) can be characterized by three distinct sequential phases: the offer, the retraction and the post-retraction reaction which contains affective elements related to the success of the tease. If successful, the teaser may act with glee, and if not, with distress. The following is an example of a narrative description used to represent one such interaction. (For further discussion of how to represent visible behaviors, see Chapter 7.)

(Continued)

(Continued)

In this interaction, Kelly approaches Eathan, who is looking away, and holds out an object toward him, a canonical offer. She makes a high-pitched vocalization as she does this (huh heh <u>his</u> <u>d</u>at?!). At first he does not respond, and she moves the object closer, almost touching his face until he turns toward her. When he sees the object, he attempts to grasp it (Figure 4.1), and she swiftly retracts it. As she is retracting it, she makes a high-pitched laugh (<u>uh</u> hih hi:h (.) hh!) and produces a little body shake (Figure 4.2). In the post-retraction reaction phase, she maintains her gaze toward him and smiles broadly as he then reaches his hand toward her in an appeal for the object (Figure 4.3).

Figure 4.1 Kelly offers the object and Eathan attempts to take hold of it

Figure 4.2 Kelly retracts the object, and produces a high-pitched vocalization and body shake as she does so

Figure 4.3 Kelly maintains her gaze toward Eathan and smiles broadly

Speech production difficulties

Representing speakers who have various difficulties in speaking can be a delicate matter. One issue this raises is whether to transcribe the sounds that are there or to transcribe what the expert hearer takes to be there. Jefferson was very clear on the importance of capturing sounds as they are produced, rather than turning the talk into the speech that the recipient can obviously understand it to be, and we agree with this.

As an example, the following data come from a corpus of calls from a mother, and her son who lives in a care home (found in Patterson and Potter, 2009). Here the candidate hearings are provided in footnotes, but could also be included in the transcript (as illustrated in 26 above):

(27)

```
A01BU002
01 Mum:      ↑HELLO:?
02           (0.2)
03 Mum:      °.hh[h°
04 Cra:          [Er on datda:y,⁸
05 Mum:      Yeah:?
06           (.)
07 Cra:      er:  wai ee:r >°nm° one nigh.<⁹
```

---

[8]'On Saturday'.

[9]'can I wait here one more night'.

```
08 Mum:        .hh No nho n(hh)o.=Ye have to come back on
09             fri:day.=uHUH ↑heh °↑heh ↑heh° [   .hhhh  ]
```

Here Mum obviously hears Craig's turn on line 4 as a preface to a request, and line 7 as its continuation. To wipe these features out by cleaning up the transcript would be to miss the interactional challenges it presents, and the highly skilled way that interlocutors make sense of such talk. More analysis of this type of material is found in Patterson (2009) and Patterson and Potter (2009).

········ **EXPERT BOX *6*** ···

Transcribing atypical interaction

Ray Wilkinson, Professor of Human Communication, University of Sheffield, UK

Atypical interaction is interaction involving at least one participant who is unable to communicate in 'typical' ways due to a communicative impairment (Antaki and Wilkinson, 2012). The impairment can result from, for example, damage to the brain or to the mechanisms of speech or hearing. While an adequate transcription of atypical interaction is often possible using conventional orthography and the standard conversation analytic symbols and conventions, on some occasions additional transcription practices are used to capture aspects of the interaction.

One such practice is the incorporation into the transcript of particular phonetic detail. Symbols from the International Phonetic Alphabet (IPA) (International Phonetic Association, 1999) may be used to represent, for example, elements of the talk that are not perceivable as 'real' words in the language. This may be the case with the talk of adults with aphasia (a language disorder acquired following brain damage) where linguistic impairments can result in the production of sound errors or of 'neologisms' ('non-words' in the language) (Wilkinson, 2007). It may also be the case with disorders such as autism, where, in addition to IPA symbols, further phonetic detail such as pitch contours may be used (Tarplee and Barrow, 1999).

For some forms of atypical interaction, the standard conversation analytic transcription symbols and conventions may be supplemented in order to represent salient features of the interaction. For example, some people with communication impairments make use of augmentative and alternative communication (AAC) devices where letters or symbols are selected to create a message presented visually on a screen and/or via synthesized speech. In order to represent visually displayed text, straight brackets around the words have been used (i.e. I hello I) (Higginbotham and Engelke, 2013). Words or sounds produced in the form of synthesized speech are represented in a form that distinguishes them from spoken talk, such as in bold italics (Wilkinson et al., 2011). Also, in AAC interaction, elements of the message production process may be salient in ways that are not present in spoken talk, and as such may be included in the transcript. For example, the 'beep' sound that is produced on some AAC devices when the user selects a letter or symbol has been included in transcripts (in the form of an asterisk: Wilkinson et al., 2011).

Most atypical interaction research is carried out using video-recording. The deployment of non-vocal resources, such as gesture and eye gaze, may be particularly salient in these interactions and as such will regularly be included in transcriptions. Various forms of visual representation of elements of the interaction may be used, including drawings, frame grabs, and photoshopped images (see, for example, Goodwin, C. 2003b; Higginbotham and Engelke, 2013; Schegloff, 2003). The representation of sign language interactions, where communication is carried out primarily via visual rather than vocal resources, may involve quite radical changes from standard conversation analytic transcription practices. For example, separate tiers may be used for eye gaze and various forms of manual activity, and glosses of conventional signs may be provided (McCleary and de Arantes Leite, 2013).

CONCLUDING COMMENTS

In this chapter we have discussed how aspects of speech delivery can be captured in a conversation analytic transcription. There is ample evidence that details of speech delivery – such as, volume, intonation and pronunciation – are interactionally significant, and as such they are crucial for performing an adequate analysis.

We continue this focus in the following chapter on aspiration and laughter, where some of the transcription symbols and conventions covered here make a new appearance, and some new ones are added.

TRANSCRIPTION CONVENTIONS INTRODUCED IN THIS CHAPTER

Symbols for turn and unit boundaries

.   falling or final intonation contour: pyjamas.

?   strongly rising intonation: it?

,   slightly rising intonation: you,

¿ ? stronger rising contour than a comma, weaker than a question mark: Statler? or Statler¿

_   continuation of same intonation throughout word: Me::_

Symbols for volume adjustments

Underlining – emphasis through all of the word: Oh:, or part of the word: Linda

Capitals or *upper case* – elevated volume: MAYBE

Degree signs – reduced volume – preceding the word: °Yeh. Or surrounding a string: °here I've godda gid°. Double degree signs indicate whispering or sotto voce: °°I hhave°°

Symbols for pitch adjustments

Up arrows – sharp rises in pitch across a string of words: ↑we pl'se bring↑

Down arrows – sharp falls in pitch across a string of words: ↓see y<u>a</u>h. Yah.↓

Single word pitch increase: ↑speak

Mid word pitch fall: <u>ma</u>tt:↓ress:.

Sharper pitch reset: ↑↑hhave

Gentler pitch adjustments

Underlining – slightly elevated pitch (may include volume) on the vowel only: Y<u>es</u>

Up to down contour – an underlined vowel followed by a colon: p<u>a</u>:ssing

Down to up contour – an underlined colon: ni<u>:</u>ght

Other elements of speech delivery

Smiley voice – £ before a word or enclosing a string of words: £cook th'm£

Creaky delivery – # before a word: #do. Or enclosing a string of words: #ma b<u>e</u>st.#~

Animated delivery – exclamation marks: ↑G[r:ea]:t!

More subtle specifics of delivery

Hardened consonant sounds – boldface consonant: the**t**

Shortened vowel sounds – two dots over the vowel: thë ('theh' not 'thee')

Fully formed vowel sounds – 'cönditioner'

Incipient sounds – parenthesized italicized letter: thë(*p*)

Unvoiced production – an italicized letter: .ha*hh*

Guttural delivery – 'gh' added into a word: '<u>ghghroun</u>' flo'

RECOMMENDED READING

For more discussion of Jefferson's transcription conventions and her own perspective on transcribing, read:

Jefferson, G. (2004) Glossary of transcript symbols with an introduction. In G.H. Lerner (Ed.) *Conversation analysis: Studies from the first generation* (pp. 13–31). Philadelphia: John Benjamins.

For interesting discussion of the way phonetic design figures in interaction analysis, see:

Walker, G. (2013) Phonetics and prosody in conversation. In J. Sidnell and T. Stivers (Eds) *The handbook of conversation analysis* (pp. 455–74). Oxford: Blackwell.

For an early overview of the role of prosody in interaction, see:

Couper-Kuhlen, E. and Selting, M. (Eds) (1996) *Prosody in conversation: Interactional studies* (Vol. 12). New York: Cambridge University Press.

For recent discussion of the role of prosody in marking emotional content, see:

Local, J. and Walker, G. (2008) Stance and affect in conversation: On the interplay of sequential and phonetic resources. *Text & Talk, 28*(6), 723–47.

Pillet-Shore, D. (2012) Greetings: Displaying stance through prosodic recipient design. *Research on Language and Social Interaction, 45*(4), 375–98.

For an interesting debate about transcription and analysis of prosodic aspects of talk, see:

Walker, T. (2014) Form ≠ function: The independence of prosody and action. *Research on Language and Social Interaction, 47*(1), 1–16.

Auer, P. (2014) There's no harm in glossing (but a need for a better understanding of the status of transcripts). *Research on Language and Social Interaction, 47*(1), 17–22.

To find out more about the concepts discussed in this chapter, see examples of real transcriptions, and test your knowledge through exercises and quizzes, visit the supporting website at
https://study.sagepub.com/hepburnandbolden

FIVE

Transcribing Aspiration and Laughter

With any luck we are all continually breathing. Most of the time we do this silently, but sometimes sounds of breathing are audible – or even produced so as to be heard by others. In other words, aspiration may be a form of social action, or action modulation, and should, thus, be captured on an interactionally sensitive transcript. In this chapter, we examine ways of representing audible sounds. We start by introducing basic principles for transcribing aspiration: we start with breathing, breathy and sighing noises, and then move on to transcribing audible laughter – one conversational activity in which aspiration plays a key role. We show how careful attention to capturing details of aspiration and laughter can serve as an entry point to understanding its diverse interactional functions. We also begin to explore some of the visual elements of laughter.

ASPIRATION: IN-BREATHS AND OUT-BREATHS

For an interactionally sensitive transcript, we need to distinguish between whether breathing sounds are done in order to be *heard* as audible by interlocutors, and whether they are simply done routinely. If the latter, for example if the speaker has a cold, or is wheezy or asthmatic, then you may want to simply note on the transcript that the speaker has breathy or wheezy delivery throughout, rather than display it continuously in their talk.

Where you can hear breathing noises as not a regular part of the speaker's delivery, then they may be of possible interactional relevance. We transcribe hearable breathing *out* with the letter 'h'. Out-breaths seem more prevalent at the end of turns, e.g., in the following example:

(1)

```
Lis: Why did Al go with you and wha' did you °say to her. hh
```

Or within words to indicate breathy delivery as in 'hhospital and 'tihday':

(2)

```
Bee: …she went to thee uh:: hhospital again tihda:y,
```

By contrast, hearable inhalation (*in-breath*) is much more common, and often occurs at the start of turns, or in places where a speaker needs to hold the floor, for example between TCUs (see Chapter 3) or in a word search. In-breaths are shown with a period/full stop (or a raised period in older transcripts) before the letter(s) '.hh'.

(3)

```
Holt:M88:1:5:12.
01 Les:      .hhh Well yes if you don't think it's too ↓late no:w,
```

```
02  Rob:      Oh: no:[no
03  Les:             [No:, okay then[.hh Well ↑when sh'll I call'n=
```

Louder aspiration, often found in gasping, panting or sighing, is marked by capital letter(s). Unlike other stretched sounds, the longer the aspiration lasts, the more h's are used.

(4)

```
Field: M88:1:5:18
Les:      [.hhhhhh     [↑Oh ye:s. Yes 'ess: that's ri:ght. Especially
          those um .tch .hhhhh °u° (.) ↓twi:ns uh:: Christopher:: uh:,
          (0.9)
Les:      wh[at's iz name.   ]
```

> **Student question:** How do I know how many h's to use?
>
> **Answer:** When transcribing aspiration of any kind, one rule of thumb for how many h's to include is to time the aspiration and add one h for every 'beat' of silence (which is usually somewhere around 0.1–0.2 seconds, depending on the relative speed of the talk).

Why should we transcribe aspiration?

Audible aspiration may be used interactionally in various ways. For instance, an in-breath may do the work of a pre-beginning – a part of turn design used to communicate that a speaker is about to take a turn and to indicate something about the character of the upcoming turn (for example, to project a longer, multi-unit turn) (Schegloff, 1996b). Both of these are evident in Bee's response in line 2:

(5)

```
TG
01    Ava:    =[Oh  my ] mother wannduh know how's yer grandmother.
02    Bee:    .hhh Uh::, (0.3) I don'know I guess she's aw- she's
03            awright she went to thee uh:: hhospital again tihda:y,
04    Ava:    Mm-hm?,
```

······· **EXPERT BOX 7** ···

Transcribing sighing

Elliott Hoey, Researcher, Max Planck Institute for Psycholinguistics, the Netherlands

Breathing is a rudimentary feature of talk-in-interaction. It not only underpins our vocal mode of communication, but also serves as an important resource in the organization of social interaction itself. The audible intake of a breath has long been recognized as a discriminate practice for the

(Continued)

(Continued)

organization of turn-taking (Jefferson, 1984b; Schegloff, 1996b; Lerner and Linton, 2004). The converse of breathing in – exhalation – has received less attention. Yet there are forms of exhalation that exhibit social-interactional use, the most conspicuous of which is perhaps the act of sighing.

The reason we may want to transcribe sighing is largely bound up with its usage as an affectively loaded social object. On its own, it acts as a kind of response cry (Goffman, 1978) or expressive vocalization that 'externalizes a presumed inner state' (p. 794). As with other such communicative emissions like laughter (Glenn and Holt, 2013) and crying (Hepburn, 2004), participants have been shown to produce and understand sighing in interaction by reference to its placement in the turn, sequence, and ongoing course of action (Hoey, 2014).

As compared to normal autonomic out-breaths, sighing is usually longer, carries greater acoustic energy, and is perceived as out of sync with normal breathing. It is also distinguished by the fact that vocalization and sighing can happen concurrently. A voiceless sigh, for instance, is different from a hummed sigh, which is different from a sighed-through speaking turn, and so forth. These differences from normal breathing are also observed visibly, as sighing is often accompanied by a characteristic heaving of the shoulders with the inspiration and expiration of breath.

Because sighing is distinct from normal breathing, special consideration should be given when transcribing it. There are some aspects of sighing that are not currently conventionalized, but should be indicated if they are treated as relevant by participants.

A first consideration relates to the public availability of a sigh. Sighing is more audible if it is done with voicing, so some indication should be given of whether a sigh is voiced or not. Similarly, sighing is visible if done in concert with shoulder movement. Marking this bodily movement is especially important if a sigh is captured by the video but not the audio, since it may have been audible to co-present participants. Something else to consider is whether sighing is done with talk or vocalization, since that likely modifies the action being done. Sighing while speaking, for instance, can impart to the turn an affective valence that might otherwise have been different. And finally, whether a sigh is produced orally or nasally may be relevant for an analysis of participation. Sighing through the mouth is acoustically and hearably distinct from sighing through the nostrils, and since mouth aperture can index a participant's willingness or availability to speak, it can also reveal that participant's analysis of the current participation framework.

TRANSCRIBING LAUGHTER[1]

Laughter is a pervasive feature of interaction. Jefferson (1984b) noted that if we assume that laughter, like crying, is an uncontrolled bodily function – a 'flooding out' that is therefore not part of the ongoing vocal interaction – we will be tempted to merely note that it occurred. Jefferson's pioneering work (1979, 1984b, 1985, 2010; Jefferson et al., 1987) has shown how laughter can be approached as an ordered interactional phenomenon. It is

---

[1]This section partially reproduces and develops elements and examples from earlier work by Hepburn and Varney (2013).

with reference to laughter more than anything else that Jefferson developed her analysis of what should be included in a transcript, and why and how it matters for the participants. Her meticulous transcription and analysis showed laughter to be typically more than an uncontrollable expression of amusement, and instead something which is closely inter-actionally coordinated and used to accomplish specific interactional tasks (e.g., Jefferson, 1985; see also Glenn, 2003; Glenn and Holt, 2013; Holt, 2010; Osvaldsson, 2004). In her paper on laughter in troubles-telling, Jefferson notes that laughter may display the teller's 'good spirits' and bravery, and so is 'troubles-resistive' (1984b: 367). Jefferson (1985) also discussed the value of transcribing laughter where it is placed in talk to manage delicate tasks, such as the saying of an obscenity. Even with shared laughter, Jefferson demon-strated that this is a highly ordered event which is coordinated by recipients in relation to rhythmic pulses of laughter (Jefferson et al., 1987). She also showed the value of attending to the exact placement of laughter in particular words, as well as its prosodic features.

In this section we lay out some of the features of laughter, and explore some reasons why it is still important to capture its often subtle interactional features.

Intriguingly, the presence of laughter doesn't necessarily indicate the presence of something 'funny' or laughable in talk. This is one of the reasons why it can be extremely useful to accurately represent its manner and delivery.

As Hepburn and Varney (2013) have noted, there are many English vernacular terms that describe different forms of laughter: for example, giggle, chuckle, guffaw, snigger, hysterical or raucous. The existence of these vernacular distinctions suggests that people routinely notice, and therefore probably orient to, different forms and gradations of laughter. Moreover, we might predict that speakers will carefully incorporate different varieties and calibrations of laughter into interaction, depending on the task at hand.

········ **BOX** *5.1* ··

Tips for transcribing laughter

Transcribing laughter can seem daunting due to the unfamiliar forms of representation, and because overlap is a common feature – there is no 'one at a time' principle as there is with actions realized through talk. As with other types of transcribing, a useful device for accurately capturing the diverse range of sounds is to add layers of detail incrementally: counting the particles, assessing their vol-ume, stretch, pitch, aspiration, listening for any voiced vowels or other sounds, marking overlaps where necessary and focusing on capturing one speaker at a time in the overlaps. This will involve returning repeatedly to a sound file to listen for different features. Some of the many different fea-tures of laughter and how to transcribe them are presented below.

··

Components of laughter

Laughter is typically made up of pulsed out-breaths, which can be delivered quite quickly, for example 'ahHAH HA HA HAH' from line 4, Extract 6 below.

Laughter may also occur as a standalone particle. Single laugh particles are common markers of action modulation in both interpolated and post-completion positions (Potter and Hepburn, 2010; Shaw et al., 2013). It may also be useful, however, to track their occurrence as standalone particles, where they are in some way responsive to some prior turn.

Each pulse or particle of laughter should be transcribed, but their speed of delivery can present a major obstacle to the transcriber. One solution (which works for transcription of all types) is to slow down the sound, which allows a more careful consideration of both the type and number of laughter particles present. Slowing the tempo also facilitates a clear sense of overlap onset and offset. Another possibility is to zoom into a sound wave, allowing a visual representation of pulses of laughter. (For a discussion of software tools to do this, see Chapter 9.)

Voiced vowels

Laughter can be combined with different voiced vowels, resulting in characteristic particles such as 'huh/hah/heh/hih/hoh'. These can be interspersed with audible in-breaths, which may themselves contain voiced vowels (e.g., 'hih' and 'ha' on line 5, Extract 6). As lines 2 and 5 below show, the same interlocutor may use a variety of forms.

(6)

```
Location, Location, Location
01   Bill:    Th[e shed-]
02   Kirsty:    [H H h i] h [h h u h    h huh   hhah   hah ]=
03   Phil:      [I don't    [think you're gonna give 'im]=
04   Hazel:               [a h H A H    H A  ↑HA  ↑HAH ]=
05   Kir:     =[hih  ha   hah hah ha .h][i.h]  h h]=
06   Phi:     =[a MO:MENT'S CHOI:CE:! ][Hh ]
07   Haz:     =[ahah   hah   ha hah .hh ][h h h    ]=
08   Bil:                        [hihyeahh]=
09   Phi:     =[.Hhugh I thi(h)nk you'll gedover it W:ON:'T you:!]=
```

The quality of 'voiced vowels' may be due to the position of the open mouth, which seems to give the expelled air a vowel-like quality, whereas a closed mouth and/or throat would more likely add consonants, e.g., 'tsshh' or 'khuh' (see below). To some extent, it's possible that vowel or consonant sound can convey the issuer's state at the time of production – for example, closed or open-mouthed, shocked or surprised. For the expert transcriber, you may also notice the presence of unvoiced vowel production – one of the more subtle features of delivery that we noted in Chapter 4. You may hear that the laugher holds their mouth in a certain position without any hearable product, so the resulting breathiness has a particular 'a' or 'e' quality to it, say. This could be indicated with an italicized vowel: 'h*a*hh'.

Vowel placement

Listening out for the placement of vowels relative to aspiration can be a challenge. Consider an example of a laughter particle in which the vowel appears prior to the aspiration, and compare with the second particle – both on line 12, below.

(7)

```
Field:J86:2:1:2-3
06 Fos:     ='t's only a (0.4) quarter'v'n hour fli:ght °but uh°
07               (0.2)
08 Les:     .hhhh expens[ive.
09 Fos:                 [interesting .hhhh
10               (0.2)
11 Fos:     We[ll I yes I s]poze ih-i-it's: uh:: it's about forty=
12 Les:       [ehh heh heh ]
13 Fos:     =pou:nds retu:rn.
14 Les:     Yes:. Yes.
```

Lesley's laughter particle on line 12 starts with a vowel sound 'ehh', and the second is given extra 'plosive' (see below) force '<u>heh</u>'. The inclusion of more vowel sounds and a plosive middle particle amplifies the delivery of the laughter, which may relate to Lesley's need to manage what turns out to be her rather problematic completion of Foster's prior turn on line 6 (see Lerner, 2004, on collaborative turn sequences).

Plosiveness and volume

When transcribing laughter, there are two elements that seem to escalate it, the 'plosiveness' of the aspiration and the volume of the vowel or other sounds within it. Underlining h's can mark more plosive aspiration, which will of course sound louder or 'emphatic' as well, but the vowel within the particle largely determines the volume. As with other types of talk (see Chapter 4), this use of underlining allows capitals to be reserved for laughter particles which are delivered at a notably higher volume. Thus in:

```
01 Jen:     [Yeh James's a little] divil ihhh ↑heh heh
```

we see the underlining marking the increased volume and plosiveness. And in line 4 from Extract 6:

```
a h H A H   H A ↑HA ↑HAH
```

the voiced vowel with marked elevated volume (possibly due both to its status as overlapping, and the management of a strongly disaffiliative turn earlier by Hazel[2]) is shown by the capital letters.

---

[2]See Hepburn and Potter (2012) for further discussion of this extract.

Decreased volume is shown in the usual way with the 'degree sign' (as discussed in Chapter 4).

Pitch

In addition to variations in the volume of each laugh particle, the pitch of laughter can also vary. Transcription of this follows Jefferson's normal conventions, for example, underlining and arrows (as discussed in Chapter 4). In Extract 8 on line 7, Lesley's laughter is high-pitched with elevated volume and plosiveness.

(8)

```
Field:M88:1:5:12
01 Les:           [Eh: ↑WE:LL eh ↑WHAT I RANG up ↓about was ehm
02          di-↑did you have ↓anybody want a photogra:ph?
03               (0.5)
04 Rob:     I'll be honest with ↑you
05 Les:     No.=
06 Rob:     =haven't a:sked ↓th'm.
07 Les:     Oh: that's alrigh[t ↑hhah hah hah hah↑[.ah
08 Rob:                      [(       )            [C'n I leave it
09          another wee:k,
```

On line 7, arrows surrounding 'hhah hah hah hah' indicate high pitch, and the underlining indicates plosive delivery as well as delivery that is moderately louder than the surrounding talk. Here Lesley preempts a dispreferred response on line 5, and her laughter manages both the interactional trouble created by Robbie's failure to grant an earlier request, and, as with Extract 7, her own problem in wrongly completing Robbie's turn for her on line 5.

To illustrate some different pitch movements, consider the following extract from a radio show. Frank is telling his listening audience and co-presenters about a photo that was recently published in a daily newspaper featuring his girlfriend Cath on her mobile phone. On lines 1–3 Frank reveals that the reason that Cath was on her phone was because she was attempting to arrange an appointment with her doctor.

(9)

```
Gastroenteritis
01 Frank:   She was actually: erm (.) phonin the do:ctor to see
02          if she could come in and see him that morning aboud
03          'er gastoenteritis.
04          (0.2)
05 Alun:    Khn[hhhuhh[  °hh-hh° ]
06 Emily:      [O::h. ]
07 Frank:          [↓She'll lo]ve me↓=
08          =[↓fer (.) telling you [that,↓]
09 Emily:   =[   Hn-hn-hn-hn       ]
10 Alun:                          [↑Hhah ] ↑hhah [°↑↑.hhih]
11 Frank:                                        [  Hhnh  ]
```

On line 7 Frank sarcastically remarks that 'she'll love me for telling you that', which both co-presenter Alun and guest Emily respond to with two different kinds of laughter (lines 9–11). The high-pitched, elevated volume and plosive quality of Alun's laughter may indicate the kind of institutional requirements of the humorous radio program, whereas Emily's laughter is much more subdued and possibly less open-mouthed, resulting in the 'hn' sound (see discussion of consonants in laughter below).

Aspiration in laughter

Laughter may contain differing degrees of aspiration, and in some cases be composed entirely of breathy sounds. For example, in the following extract, laughter is hearably present, but without the vocal features.

(10)

```
Hyla and Nancy
01  Nancy:     Didja a'ready get the mai:l,=
02   Hyla:     =.hhhh Yes, hh-hh-h[h,
03  Nancy:                        [Oh, hhhmhh[hh
04   Hyla:                                   [hh-hh
05                     (.)
06  Nancy:     Sorry I brought it uhhhp
```

Hyla's response on line 2 reveals a painful lack of correspondence from her boyfriend, largely through the particulars of its delivery. Rather than simply confirm that she had received mail that day, she prefaces her turn with a long in-breath (.hhhh) and follows the confirming 'yes' with voiceless laughter. This is marked by 'hh' without a voiced vowel, and the cut-off indicates that the particles are clearly separated – 'hh-hh-hh'. Compare this with Nancy's breathy laughter in the post-completion slot on line 3. Here a single extended breathy particle is hearable. The value of this type of delivery may relate to Shaw et al.'s (2013) suggestion that more muted delivery seems more appropriate when mitigating actions that have the potential for being in some way interactionally delicate or troublesome. Were Nancy to do something louder or more raucous here she would risk sounding callous, or as if she was reveling in her friend's discomfort. This segment is a nice illustration of the importance of capturing aspiration and laughter in all of its detail – without it, Nancy's 'Oh sorry I bought it up' would make little sense.

How many h's?

As mentioned above, when transcribing aspiration of any kind, one rule of thumb for how many h's to include is to time the aspiration and add one h for every 'beat' of silence (which is usually somewhere around 0.2 seconds, depending on the relative speed of the talk). Where laughter is very breathy, this may be a useful guide. Another strategy would be to compare different examples of laughter that have been transcribed by experts. For example, compare Jenny's post-completion laughter managing her troubles-telling:

(11)

```
Jen:    No I've gotta pimple on my chin en one on my eyebrow
        so ah ha ha ↑ha
```

with Charlie's breathier laughter below, managing what will become, following various hedges and false starts, the delivery of bad news:

(12)

```
Cha:    Hi howuh you doin.
Ile:    Goo::[d,
Cha:        [hhhe:h heh .hhhh I wuz uh:m:  (.)  .hh I wen' ah:-
```

And also in Hyla's laughter in Extract 13, compare her particles in line 6 with the later ones in line 12, which are delivered with marginally less aspiration:

(13)

```
Hyla and Nancy 12.01: 18
01 Nancy:    It wasn't fu(h)u(h)nn(h)y
02                     (0.2)
03 Nancy:    [.hhhhhhh
04 Hyla:     [I'm not laughing.[.hhhh
05 Nancy:                      [I kno:w,hh[hhh
06 Hyla:                                  [he:h huh,
07                 (0.2)
08 (Nancy):  .hhh
09                     (0.5)
10 Nancy:    A::nywa::y,
11                 (.)
12 Hyla:     eh-eh .hhhhhh Uh::m,
```

On line 6 the laughter particles are enclosed by 'h' and in the turn-initial particles on line 12, they aren't.

Audible in-breaths can also accompany episodes of laughter, and seem related to the plosive exhalations that precede them, as the above example shows. For example, line 3 sounds like the inhalation from Nancy's laughter particles through 'funny' on line 1, and similarly Hyla's in-breath on line 12 sounds like the aftermath of her bout of laughter that starts on line 6, and is finished on line 12, although it's difficult to hear any intervening laughter.

Student question: Sometimes I am not sure if the transcript shows laughter. How can I distinguish laughter from other sounds?

Answer: When a transcript is our only guide, it can be hard to tell laughter from other practices[3], such as crying or coughing, for example:

(14)

FAN: Yeah. .hh uh-hhu-uh: how d'd they <u>live</u> uh lately.=

Here the speaker has a couple of aborted attempts at 'uh: how' – we can hear the cut-off sounds and the breathy hhu- sound headed for 'how'. The result is something that looks like laughter, but sounds very different. Sometimes the only way to check is by listening to the recording, or here analysts might rely on features of the context – speakers are discussing the death of a mutual acquaintance, and the sounds are compatible with a word search.

　　Laughter composed solely of aspiration is also in danger of not being seen as laughter by analysts working with transcript alone. If this runs the risk of generating confusion then it may be important to add a description, such as ((breathy laughter)). In order to distinguish breathy laughter from out-breaths where it has the characteristic 'staccato' delivery, separate out the particles with the 'cut-off' symbol, as with Extract 9, line 9 'Hn-hn-hn-hn' and Extract 10, line 2: 'hh-hh-hh,'.

Consonants

Laughter isn't simply composed of voiced vowels such as 'huh/hah/heh/hih/hoh'. These sounds are often transformed into sounds that are more like consonants through the speaker's use of some combination of voicing, various levels of mouth tension and nasal involvement.

　　A less common feature of laugh particles is a distinct back of the throat guttural quality that modifies the resulting laughter, such as the 'gh' in Phil's '.hhugh' in Extract 6, line 9 (see Jefferson, 2010).

　　A 'k' can be used for back of the mouth quality in laughter; below the 'k' with the 'n' in Extract 9, line 5 makes the laughter sound 'snorty' as if displaying something suppressed or surprising about what is laughable:

05 Alun: Khn[hhhuhh[°hh-hh°]

In Extract 10, we noted that Nancy's laughter was managing the delicacy of responding to Hyla's uncomfortable situation. We noted the lack of voiced vowels as a useful device to deliver laughter in a more downplayed way.

　　Whereas breathy aspirational elements can be produced by the nose or mouth, which may be open to deliver vowel sounds, a more closed or tensed mouth makes other consonants such a 'n' or 'm' or 'l' hearable, often displaying a more stifled quality:

03 Nancy: ⌊Oh, hhhmhh⌈hh

---

[3]See Hepburn (2004) for a discussion of laughing and crying in transcription.

Laughter particles within talk

Laughter may interlace speech so that laughter particles are produced simultaneously with talk, or there may be a small number (typically 1–3) of particles in pre- or post-completion position. Interpolated laughter particles may be produced in different ways, which is important to indicate on the transcript (Potter and Hepburn, 2010). The plosiveness of laughter particles – how 'explosive' they sound – is marked by placing h's in *parentheses*, such as in 'thi(h)nk' in Extract 6, line 9:

```
9    Phi:      =[Hhugh I thi(h)nk you'll gedover it W:ON:'T you:!]=
```

Interpolated laughter may also come across as *breathy*, as in 'yeahh' in Extract 6, line 8. In this case, no parentheses are used:

```
8    Bil:      [hihyeahh]=
```

Small particles of interpolated laughter work to modulate the action in which they reside (Potter and Hepburn, 2010), so they are often found in particular words that carry descriptive trouble, such as descriptions of people that could be heard as complaints (e.g., note the complainable: 'you(h) hhad t(h)ih g(h)o a(h)wa(h)a(h)y' on lines 7–8 below), or as derogatory.

(15)

```
Field: 88U:2:2:8
01 Kev:      We invited you o:ver[didn't we 'n[: (              )]=
02 Les:                          [.hh .hhh    [We:ll (.) e-that's]=
03 Kev:      =[(          )
04 Les:      =[alright uh i-it all got a bit um .hhhh fraught (.) the
05           holiday didn't it a lot t'do an:d hh the kids were
06           dashing about 'nd .hhhhhh I've forgotten what happened
07     ->    now Oh 'n Skip had tih go awa::y 'n you(h) hhad t(h)ih
08     ->    g(h)o a(h)wa(h)a(h)y .hhhh e-an:d uh (0.2) We'll do it
09           again sometime.
10                (0.3)
11 Kev:      Yes it wz uh (0.4) uh: a bit nau:ghty altogether
```

Laughter and smiling

Where visual information is available, it may be interesting to track the occurrence of facial features that accompany or precede the laughter. There is some interesting research evidence that points to smiling as a 'pre-laughing device' Haakana (2010) – i.e. something that prefigures the occurrence of laughter. Haakana also notes the occurrence of smiling in response to laughter. Similarly, Auburn and Pollock (2012) note that smiling can convey 'an ironic, joking stance' (p. 143).

Laughter in emotion displays

Laughter can inflect a range of actions and emotion displays, which demonstrates its use-
fulness as a resource for action and argues for the importance of being able to represent
how it is delivered with a high degree of granularity. For example, a laughter-induced
sympathy particle 'aw' is hearable in Nancy's uptake to Hyla's confession (that she called
her maybe boyfriend and hung up) on line 4:

(16)

```
Hyla and Nancy
01   Hyla:    Hu:h?
02   Nancy:   C'djih tell iz vo[i:ce,]]
03   Hyla:                    [Y e a]:h, I knew iz voice,=
04   Nancy: →   =Oha:::[w,
05   Hyla:          [hhhih .hh=
```

The laughter works here because sympathy on its own would have cast Hyla too far into
the role of rejected girlfriend.

For a more exaggerated example of the interplay between sympathy and laughter, see
Mum's turn in line 5 of Extract 17, where she is responding to Sarah's story about how
her young son (Mum's grandson) became upset:

(17)

```
Shaw PC
01   Sarah:   And he got him£self all upset£='cause he thought I'd
02            tell him off=[because he didn't have his jum]per,
03   Mum:              [Oh~:: bless °him        ]
04   Sar:     Hh[hh    ]
05   Mum: ->    [Tch ohhh] hoh hoh hoh hoh [.HiUHH
06   Sarah:                             [.HHH
```

In the following extract, laughter inflects displays of disbelief or shock. Several friends,
one of whom is from India, are watching television.

(18)

```
Shock
06 TV1:    =You take the phone for a bit and let me know if any re:al
07         people come on.
08              (.)
09 TV3:    Indians are real people dad.
10         ((Doorbell rings on-screen))
11 Barb:   Mphuh
12 Carol:  ↑Ehohh!
13 Denise: Ohkh=
14 Anne:   =↓Owh>hoh hguh [hooh<]
15 Carol:            [hhh  ] wh↑(h)howh! .hhh
```

Figure 5.1 Caroline's shocked laughter at line 12, from Hepburn and Varney (2013)

Here laughter is mixed with 'oh's in lines 12–14 (see Figure 5.1 for illustration of accompanying open-mouthed facial features) and a 'wow' in line 15. It is useful in displaying both disbelief and a non-serious orientation towards TV1's racist utterance.

Post-completion particles

Sometimes, laughter particles are produced at the end of a turn (or post-completion). As Shaw et al. (2013) show, it is also important to capture the quality of delivery in post-completion position, as sometimes laughter particles can be designedly 'raucous' or minimal, depending on the interactional work being done. Post-completion plosiveness can be represented through such devices as underlining to show the sound as 'punched up'. For example, line 1 below:

(19)

```
Rahman B.2.IV; 1.10, P2 (Raymond and Heritage, 2006)
1 Jen:    [Yeh James's a little] divil ihhh  ↑heh heh
2 Ver:    [That-
3 Jen:    [huh .HH[H He:-
```

Shaw et al. note that Jenny's post-completion laughter on line 1 is produced as plosive via the underlined 'h': '↑heh heh', and it also contains elevated pitch and 'voiced vowels'. By contrast the laughter particle on line 3 'huh' has a less plosive and more breathy sound.

> **Student question:** When laughter is produced simultaneously with talk, plosiveness is marked by placing h's in parentheses. Should I be using the same rule for post-completion laughter?
>
> **Answer:** No, because using parentheses can lead to confusion when transcribing standalone particles, given that they mark uncertain hearing in other contexts (see Chapter 2). Instead, transcribe the laughter particles in the usual way, as in Extract 19, line 1 above.

CONCLUDING COMMENTS

In this chapter we set out to consider when and how to include sounds of breathing in a transcript. This gave us a basis for exploring the design and delivery of different forms of laughter and seeing how a careful transcription allows us to notice the many different ways that laughter can be delivered. While transcribing laughter is a time-consuming process that requires quite a bit of patience and practice, it has tremendous payoffs for our understanding of social interaction. A significant body of research into laughter, made possible by its granular transcription, has demonstrated that even when laughter appears to be 'flooding out' (Jefferson, 1985), it is still organized in orderly ways, modulating actions or managing some perceived insufficiency, delicacy, or trouble or adjusting emotional displays, such as shock and sympathy. Once we start to transcribe laughter in detail, we can begin to understand the variety of interactional features of laughter in different contexts. This leads us to suspect that a more careful exploration of some of the many sounds that accompany talk will bring similar benefits.

TRANSCRIPTION CONVENTIONS INTRODUCED IN THIS CHAPTER

Aspiration: In-breaths and out-breaths

Hearable aspiration (out-breath): h

Hearable inhalation (in-breath) – period (or raised dot) preceding h's: .h

Stretched aspiration – multiple h's rather than using colons: hhhh or .hhhh

Elevated volume of aspiration: HH .HHH

Decreased volume of aspiration – degree signs: °hh

Components of laughter

Voiced vowels: huh/hah/heh/hih/hoh/ha/ehh

Voiced consonants, e.g.: tsshh or khuh

Plosiveness in standalone particles – underlining: <u>h</u>eh

Plosiveness in words – enclosed particles in parentheses: a(h)wa(h)ay/thi(h)nk

Breathy laughter for discrete particles – cut-off symbol: hh-hh-hh

Breathy laughter with voiced vowels/consonants: hhhmhhhh

Breathy laughter in words: uhhhp

RECOMMENDED READING

For further discussion on the transcription of laughter see:

Jefferson, G. (1985) An exercise in the transcription and analysis of laughter. In T.A. v. Dijk (Ed.) *Handbook of discourse analysis* (Vol. 3, pp. 25–34). New York: Academic Press.

Hepburn, A. and Varney, S. (2013) Beyond ((laughter)): Some notes on transcription. In P.J. Glenn and E. Holt (Eds) *Studies in laughter in interaction* (pp. 25–38). London: Bloomsbury.

For a volume that includes a number of cutting edge developments on conversation analytic research into laughter, see:

Glenn, P.J. and Holt, E. (2013) *Studies of laughter in interaction.* London: Bloomsbury Publishing.

Jefferson's research on laughter in troubles-telling is one of the classic papers on the interactional role of laughter:

Jefferson, G. (1984) On the organization of laughter in talk about troubles. In J.M. Atkinson and J. Heritage (Eds) *Structures of social action* (pp. 346–69). Cambridge: Cambridge University Press.

To find out more about the concepts discussed in this chapter, see examples of real transcriptions, and test your knowledge through exercises and quizzes, visit the supporting website at
https://study.sagepub.com/hepburnandbolden

SIX

Transcribing Crying, Expressions of Pain and Other Non-speech Sounds

CHAPTER CONTENTS

A great deal of social and clinical research is focused around various aspects of human suffering. But if you had to detail how to most effectively soothe someone in pain or distress, would you know how to do it? One basic problem in specifying the interactional techniques for managing distress is that there are very few studies that have attempted to capture episodes of human suffering as they happen, in a way that allows analysis of their interactional unfolding. In this chapter we provide some basic tools that facilitate researchers in taking up that challenge. Following from the previous chapter, we further develop our understanding of how to clearly represent hearable elements of aspiration, with a focus on crying and other forms of embodied and hearable upset and pain. Towards the end of the chapter, we turn to transcription of other (potentially) interactionally relevant non-speech sounds, such as throat clearing and 'tutting'.

TRANSCRIBING CRYING[1]

Crying is probably the first communicative act that any of us performed. Those who conduct research in institutional settings will know that for many practitioners, the number one request is for communication training in how to manage upset more productively. An interactionally sensitive transcript gives us an important tool with which to provide such help. To explore the interactional organization of upset and crying, it is useful to try to capture its audible components.

By way of a demonstration, we begin with a lengthy example that contains a number of characteristic features of upset. It comes from the live transmission of a UK 'reality TV' program *Pop Idol* from 2003, where aspiring musicians are having their singing performance evaluated by a panel of experts who give direct and often quite scathing feedback. Ant and Dec are the hosts; 'Cont' is the contestant who has just performed.

(1)

```
Pop Idol Crying
01 Cont:      [((mouthing, shakes head, [smiling))
02 Dec:                                 [((puts hand on
03 Dec:      [  Cont's shoulder)) ]
04 Cont:     [((thumb wiping eye))]
05 Cont:     [°.snih]
06 ??:       [ (    ]      )      ]
07 Dec:      [Y'er['t.  ]
08 Ant:      [     [(°↓Ar]ight.°)
09           (0.3)                                   Silence
10 Cont:     ↑↑Yeah,
11           [          (1.2)                     ]
```

---

[1]Some elements of this section have been reproduced and developed from materials in Hepburn (2004) and Hepburn and Potter (2012).

```
12 Cont:    [((thumb stays on eye, looking down))]
13 Cont:    °.hh° (.) .SHHIH ─────────────────────────     Sniff
14 Ant:     Take ye time there don't worry.
15          (0.4)
16 Cont:    I'[ve ↑never  ] ↑had that e- in my life
17 Dec:       [Don' worry.]
18 Ant:       [(A'↓right.)]
19 Cont:    performin.=I've gone on sta:ge ((touches eye))
20          (.) bin character ((touches nose)) ~all that
21          sorta stuff an~ (.)                              Elevated
22 Dec:     Mm.                                              pitch
23 Cont:    ah've- it's ~↑weir:d °↑it's ↑↑weird an°~
24          [((camera pans to other Cont wiping her eye))]
25          [               (0.7)                      ]
26 Dec:     An you've worked har:d fer this haven't you.
27          Up- up to this point [ah mean] you knaw: ye've
28 Cont:                         [Hhh  .h]                   Creaky
29          (0.4)
30 Cont:    ~THAt wasn' #ma best.#~  That wus the one
31          thing ah ~wanted to #do,~ (.)                    Tremulous
32 Cont:    [((touches eyes, faces camera] hand down))
33 Cont:    [ .hh h HHh (0.2) HHHh        ]                  Aspiration
```

We will consider features of crying roughly in the order that they appear in Extracts 1 and 2.

Silence: Common features of crying are extended pauses, missing uptake and unfilled places in adjacency pairs. Under certain interactional conditions (especially phone calls where there are no visible indications) silence can be treated by recipients as suggesting that the speaker is seriously upset. Note, for example line 11 where the recipient might have been expected to elaborate; the 'take your time' from the presenter on 14 orients precisely to the failure to speak in a relevant slot.

Sniffs come with varying degrees of volume and stretch, represented as inhalation, with the addition of various voiced vowels and consonants, caused by nasal or 'wet' sounds – see, for example, lines 5 and 13 in Extract 1, '°.snih' (a quiet nasal sniff) and '.SHHIH' (loud 'wet' sniff).

One role for sniffing can be to signal the incipience of the crier's next turn, which can give it a floor-holding role in the interaction, similarly to a hearable in-breath (Hepburn, 2004). This can be seen, for example, in Extract 2, line 6 from a child protection helpline, where a turn from the crier has been due from line 4 onwards:

(2)

```
JK Distraught dad 29.4.01
01 Cal:    >.Hhih .hhihhh<
02 CPO:    D'you want- d'y'wann'ave [a break for a ] moment.=
03 Cal:                             [ Hhuhh >.hihh<]
```

```
04              =>hhuhh hhuhh<
05              (0.6)
06  Cal:        .shih ((sniff))
07              (0.3)
08  Cal:        ∘∘khhay∘∘
```

Sniffing can also serve as a hearable display (combined with silence) of interactional incapacity, or signify that a bout of more disruptive sobbing has not completely passed. These sound differences and the sense in which sniffs are interactionally relevant suggest the importance of transcribing rather than just describing the sound.

Elevated pitch can occur when the speaker is continuing talking through a crying episode, probably caused by muscle constriction in the throat and vocal chords. In Extract 1, the speaker struggles with delivery of the description of his problems, becoming increasingly high-pitched on lines 16 and 23. This pitch shift (marked with upward arrows and double arrows indicating a more extreme shift), typically accompanies talk that begins to break down into sobbing. Here the speaker's upset inflects a description where an account for being upset is offered.

Tremulous or wobbly delivery is represented by enclosing the talk in tildes (~) (e.g., Extract 1, lines 20 and 31). This can be less disruptive than sniffs, sobs or high-pitched delivery, as speakers can continue speaking in a tremulous manner for extended periods. As with many of the individual elements of upset, tremulous delivery alone can be treated by recipients as a sign of distress (Hepburn, 2004).

Aspiration particles during words have been represented by one or more h's. As with laughter (see Chapter 5), parentheses – (h) – are used to represent plosive breathing; outside of parentheses the h represents a more 'breathy' sound. It is different from sobbing in that the aspiration occurs during or directly before or after speech.

Like tremulous voicing and high pitch, aspiration is a feature of speakers' attempts to talk through a crying episode. This can be seen in Extract 2, above, in line 8. Aspiration of this kind, like tremulous delivery, can also be an initial cue to recipients that their interlocutor is upset in some way (Hepburn, 2004).

Sobbing is represented with normal in- and out-breaths, and like laughter, may include 'voiced vowels' (e.g., huh .hih), and can be elevated in pitch, and done with more or less aspiration. When sobs are sharply inhaled or exhaled or spasm-like, this is represented by enclosing them in greater/less than symbols (>huh huh< >.hihh<), which borrows from their indication of a faster pace, and marks them out visually from laughter. Sobbing is probably the most familiar and recognizable feature of crying, and is usually the most disruptive to ongoing interaction. Extract 2 (above) provides some examples (e.g., lines 1, 3 and 4) and also illustrates different vowel sounds and degrees of aspiration.

Further problems with delivery are evidenced by *'mouthed'* (Extract 1, line 1) or *whispered* talk (e.g., Extract 2, line 8) enclosed in double degree symbols (∘∘). Both may result in talk that can be very difficult to hear, which may be due to physiological changes in the muscles around the vocal chords. Due to the lack of sound, mouthing requires video-recording to identify it clearly. We can also see the representation of barely audible talk in Extract 2, line 8, and here transcription is often facilitated by amplification settings on software (see Chapter 9).

Additional features of voice quality may be part of recognizable upset, such as creaky delivery (represented with #) or staccato delivery (represented with the iteration of a 'cut-off' symbol (e.g., 'it-is-cut-off-')). Activities such as swallowing and throat clearing may also accompany upset.

Visual features of upset may include trembling face and/or hands; tears; touching eyes or face (e.g., Extract 1 above, lines 4, 12 and 32); looking down/hiding one's face/turning away (Extract 1, line 12); combined with more characteristic facial features of screwed up eyes; downturned mouth with eyebrows drooping down from the middle of the face; flushed appearance especially around the eyes and nose. (See Chapter 7 on transcribing visible conduct.)

Student question: In some transcripts, the transcriber simply notes that crying has occurred. Why is it important to mark all of these different elements of crying?

Answer: As with laughter, an interactionally sensitive transcript allows us to spot the organization of upset in interaction in ways that haven't been done before. As we saw in the previous chapter, Jeffersonian transcription conventions have given rise to some important research on the interactional role of laughter. The examination of interactional features of upset is still in its infancy, but initial work by Hepburn and Potter suggests that various signs of possible distress can appear in isolation, and/or accumulate, sometimes with considerable subtlety. These may appear as an inflection of one or more elements of crying into the ongoing interaction without disrupting it, at least initially. Crucially for us as transcribers, interlocutors will tune into these small signs and respond (see section below on expressing sympathy) or simply leave longer than normal silences. Crying can therefore result in sequences of talk that break away from ongoing activities and are instead occupied with the crying itself, such as apologies from the crying party, soothing, reassuring, sympathetic, empathetic and diagnostic moves from the crying recipient (e.g., Extract 1, lines 2, 3, 7, 8, 14; Extract 2, line 2). The crying recipient can continue to orient to the ongoing talk, or can orient to the disruption of the talk (in institutional settings 'take your times' may be more common; Hepburn, 2004; Hepburn and Potter, 2007; and see Extract 1, line 14, and Extract 2, line 2) or they can respond more directly to the upset evidenced by the speaker (e.g., Extract 1 above, lines 26–27). The nature of recipients' responses can tell us interesting things about the kind of relationship interlocutors have, or the kind of activities they are engaged in (e.g., a therapist may respond very differently to a friend or a police officer; see also Box 6.1). Analysis of sequences involving upset can then reveal important insights that can be used in applied workshops (e.g., see Hepburn et al., 2014).

------- **BOX 6.1** ---

Extreme upset and hysteria in citizen–police interactions

Whalen and Zimmerman (1998) examined the role of extreme upset in managing institutional requirements of 911 emergency calls. Call takers (CT) are required to collect detailed information

(Continued)

(Continued)

about the nature of the emergency the caller is calling about. When the caller is too upset to provide that information, call takers may use the term 'hysteria' to account for failing to collect required information. For instance, the caller (C) in this call was subsequently classified as 'hysterical':

(3)

```
Whalen and Zimmerman (1998: 148)
1   CT:  Nine=one=o[ne, what is your emergency?
2   C:             [HUHHHHH .HHHHHH HHHHHHH .HHHHH
3        HUHHHH .HHH ((loudly gasping/out of breath))
4   CT:  Hello?
5   C:   we(HHH)- .HHHH we've(HHH)- HUHHH .HHHH HEEHHH-
6        the address- HHHHH .HHH we need (ambu-ln-) .HHH
```

Different sorts of institutional contingencies may be at play when police officers interact with upset or hysterical citizens face to face. Kidwell (2006) relies on detailed transcripts of embodied behaviors to examine interactional processes involved in managing hysteria in this setting. (See Chapter 7 for a discussion of transcription of visible conduct.)

Transcribing responses to crying and upset

With the help of an interactionally sensitive transcript, it is possible to track a distinction between, on the one hand, claims or displays of understanding of the other's perspective (what Hepburn and Potter, 2007, suggested might be 'empathic' turns), and on the other sympathy tokens that may or may not be propositional. Sympathy is clearly identifiable by the prosodic delivery of the turn: it is usually stretched, sometimes with elevated or rising-falling pitch and/or creaky delivery, sometimes involving a sympathetic token such as 'oh' or 'aw'. Sympathy can also carried via a 'softened' delivery that includes decreased volume and increased aspiration. Although they can mirror prosodic elements of crying, sympathetic tokens are hearably specific to the action of sympathizing or soothing. The ability to vary calibrations of sympathetic prosody can be especially useful in institutional environments where maintaining appropriate institutional neutrality is a fundamental requirement.

To illustrate, in the following example, which involves a child custody issue, Hepburn and Potter (2007) suggested that the call taker's display of sympathy on lines 3 and 5–6 allowed her to maintain a level of affiliation that avoided 'on the record' empathizing with the caller's difficulties.

(4)

```
NSPCC AD Grandson black eye
01 Caller: An she won't ~answer my phone or anythin' and
02         I'm jh's s(h)↑o whorri[ed th't some'ing c'd]
03 CPO:                         [ °O h :    m y   ° ]
04 Call:    ↑hhappen [↑to ↑↑'im >.HH<] h
```

```
05 CPO:                    [ °g o : s h :   ]
06 CPO:     #Oh: go:s[h# ]
07 Call:                   [°.S]hih°
08          (0.5)
09 CPO:     .HHhh
10          (0.5)
11 Call:    °.Shih°=
12 CPO:     =I mean is your relationship with her normally-
13          is it (.) e-normally okay,=or is it normally
14          a bit (.) rocky anywa:y.
```

The call taker's (CPO – child protection officer) response ('oh my gosh' lines 3 and 5) to an emotionally delivered problem presentation by the caller is in the form of a combined news receipt and marker of surprise, which also acknowledges that something untoward has been described. The CPO's turn is stretched, quieter than normal (perhaps in acknowledgement that it is persisting in overlap across the caller's turn), and repeated with stretched and creaky delivery on line 6. This type of sympathetically inflected turn acknowledges the feelings of the other, without topicalizing them or going on the record with propositional content. Weiste and Peräkylä (2014) found a similar phenomenon and called it 'prosodic continuity'.

This section has shown the importance of attending to the details of delivery, not simply in the identification and representation of upset in talk, but also in transcribing the specifics of how interlocutors respond to upset. As Hepburn et al. (2014) noted, this attention to specifics allows us to engage with call takers in knowledge exchange workshops, and help them to reflect on what constitutes good practice in the challenging interactional arena of responding to upset.

EXPRESSIONS OF PAIN AND DISCOMFORT

Not unlike crying, expressions of pain are interactional objects; their delivery and uptake are shaped by the exigencies of ongoing interaction. Interactional organization of pain has been explored in medical settings and everyday family interactions. Early research by Heath (1989) showed that patients' expressions of pain are interactionally organized and sensitive to local frameworks of diagnostic activity (see also Expert Box 8). The importance of close transcription of embodiments of pain and their uptake has been demonstrated in Jenkins and Hepburn's (2015) work on family interactions. They describe a constellation of features characteristic of children's expressions of pain and physical discomfort: (i) prosodic features embedded in the delivery of pain cries, including heightened pitch, changes in volume, such as sharp elevated volume or aspirated whispering, and tremulous and creaky voice; (ii) pain cries produced with recognizable utterances such as 'ouch', 'ow', 'owa', 'ah' or more discrete moans; and (iii) embodied actions, such as facial contortions, agitated movements, and placing a hand on the site of the pain. This analysis documents how these actions encode both informational content pertaining to the nature and severity of the sensation, and emotional content in terms of the distress, upset and discomfort the pain is causing.

<hr>

····· **EXPERT BOX** *8* ··

Transcribing distress

Ignasi Clemente, Hunter College, CUNY, USA

Transcription has the power to make us see and hear elements of an interaction that would otherwise go unnoticed. At the start of his/her analysis, a transcriber works like a spy cracking a code: in the chaos of multimodal communication, patterns and cues begin to emerge and suddenly, the moves and countermoves of participants are clearly observable.

In Clemente (2015), I analyze one such ostensibly chaotic instance. Fifteen-year-old Pedro, from a pediatric cancer clinic in Spain, has just been told he has cancer and is crying profusely. At a first glance, Pedro may appear to say nothing and to do nothing, other than expressing his distress. He is overcome by emotion, looks down, withdraws from the interaction, and cries. However, after a close transcription of where and how Pedro cries, we find that the crying has a specific sequential location, development and distribution. Pedro does not cry immediately after the doctor's delivery of bad news. Instead, he begins to cry when his doctor and his mother engage in multiple and extensive rounds of optimistic reassurances. Furthermore, Pedro's crying tends to occur during transition relevant places (see Chapter 3, Box 3.2). Moreover, Pedro changes the type and length of his crying and modulates it as he participates in the progress of the interaction. His doctor and his mother are reassuring Pedro in overlap, which leads to a competitive increase in the loudness of the talk. Pedro's crying also becomes louder, with elevated pitch, which in turn, leads to louder talk. Before the overlap of reassurances, Pedro cried with short and sharp sniffs, but during the overlap, Pedro cries wailingly with long sobs that contain multiple vocalic sounds. The more Pedro is reassured his treatment will be unproblematic, the more Pedro intensifies his crying.

The close transcription of expressions of pain and distress has other analytic payoffs. I would like to highlight two. First, transcription reveals how emotion and action are not opposites. Whether we consider crying as solely an expression of an inner state, it happens in a social lived world and has consequences to the shaping of that social lived world. Pedro is distressed, and he also is manifesting his misalignment with the activity of reassuring, which indeed stops soon afterwards. Second, Pedro emerges as a social actor who participates in and actively seeks to influence the progress of an interaction. The transcription of how and where Pedro cries is evidence that children and young people, even when they seem to say and to do nothing, are competent social agents.

<hr>

Prosodic features of pain

Many expressions of pain contain prosodic features associated with upset and crying. These features include elevated pitch, tremulous or creaky delivery, sobs, increased aspiration and changes in volume:

Elevated pitch can convey distress. The shift may affect the whole formulation as below:

```
Edwards 2:00.00
~↑↑my: hea:d hur:ts↑↑~.
```

Or the pitch may mark a specific word as below in the words 'tooth' and 'it'.

```
Crouch 4
OW::: MY:: ↑↑~TOO:TH it rea:l↑ly hur:::ts.

Jepchott ?. 17.13
↑↑°It° s:ti:ngs me::.
```

Tremulous delivery may mark a single word (as in 'tooth' above) or the whole turn.

   Creaky delivery (marked by a hash sign, see Chapter 4) seems to be another character-istic feature of displays of pain and discomfort.

```
Edwards 5:15.40–17.30
#My tu:mmy hur:ts:.#
```

Some studies of creaky voice (or laryngealization) in responsive turns has shown that it can convey lack of affiliation (e.g., Grivicic and Nilep, 2004; Pittam, 1987). This seems to contrast with our earlier observation of its use in sympathy expressions. However, this makes more sense when we consider that sympathy expressions are probably also conveying pain and discomfort with the caller's upset. Creaky delivery seems to be a by-product of not fully opening one's throat and engaging vocal chords – perhaps con-veying that one is either occupied with discomfort or pain, or simply 'running out of steam', which tallies with Ogden's (2001) finding that it can mark turn endings.

   Changes in volume can go in either direction in pain expressions. Extremely quiet vol-ume, marked by double degree signs, may also have a 'breathy' quality (marked by extra h's) and can occur when a child is talking through crying or pain. The whispers may mark particular words or the whole turn.

```
Edwards 2:02.11–2.28
°uh° m:::↓y (0.5) tummy (0.8) °°#hurts:°° (0.3) °°me::°°
```

Alternatively, a marked heightening of volume (shown in capital letters) can display the sudden onset of the expressed experience, and display significant levels of upset.

```
Crouch 4
OW::: MY:: ↑↑~TOO:TH it rea:l↑ly hur:::ts.
```

Stretched delivery is a prevalent feature of expressions of pain, as the above examples demonstrate. Stretching extends the interactional space a turn holds, which may serve to override existing conversational projects, and/or convey the ongoing nature of the suffering.

Sobbing is perhaps the most characteristic feature of both pain and upset, and sequences in which children, rather than adults, express pain are probably more likely to contain sobs:

(5)

```
Jepchott 6: 17.13
11 Isa: [ >H(h)eh< ][.HH ~Don't touch]it.~ .hheh[hiheh]
12 Mum:                                          [Okay.]
13 Dad:                  [((looks over chair)) ]
14 Isa: ↑↑°It° s:ti:ngs me::.
```

In this interaction, Isabelle has already delivered a pain cry, and here produces in-breaths and out-breaths with characteristics of sobbing, differing volume to the surrounding talk and voiced vowels produced with tremulous voice. Rather than being embedded in the formulations, the sobs are separate, preceding and following the talk, a quality shared with pain cries.

Jenkins and Hepburn (2015) also discussed some indicative findings around the *embodied elements* accompanying expressions of pain, such as facial grimacing, agitated movements, and placing a hand on the site of the pain. Such research needs further development.

Pain cries

Pain cries often contain voiced vowels such as 'ow' or 'ah' or the more lexicalized 'ouch' and do not appear to be produced subsequent to a lexical assertion in the form of, for example, 'my tummy hurts ouch'. See the following for some examples of children's pain cries:

```
Jephcott 11: 1:41
Ou:ch ou:ch ou::tsch::
```

```
Hawkins 11:10.05-12.29
a. #ah::¿ hh
```

```
Edwards 2:02.11-2.28
a. .hhhh u::(h)h::
b. .hhhh ow:a: .hhh
```

```
Jepchott 6: 17.13
↑o::: ↑↑::::W.
```

```
Jephcott 9:6.15
↑↑aa:::o:::w.
```

Rather than being embedded in a verbal formulation, pain cries are typically separate utterances often delivered in sequences in which pain is expressed. Pain cries and their associated descriptions are often stretched and delivered with creaky voice, elevated pitch, and aspiration (Jenkins and Hepburn, 2015). Pain cries may allow the speaker to draw a sharp intake of breath, as if it simultaneously serves the physical need for oxygen (Heath, 1989). They may be preceded or followed by labored inhaling and exhaling, or be infused with breathiness.

INTERACTIONAL ORGANIZATION OF CRYING AND EXPRESSIONS OF PAIN

With a sophisticated system of transcription to underpin analyses of episodes of upset in interaction, we can begin to draw some conclusions about their interactional organization. Analyses of upset across a range of projects (see Hepburn and Potter, 2012, for an overview) suggest that crying is something that typically inflects talk, sometimes interferes with, dramatizes or underscores talk, and sometimes replaces talk altogether. In our discussion of expressions of pain and discomfort, we discovered that they contain prosodic features associated with upset and crying. These features include elevated pitch, tremulous or creaky delivery, sobs, increased aspiration and changes in volume. The link between heightened emotion and pitch is borne out by interactional studies of prosody (e.g., Couper-Kuhlen and Selting, 1996). For instance, in their discussion of doctors conveying bad news, Freese and Maynard (1998) noted that such turns were characterized by stretched vowels, and creaky and/or breathy voice quality, and these were associated with expressions of sorrow (during which they also noted the presence of falling pitch contours).

Differences between the expressions of pain and upset will clearly relate to whether they are communicated by adults or children, and in what context. The research we have discussed suggests that increased volume is more common in pain expressions, and this, combined with the increased prevalence of stretching out pain expressions, matches the sense that they can potentially take interactional priority over more mundane matters. Upset, at least in adult interaction, often involves some attempt to conceal or minimize it (Hepburn and Potter, 2012), whereas expressions of pain can be more indicative of some immediate problem for which further elaboration may be required so that a remedy can be sought. Further differences appear to entail a reduced level of sobbing and general aspiration during expressions of pain, and an increase in creaky and stretched delivery.

TUTTING

In this section, we offer 'tutting' as an illustration of the utility of noticing and transcribing smaller, and often seemingly inconsequential, sounds. Consider the following extract from a child protection helpline. The caller is complaining about her neighbors, and in line 8, the call taker (CPO) responds to the complaint with '.tch Ri:ght,':

(6)

```
AD Girl Shut In
01 CPO:      D.hh al↓ri:ght then so e- w- ↑what was your
02           concerns a↓bout these children.
03 Caller:   R:ight.=Erm I think it's er:: (0.2) juss one
04           o' their childre:n, (0.2)
05 CPO:      Mm:[:.]
06 Call:        [E:]m:: (0.2) I think she's bein locked in
07           a room:, (0.3)
08 CPO:      .tch Ri:gh[t,]
09 Call:               [ E]n she- an her ~crie::s (0.3) are
10           really distressin:.
```

The initial sound (.tch) of the CPO's turn in line 8 can be characterized as a tut. Tut particles may display an orientation to the kinds of censure that might happen in more everyday interactions (such as reporting this type of thing to a friend) (Potter and Hepburn, 2015). On a helpline, tutting may convey a sense of supportive recipiency to callers, despite the institutional requirements for neutrality. In this sense, tutting functions in a similar way to prosodic displays of sympathy discussed above.

It is important, however, to be sensitive to the interactional contexts in which non-speech sounds occur. An analyst should remain alert to the interactional distinction between tut-particles and similar turn-initial sounds, such as 'lip smacks', which do not convey the sense of censure or sympathy. For some examples of other turn-initial sounds, see the range of sounds at the start of Gordon's turns in the following:

(7)

```
Field: SO88:1:5.1
01 Sus:   [.hh ↑Barmington are you:, a[h:::[::.
02 Gor:                               [.t  [.puh I am indee:d.
03           h[h
04 Sus:   [You're gunna pla[: y .]
05 Gor:                    [.pl.h]hhhhh[h
06 Sus:                               [(0.5)[Okay,hh well 'at's all I
07           wanted to know,
08               (0.2)
09 Gor:   .k.k Why's that.
10               (0.6)
11 Gor:   .mp[t
```

MISCELLANEOUS NON-SPEECH SOUNDS

A range of other sounds might be relevant for participants in analyzing one another's talk. Let's take the example of a *throat clear*. Often simply marking on the transcript (in double parentheses) that it has happened is enough: ((clears throat)). However there may be times when you want to represent the sound as well, due to its position, volume, or other interactionally relevant qualities. Generic advice in this situation would be to first have a go at the basic sound. For instance, for a throat clear one would expect an out-breath element, a guttural element, 'g', 'gh', 'uhg', etc., sometimes a 'k' sound, all of which is often done through closed or sealed lips, giving a possible 'm' sound, so 'hgm' or 'mhgmhm'. Think about whether the noise starts with a consonant or vowel sound like 'uhghm'. Then add in volume, length, emphasis, cut-off sounds, and any overlap or other elements of delivery (e.g., 'MHGHM!'). Here is an example from Gail Jefferson's transcripts:

(8)

```
Rahman:C:1:IK(17)
Ker:     I[t's me:.[<Kerry.=
Ida:      [Ih-     [mh-
Ida:     =mgh-mgh-mghhm Kerry,
(0.4)
```

Here, there are particles that run together but are divided by cut-off symbols and these are delivered as short bursts in quick succession. In the following instance, however, there are two clear standalone particles of throat clearing:

```
Field SepOct88-1-04
Skip:    khgz mghhm ((fidget)) .mtk .kn .khh[hhh
```

Note also the different sounds appearing with a 'k' and 'z' sound added in. This case also provides a useful example of a lip smack '.mtk' and 'k' sounds preceding inhalation sounds – another item that often appears when speakers are gearing up to speak.

······· **EXPERT BOX 9** ···

Transcribing 'disgust'

Jenny Mandelbaum, Rutgers University, New Brunswick, NJ, USA

Research on disgust suggests that the disgust reaction tokens that we produce (e.g., 'ogh', 'eeyew', 'Yu::ck!') are evolutionarily vestigial sounds of actual vomiting. Historically, when faced with food that is spoiled, and therefore dangerous, in the spirit of self-preservation, our bodies reacted (literally) viscerally, physically rejecting the food by expelling it. The sounds of disgust, then, are token vomit sounds, often produced in the throat, and sometimes accompanied by facial expressions that mimic vomiting.

This line of thinking suggests that disgust sounds may be physiologically generated by encountering something disgusting. However, as Wilkinson and Kitzinger (2006) found with surprise, expressions of disgust are not merely visceral emotional eruptions, but rather are socially constituted

(Continued)

(Continued)

performances. This discovery was made by writing precisely the sounds of disgust (usually produced in the throat), their exact placement, and indicating on the transcript and in written work the facial contortions and other embodied actions that may precede, accompany, or be produced in response to these sounds.

The following extract is from a conversation that takes place on the phone. In response to Leslie's report in line 5 of UHU (a kind of glue) 'dripping down the cooker', Mum produces a disgust sound in line 6, followed by a short burst of laughter.

```
D01_uhu_Holt:1:8
01   LES:  I'm sorry tuh keep you, I've jus'been sticking .h something
02         on the front a'the: uhm (0.3) cooker .h because:: uh:(.)
03         the top a'the knob fell off.
04   MUM:  Oh: I see[:,
05   LES:           [A:nd uh I've got (.) UHU dripping down the cooker.
06   MUM:  eu:kh hih-hih-hih
07         (1.0)
08   LES:  How are you:?
```

Unlike laughter, which occurs in distinguishable bursts of recognizable sounds that often can be translated into representative letters, disgust sounds are predominantly produced in the throat. Transcribing the sounds as they are produced in line 6 involves using letters to capture non-verbal guttural sounds, and so involves some poetic license, particularly since there is no standard English representation for guttural sounds. This extract is relatively straightforward though, in that it occurs in a telephone conversation, between two participants, without overlap. In the next extract, four roommates are together in a dorm room, talking and looking at their computers and mobile phones. In response to a loud burp produced by Amy at line 6, two participants react with disgust in lines 7–10.

```
D32_8RISp14EC_7-34
01     AMY:      The day that I get entered into the twenty one
02               an-groupchat °I'm gonna be so excited°
03               (0.7)
04     AMY:      One day
05     DON:      One day (.) °dot dot dot°
06     AMY:      ((lifts finger and pulls back head)) E::HEUGH*
07     DON:      [(((turns head away from AMY & screws up face))
08     DON:      [Ogh A[::w Amy::.          ]
09     JEN:            [No::a::uh           ]
10     JEN:          [(((grimaces in disgust))]
11     AMY:      I'm so:rry=
12     DON:      =It makes me wanna throw up.
*Loud burp
```

Jen's grimace in line 10 is noticeable and distinctive in the course of its production. Donna's head movement and disgust sound (lines 7 and 8) are produced immediately after Amy's burp. Jen's grimace and 'No::a::uh' occur in overlap with Donna's response, but start just a little bit later. This may indicate that while Jen's embodied and verbal responses may come off as produced in response to Amy's burp, they may be generated interactionally in response to Donna's response. Their precise production and placement relative to Amy's burp, to Donna's response, and to one another, are important for investigating the interactional construction of disgust.

CONCLUDING COMMENTS

This chapter began by noting the paucity of interactional research focused on episodes of human suffering. Such work as there has been has suggested the benefits of working with a careful transcript, in particular of expressions of upset and pain, in order to begin to make sense of its complex interactional functions.

Speakers routinely incorporate and orient to non-lexical elements of talk, and the study of these elements is still in its infancy. In order to pin down the systematic ways in which these features are achieved, we need to develop advanced transcription skills that exploit the agreed-upon conventions for their representation in our transcripts. One payoff, as various applied studies in conversation analysis and related fields have shown, is that we have examples from everyday materials that facilitate sophisticated discussions with practitioners about their own practices for managing other people's suffering.

TRANSCRIPTION CONVENTIONS INTRODUCED IN THIS CHAPTER

Signs of upset

Sniffs – inhalation, with possible voiced vowels and consonants: °.snih (a quiet nasal sniff). And: .SHHIH (loud 'wet' sniff)

Silence: may be unusually long

Sobbing – sharply inhaled or exhaled – enclose in greater/less than symbols: >huh huh< >.hihh<

Swallowing: can be described in ((transcriber comments)) unless it appears interactionally significant

Where talk is attempted through upset

Elevated pitch – may be unusually high-pitched: ↑↑Yeah

Tremulous or wobbly delivery – enclose in tildes (~): ~THAt wasn' #ma best.#~

Aspiration particles in words: parentheses (h) represent plosive out-breath; h represents 'breathy' delivery

Volume – may be reduced to the point of 'mouthing' or whispering: °°khhay°°

Creaky delivery: represented with #

Staccato delivery: represented with the iteration of a 'cut-off' symbol (e.g., it-is-cut-off-)

Visual features of upset

Facial features: screwed up eyes; tears; downturned mouth with eyebrows drooping down from the middle of the face; flushed appearance especially around the eyes and nose

Bodily elements: trembling face and/or hands; touching eyes or face; looking down/hiding one's face/turning away

Expressions of pain and discomfort

May include elements of upset as described above, often through pain cries, e.g.

Sobbing – sometimes within moans or pain cries: u::(huh)h::

Elevated pitch: OW::: MY:: ↑↑~TOO:TH

Tremulous delivery: ~Don't touch it.~

Creaky delivery: #My tu:mmy hur:ts:.#

Changes in volume – may be reduced or elevated: °°#hurts:°° / OW:::

Stretched delivery: ou::tsch:: ↑O::: ↑↑::::W

Other non-speech sounds

Hysteria – words interspersed or replaced by gasping sounds: we(HHH)-.HHHH we've(HHH) HUHHH

Lip smacks – precede with a period to indicate their inhaled quality: .pl.hh or .kh or .mp[t

Tuts – as with lip smacks precede with a period to indicate their inhaled quality: .tch or .TCH

Throat clear: hkm or mhgmhm or MHGHM! (e.g., to attract attention)

RECOMMENDED READING

For an overview of their research into crying in both mundane and institutional contexts, see:

Hepburn, A. and Potter, J. (2012) Crying and crying responses. In A. Peräkylä and M.-L. Sorjonen (Eds) *Emotion in interaction* (pp. 194–210). Oxford: Oxford University Press.

For the classic work on expressions of pain and their diagnostic work in medical consultations, see:

Heath, C. (1989) Pain talk: The expression of suffering in the medical consultation. *Social Psychology Quarterly, 52*(2), 113–25.

For more contemporary studies on the interactional role of expressions of pain, see:

Jenkins, L. and Hepburn, A. (2015) Children's sensations as interactional phenomena: A conversation analysis of expressions of pain and discomfort. *Qualitative Research in Psychology, 12*(4), 472–91.

Clemente, I. (2009) Progressivity and participation: Children's management of parental assistance in paediatric chronic pain encounters. *Sociology of Health & Illness, 31*(6), 872–88.

To find out more about the concepts discussed in this chapter, see examples of real transcriptions, and test your knowledge through exercises and quizzes, visit the supporting website at
https://study.sagepub.com/hepburnandbolden

SEVEN

Transcribing Visible Conduct

Conversation analytic transcription conventions were developed primarily on audio-recorded data (such as telephone conversations) and, thus, capture interlocutors' vocal conduct. However, the use of video in conversation analytic research, pioneered by Charles Goodwin in the 1970s (C. Goodwin, 1981), is widespread today (see, e.g., Heath et al., 2010 for a recent overview). In face-to-face interactions, participants' visible conduct – including their gestures, eye gaze, body positioning, posture and movement, facial expressions, etc. – can be instrumental to how social actions are accomplished and coordinated, which means that there will be times when it has to be represented on a transcript. In his discussion of issues involved in visual analysis, Goodwin writes:

> The task of translating the situated, embodied practices used by participants in inter-action to organize phenomena relevant to vision poses enormous theoretical and methodological problems. Our ability to transcribe talk is built upon a process of ana-lyzing relevant structure in the stream of speech, and marking those distinctions with written symbols, that extends back thousands of years, and is still being modified today … When it comes to the transcription of visual phenomena we are at the very beginning of such a process. (C. Goodwin, 2000b: 161)

The Jeffersonian transcription conventions for transcribing vocal conduct (discussed in Chapters 2–6) have been widely accepted and used. However, there is currently no one agreed-upon system for transcribing visible conduct. In this chapter, we discuss the main approaches to capturing visible behaviors on a transcript, present a number of relatively well-known transcription systems, and offer guidelines for their use. We also explicate how a detailed examination of visible conduct, facilitated by thorough transcripts of non-vocal behaviors, has contributed to a more nuanced and comprehensive under-standing of social interaction.

The chapter will start with a discussion of basic issues that need to be considered when transcribing visible conduct, such as: What are some fundamental differences between vocal and non-vocal behaviors and how do they impact transcription? We will then pre-sent three main approaches to transcribing non-vocal conduct: transcriber comments, specialized notational systems and visual representations. The chapter will offer sugges-tions on when and how a researcher might adopt one (or several) of these approaches. Additionally, we discuss how the use of a particular transcription system has advanced the study of social interaction.

THE BASICS OF TRANSCRIBING VIDEO-RECORDINGS

Here we introduce some basic issues involved in transcribing visible conduct and provide guidelines for getting started.

Is a picture worth a thousand words?

Although the transcription of both talk and visible behavior is necessarily selective, the transcription of visible behavior is even more so. In fact, no transcript of visible conduct, however detailed, will amount to a complete record of a video-recorded interaction. There are several fairly transparent reasons for this. First, the sheer number of visible behaviors that could potentially be captured on a transcript and the level of detail with which they can be represented are virtually limitless. (As an experiment, try making a comprehensive description of just one frame of a video-recorded face-to-face interaction. You will soon discover that your description is never exhaustively complete or detailed. This problem is of course exacerbated once the video is unfrozen.) Furthermore, unlike talk, which is produced sound bit by sound bit and can, thus, be represented linearly on a transcript with relative ease, visible behaviors occur simultaneously and in overlap with talk. In other words, people can move parts of their bodies, shift direction of their gaze, make facial expressions, etc., all at the same time as they talk or listen to others. This makes a strictly linear transcript difficult, if not impossible. Finally, how *does* one represent all this continuous visible movement in a written form? What form should such a record take? In describing the impossibility of translating a video-recording into a static record, Schegloff notes:

> Still pictures, tracings, stick figures, and the like all lose ... the shape and pace of movement. Discursive description preempts the very analysis the material should bear on contingently ... Quasi-anatomical and topographical descriptions give a false sense of objectivity and precision, and are not the relevant terms of descriptions for the analysis; metaphorical and analogical descriptions 'capture the flavor' but are not detailed accounts; in any case, the reader is disallowed an independent judgment of the adequacy of the account to the materials. (Schegloff, 1984: 294–5)

While all these may seem like insurmountable obstacles to transcription, it is, in fact, possible to produce a *serviceable* transcript of visible conduct, i.e. a written record that will more or less adequately serve the goals of a particular research undertaking. Here, we discuss how and why one may choose a particular transcription system, with the understanding that no transcript can substitute for the data – i.e. a video-recording of the interaction.

······ **EXPERT BOX *10*** ··

How I transcribe embodied interaction and why

Charles Goodwin, University of California, Los Angeles, USA

In the summer of 1973 Gail Jefferson worked with Candy (Marjorie Goodwin) and me to try to develop methods for transcribing the organization of the body in face-to-face conversation. She taped

(Continued)

(Continued)

a clear plastic overhead on the front of a TV monitor and drew an outline of the participants' bodies, faces, gestures and things in the environment that were relevant to their actions. This is, in essence, what I have done ever since (now with the computer). Frame grabs work as well as drawings, but I erase the background to highlight bodies and action.

There are, I believe, powerful reasons for transcribing the body with cartoon-like renderings of interacting bodies rather than linguistic glosses. Despite the pervasive logocentricism of much conversation analysis (a position clearly not shared by Gail), the body in interaction is organized in ways that are quite different from either talk or language. Rather than being discrete and segmental, the units that build embodied action are continuous, frequently frame what is being said rather than contributing to its semantic content, etc. The embodied phenomena that participants attend to are intrinsically heterogeneous and operate on multiple time scales simultaneously.

In face-to-face interaction, both states of talk, and the utterances that emerge within them, are built not through talk alone, but by joining together different kinds of meaning-making practices where the unique properties of each can mutually elaborate the others. Facial displays can inflect what is being said with powerful, transformative stance. The mutual orientation of participants' bodies creates a shared focus of attention where talk, gesture, indexical grounding and other kinds of meaning-making practices can flourish. Speaker's orientation to the silent, but most consequential embodied displays of hearers, can lead to changes in an emerging utterance. Indeed a focus on embodied interaction is too limiting. Typically, participants are also attending to diverse phenomena in the environment: cigarettes, food, hopscotch grids, etc.

I find that words alone are not adequate to present to the reader, or myself, how action in interaction is cooperatively built through the simultaneous orchestration of these very different resources. However, they can be seen with clarity in an analytic sketch that brings into a single visual field both the diverse activities of multiple bodies, and the talk in progress. I also frequently add annotations, creating what Tufte (2006) calls *mapped pictures*, images that simultaneously provide evidence and explanation. The hopscotch dispute in 'Action and embodiment' (Goodwin, 2000c: 1502) provides an example. I call such a transcription (for an example, see Figure 7.1) an analytic sketch because, like the map of a geologist, it is not designed to simply copy what is present, but to clarify, and render visible, the complex organization of the action in progress. Indeed these sketches shape my developing analysis of the sequences I am examining.

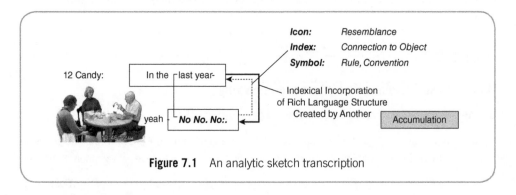

Figure 7.1   An analytic sketch transcription

In working this way I try to continue to develop Gail Jefferson's original vision for how talking, interacting bodies might be transcribed with the clarity necessary for fruitful analysis.

Getting started

When starting to work with a video-recording of an interaction, it is often advisable to first produce a transcript of participants' vocal conduct (following the conventions discussed in Chapters 2–6). There are several reasons for this recommendation. The process of transcribing talk affords the transcriber analytic advantages of close listening and observation (see the discussion in Chapter 1). Further, starting with talk is a relatively easy and quick way into the data, which postpones (more) difficult decisions about representing visible conduct until the researcher has a better grasp of what is analytically important or interesting. Finally, visible behaviors can be subsequently mapped vis-à-vis talk – which is how much of visible bodily conduct appears to be organized (e.g., C. Goodwin, 1981; Kendon, 1972; Rossano, 2012; Schegloff, 1984; Streeck, 1993). While transcribing talk, you may also want to record the most noticeable and obviously consequential non-vocal behaviors; for example, those that replace speech (such as, a head nod in place of a vocal response). The simplest way of doing it would be via transcriber comments in double parentheses (see the discussion below).

As an illustration, see Extract 1, which represents a transcript of a face-to-face interaction, with no information about the participants' bodily conduct. This record gives some sense of what is going on in the conversation and can serve as a starting point for further transcription and analytic work.

(1)

```
Tickets - A transcript of vocal conduct
01  Al:      I tried yesterday: the who:le day, (.)
02           to get tickets for the Van[Gogh]
03  Bob:                                [heh ]heh
04           .h[heh
05  Al:        [°(exhibition)°
06           (0.8)
07  Al:      I am getting cra:zy.
08           (3.8)
09  Al:      But (0.2) the ↑whole ti:me, the
10           telephone number (.) was busy.
11           (1.5)
12  Bob:     Every time?
13  Al:      ↑Every time.
14           (3.5)
15  Al:      It- (.) was: (.) ↑s:o ↑crazy.
```

With this basic record of the interaction in hand, the researcher will decide how to proceed with the transcription task – a decision that will be informed by the stage and the goals of the research project. (We will discuss different transcription systems and what they are most useful for in subsequent sections.) At early, exploratory stages of a project, producing a detailed working transcript of everything one sees can be an especially useful and illuminating exercise (Heath et al., 2010). To do this exercise, choose a very short – ten seconds or less – segment, print out the transcript of the vocal conduct you have created (with ample space between lines), and carefully map what you see onto it. Any sort of notation will do at this stage; it is the level of detail and careful observation that are important. This exercise will allow you to tap into the relationships between talk and non-vocal behaviors. The resulting transcript (what might be called a *working transcript*) will be too complex for public presentation, but is an important analytic step for examining the organization of face-to-face interaction.

A *presentation transcript* that can be effectively shared with others will necessarily be selective. In preparing a presentation transcript, the transcriber will be guided not only by what can be seen on the video, but also by the analytic points being made on the transcript's basis. As Goodwin puts it:

> [A]ny transcription system must attend simultaneously to two separate fields, looking in one direction at how to accurately recover through a systematic notation the endogenous structure of the events being investigated, while simultaneously keeping another eye on the addressee/reader of the analysis by attempting to present relevant descriptions as clearly and vividly as possible. In many cases different stages of analysis and presentation will require multiple transcriptions. There is a recursive interplay between analysis and methods of description. (C. Goodwin, 2000b: 161)

In other words, the process of creating a transcript of visible conduct is intertwined with the process of analysis.

····· **BOX 7.1** ···

Tips for transcribing video

- Prepare short clips of video segments you are interested in. See Chapter 9 for a discussion of useful software for doing this.
- Start by transcribing vocal conduct following the conversation analytic conventions.
- Produce a *working transcript* of visible conduct. You can do this by hand over a printout of the transcript of talk.
- As the analysis develops, consider how to represent visual aspects of interaction in a way that would make your arguments most accessible. *Presentation transcripts* may use a combination of methods discussed in this chapter. The same extract may need to be represented in multiple ways.

···

METHODS FOR TRANSCRIBING VISIBLE CONDUCT

Visible conduct can be captured using three main approaches: (1) via transcriber comments, (2) with specialized notational systems for marking particular visible behaviors (e.g., eye gaze or gestures), and (3) by incorporating visual representations, such as video frame grabs and drawings, into transcripts. These approaches may also be used in combination. Here, we will explicate and illustrate the use of these approaches and discuss their advantages and disadvantages as analytic and presentational tools.

Transcriber comments

Using transcriber comments – in double parentheses – is, perhaps, the simplest and quickest way of transcribing visible conduct. Transcriber comments gloss what can be seen on the video, in more or less detail (as illustrated in Extract 2 below). Of course, what behaviors are selected for glossing and how they are described are products of the analysis. Just as with any transcript of visible conduct, transcriber comments are highly selective, typically highlighting only those aspects of behavior that the researcher deems relevant.

Transcriber comments are typically timed vis-à-vis speech, as in Extract 2. Square brackets can be used to indicate visible conduct that takes place simultaneously with speech (see, for example, line 1). However, in transcripts containing a lot of overlapping talk, the onset of visible behaviors may need to be indicated with different symbols (e.g., asterisks *, or vertical lines |) for better readability. Visible behaviors that occur during silences can also be timed (as in lines 6, 11 and 14). Different fonts (e.g., *italics* or **bold**) can be used to set off talk from descriptions of visible conduct.

(2)

```
Tickets – Transcriber comments

((Al is sitting at the desk, working. Bob is standing a few feet
away, picking up papers to bring to his office))
01  Al:    [I tried yesterday: the who:le day, (.)
           [((Al turns to look at Bob; Bob looks at Al))
02         to get tickets for the Van[Gogh]
03  Bob:                               [heh ]heh
04         .h[heh
05  Al:      [°(exhibition)°
06         (0.8) ((Al turns back towards his desk))
07  Al:    I am getting cra:zy.
08         (3.8) ((Bob walks to his office after 1.8s))
09  Al:    But (0.2) the ↑whole ti:me, the
10         telephone number (.) was busy.
11         (1.5)((Bob walks out of his office and looks at
                Al; Al turns to look at Bob))
```

```
12   Bob:   Every time?
13   Al:    [↑Every time.
            [((lateral headshake))
14          (3.5) ((Al turns to his desk after 1.5s; Bob waits,
                   then starts moving towards his office))
15   Al:    It- (.) was: (.) [↑s:o ↑crazy.
                             [((Bob glances at Al))
16          ((Bob moves into his office; Al works at the desk))
```

The transcriber's overall goal is to make the transcript as readable as possible given the analytic points the transcript is used to make.

Transcriber comments may be a useful tool for representing visible behaviors that are crucial for understanding the interaction when visible conduct and its temporal unfolding are *not* the foci of the analysis. For instance, in a multiparty interaction, participants may rely on gaze to explicitly address and select as a next speaker another interlocutor (Lerner, 2003). Even when addressing is not the primary focus of the analysis, it is a central feature of turn design (see also the discussion of C. Goodwin, 1979, below), which suggests that indicating who is being addressed may be crucial for understanding a particular stretch of interaction. The simplest way to do this is via transcriber comments, as in Extract 3. This segment is from a conversation between four people living in a multi-building complex for the elderly. Hank has been talking about the advantages of the building he had recently moved into (data not shown). At line 1, Betty asks a clarifying question, addressing it via gaze (as well as tacitly; Lerner, 2003) to Hank.

(3)

```
Building D (Coffee chat; 12:15)
1   Betty:   What- what- what [building. ((to Hank))
                             [((Rich turns to Betty))
2            (.)
3   Rich:    D.
4            (0.3)
5   Betty:   D[::? ((to Hank; Rich turns to Hank))
6   Hank:     [Right der.
7   Betty:   That's where I am.
```

Note that (in line 3) Rich intervenes to provide a response even though it is Hank who was selected to do so (Lerner, 2002). Further, in line 5, Betty pursues a response from Hank by initiating repair on Rich's answer (Schegloff et al., 1977). The transcriber comments that indicate who is being addressed via gaze help us (the readers) see that, first, in line 3 Rich responds 'out of turn' (Lerner, 2002); and, second, Betty resists Rich's intervention and continues to address Hank rather than Rich (in line 5), thereby maintaining that Hank has primary epistemic rights to speak to the matter at hand (Bolden, 2011). These interactional dynamics would be invisible on a transcript of vocal behaviors only, and transcriber comments provide readers access to these important features of action design.

A wide range of visible, embodied actions can be transcribed by using transcriber comments, such as head nods and headshakes, shoulder shrugs, eyebrow flashes, etc., all of which play an important role in interaction. For instance, vertical and lateral nods, even without a vocal component, may constitute a conditionally relevant response following a sequence initiating action. This can be seen in Extract 4 taken from a lunch conversation between college students. Candice is moving to an apartment complex where Annabelle lives and is asking Annabelle's opinion on how to deal with various amenities. Just prior to this extract, the women agree that the internet can be split between the apartment mates, and, in line 1, Candice proposes that she can 'do that' for 'ca:ble' as well. In response, Annabelle repeatedly nods (line 3) to indicate her agreement with Candice's proposal. (Annabelle is chewing her food, which probably explains her choice to respond non-vocally.) The nodding starts as Candice repairs her reference from 'ca:ble' to 'cable television' (at line 2) and contin- ues in the following silence, as marked on the transcript. Annabelle then confirms vocally (line 4) and goes on to elaborate on her response (not shown).

(4)

```
Cable (GB07-7; 7:20)
1       C:      I was thinking for ca:ble we could do that too.
2               <F[or cable television? (1.2)]
3 ->    A:        [   (( N o d d i n g ))       ]
4       A:      Mm:.
```

There is ample interactional evidence that speakers closely monitor recipients' non- vocal actions (such as, vertical and lateral headshakes) as they speak and may adjust the turn-in-progress in response to such actions (e.g., M.H. Goodwin, 1980). A clear exam- ple of such adjustment comes from an exchange between a journalist (Tom Brokaw) and 1988 US vice-presidential candidate Dan Quayle during a televised debate (for a full discussion, see Clayman, 2001). Leading up to the following segment, Quayle has been repeatedly attempting to deal with the question about what he would do if he had to assume the office of the president. After several attempts to get away with evasive responses in which Quayle veered off to discuss his qualifications for the position, the following takes place:

(5)

```
US 5 Oct 1988 Bentsen-Quayle Debate (Clayman, 2001: 436)
01 DQ:          ... and I'll try to answer it again for ye.
02              (0.2)
03 DQ:          as clearly as I can.
04 DQ:          (0.6)
05 DQ:          .hh Because the question you're a:sking. (1.3)
06              is <what ki:nd> (0.2) of qua:lifica:tions, .hh
07              [ does Da:n Qua:yle have to be president. (0.5)]
08 JRN: ->      [   (( H e a d s h a k i n g ))                ]
09              (0.5)
```

```
10 DQ:        tch What kind of qualifactions do I have
11            and what would I do:.
12            (1.0)
13 DQ:        in this kind of a situa[tion. (0.4)]
14 JRN: ->                          [((Nodding))]
15 DQ:        And what would I do in this situation, .hh
16            I would (1.9) make sure. (2.1) that the people
17            in the cabinet, ...
```

In lines 1–7, Quayle makes another attempt to shift the agenda of the question from his plans for assuming the office of the president to discussing his qualifications for the presidency. On hearing where Quayle is going with his response, the journalist starts shaking his head laterally and continues shaking his head through the possible completion of the turn constructional unit in progress (line 8). The headshaking conveys the journalist's rejection of Quayle's attempt to evade the question yet again. Quayle's monitoring of the journalist's visible behavior is evident when he abandons his attempt to evade the question and returns to the question's agenda at lines 11–13. When he does, the journalist nods in approval (line 14), and Quayle continues to respond to the question he'd been asked. Note that without marking the journalist's conduct on the transcript, the dynamics of Quayle's response would be completely opaque.

Head nods and headshakes are distinctive forms of recipient uptake. For instance, M.H. Goodwin (1980) showed that, when producing evaluative descriptive statements, speakers treat recipient head nods as simply acknowledging the information (and thus as insufficient uptake to an evaluation) and treat lateral headshakes as displays of appreciation and agreement. Furthermore, as Stivers (2008) argues, in story-telling episodes, nods by recipients are treated differently from vocal continuers (such as, 'mm hm'). In a middle of a story, vocal continuers by story recipients may display alignment with the activity of telling, but not affiliation with the teller's stance. In contrast, as Stivers shows, in the same sequential environment, recipients' nods claim affiliation with the teller's expressed position. These findings point to many complex ways in which recipients' non-vocal conduct informs the production of talk and indicate the necessity of representing such behaviors in transcripts.[1]

As we have seen, transcriber comments allow the transcriber to indicate the rough timing of visible behaviors vis-à-vis talk. However, only limited information about how visible behaviors unfold incrementally over time can be effectively presented in this way. While expedient, these comments are not flexible enough tools to indicate gradual unfolding of visible behaviors; for example, the movement of eye gaze from one direction to another; the beginning of a gesture, its hold and release, etc. Thus, researchers may need to supplement (or replace) transcriber comments with more sophisticated methods for capturing visible conduct.

---

[1]For a discussion of interactional functions of head nods by the speaker, see Aoki (2011). Aoki uses upward (↗) and downward (↘) arrows above talk to indicate head movements and colons (e.g., ↘::) to indicate slow movement.

Using specialized notational systems

Specialized notational systems – such as those developed for eye gaze and gesture – are designed to capture details of how a particular visible behavior gradually unfolds over time. While quite difficult to implement and read, specialized notational systems may be required when the precise unfolding and coordination of visible behaviors is the focus of the research. Here we discuss several notation systems for representing gaze and gesture that are relatively commonly used by social interaction researchers.

Transcribing eye gaze

Probably the most commonly used system for transcribing eye gaze is the one developed by Charles Goodwin in the 1970s during his work on the role of gaze in the organization of speaker and hearer activities (C. Goodwin, 1981). Goodwin's notation system indicates not only the *direction* of the gaze once it reaches its target (e.g., another interlocutor) – which can be quite easily done through transcriber comments, as in Extract 2 above – but also the *movement* of gaze towards and away from the target. In other words, the system emphasizes and brings to light the temporal organization of eye gaze. Further, it is designed to indicate both the speaker's and the recipient's gaze directions by reference to the speaker's talk. The basic conventions are summarized in Box 7.2.

------- **BOX 7.2** ....

Goodwin's conventions for transcribing gaze (adapted from C. Goodwin, 1981)

Speaker's gaze is marked with a line above (‾‾) the transcribed utterance. Recipient's gaze is marked with a line below (__) the utterance. A transcript of an interaction between two people will look like this (re-transcribed from Extract 2):

```
01      Al:      .... X_____
                 I tried yesterday: the who:le day, (-)
        Bob:          . X_____
```

Dots (....) indicate a movement that brings the participant's gaze to the interlocutor. X is placed where the gaze reaches its target. The transcript above thus shows that the speaker Al moves to look at Bob as he (i.e. Al) starts talking, his gaze reaching Bob at the end of the word 'tried'. The recipient Bob moves to look at Al at the very end of 'tried', his gaze quickly reaching Al on the first sound of 'yesterday'. From that point on, Al and Bob continue to look at each other.

Goodwin's conventions also mark a movement of gaze away from the target via commas (,,,), as in line 5 below:

```
02      Al:      _____
                 to get tickets for the Van[Gogh.]
        Bob:     _____
```

(Continued)

(Continued)

```
03                                              [heh ] heh

04                   .h[heh

05      Al:         _____ ''''
                    [°(exhibition)°  (- -)
        Bob:        _____

06      Al:
                    I am getting cra:zy.
        Bob:        _____
```

At line 5, Al moves his gaze away from Bob (see the commas), while Bob continues to look at Al (as shown by the line). In line 6, while saying 'I am getting cra:zy' Al continues to *not* look at Bob (as indicated by the absence of the line above the utterance).

Because gaze shifts may occur during silence, silences are often indicated via dashes (-) rather than numerically: each dash marks a tenth of a second silence. For silences longer than a second, a plus sign (+) is used at each second. Here is a representation of a 3.8 second silence that follows:

```
07              (----------+---------+---------+--------)
        Al:
        Bob:     _''                  .X_,
```

In line 7, Al is looking away from Bob throughout. In the beginning of this silence, Bob continues to look at Al, then looks away. Just over a second later, Bob again briefly glances at Al.

When transcribing a multiparty interaction, the name of the person gazed at appears above the line that indicates gaze. Further, each recipient (or subset of recipients) is shown on a separate line below the speaker. The following is a conversation between three participants (A, B and C). A is speaking, primarily addressing her talk via gaze to C; C continues to look at A throughout this excerpt; B looks at A during the silence at line 2:

```
1       A:     C_____
               he's a chihuahua
        B:
        C:     A_____

2       A:     ''                              .C___
               but he's- this (--------) like wi:de.
        B:                            . A_____
        C:     A_____
```

At line 2, the speaker (A) looks away from C to the gesture she is making while speaking. Goodwin's standard notations can be slightly modified to indicate this:

```
2       A:     ,,Gesture_____  .C___
               but he's- this (--------) like wi:de.
```

```
B:                              . A _____
C:        A _____
```

Goodwin (C. Goodwin, 1981) occasionally uses other symbols, such as, Θ for a 'mid-distance' look. He also provides descriptions of visible behaviors (e.g., 'eyebrow flash') when analytically necessary.

Goodwin writes that his 'decision to describe gaze in terms of the speaker–hearer framework is itself a major analytic one, and by no means simple, neutral description' (C. Goodwin, 2000b: 161). As with any transcription system, Goodwin's approach to transcribing gaze carries with it a number of theoretical assumptions, of which the transcriber should be aware. First, it implies that gaze by speakers and recipients is temporally organized by reference to talk and, specifically, by reference to talk within an utterance (or turn-constructional unit) in progress. Second, it suggests that minute changes in gaze direction – beginnings of movements towards and away from the target – are analytically important. Third, because the system is primarily designed to indicate gaze at other *interlocutors* (though this can be altered, as shown in Box 7.2), it foregrounds the analytic importance of two basic values for gaze: gazing *at* and *away* from the speaker/recipient. This 'speaker–hearer' framework backgrounds other gaze configurations, such as gazing at someone's gestures or at objects in the environment. (In his later work, Charles Goodwin shifts away from using this transcription system to transcripts that incorporate visual representations, as discussed below and in Expert Box 10.)

While widely adopted, Goodwin's is not the only system that has been used for transcribing eye gaze. More recently, Rossano (2012) developed an alternative approach for transcribing gaze (see Box 7.3 for an explication of Rossano's conventions). Rossano's system is designed for dyadic interaction. It makes use of iconic representations, meant to be easily interpretable by a reader. Rossano's conventions are designed to convey a lot of information about where participants are looking when they are not looking at their co-interlocutors: e.g., away, at objects, eye closing, etc. Further, unlike Goodwin's conventions, Rossano's system does not systematically decompose gaze movement (towards, at, away), though it is possible to represent such movements as well.

···· **BOX 7.3** ···

Rossano's conventions for transcribing eye gaze (adapted from Rossano, 2012; Rossano et al., 2009)

Rossano uses a large set of symbols, which can be further extended to account for more gaze configurations. Extract 6 illustrates the use of these conventions. Note that similarly to Goodwin's system, the gaze is timed vis-à-vis talk, and dashes are used to represent silences.

(Continued)

(Continued)

(6)

Tickets – Rossano's conventions

```
01  Al:  I tried yesterday: the who:le day, (.)

02       to get tickets for the Van[Gogh]
03  Bob:                       [heh ] heh
04       .h[heh

05  Al:  º(exhibition)º (- -)

06  Al:  I am getting cra:zy.

07       (- - - - - - - - x- - - - - - - - - - - x - - - - - - - - x

         - - - - - - -)
          (3.8)

08  Al:  But (0.2) the ↑who̲le ti:me,

09       the telephone number (.) was busy.
```

While some of the symbols are transparently iconic, many do need an explication. Here is how Rossano explains the symbols used in this transcript:

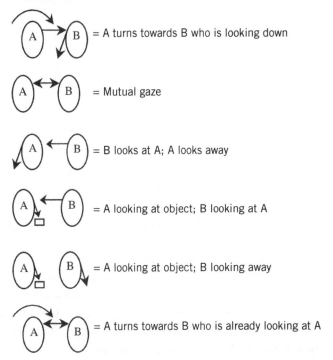

= A turns towards B who is looking down

= Mutual gaze

= B looks at A; A looks away

= A looking at object; B looking at A

= A looking at object; B looking away

= A turns towards B who is already looking at A

In lines 7–9, another symbol was used, which is not part of Rossano's set:

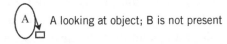

A looking at object; B is not present

The fact that the transcriber can easily supplement the symbols as necessary illustrates the flexibility of the conventions.

Why should we transcribe eye gaze?

Goodwin's and Rossano's conventions for representing eye gaze facilitate the analysis of the coordination of gaze and talk, and the coordination of gaze between the participants (for a review, see Rossano, 2013). For example, by using a detailed transcript of gaze movement by speaker and recipients, Goodwin (C. Goodwin, 1979) demonstrated that a single sentence may be constructed incrementally as the speaker shifts his gaze from one recipient to another, thus changing the addressed recipient of his talk. In the following extract from a dinner conversation between two couples, John and Beth and their guests Don and Anna, John makes an announcement, initially addressing it to Don (line 1). Don is a proper recipient of the announcement, as the announcement can be expected to inform John of something he does not know.

(7)

Adapted from C. Goodwin (1979):

```
1       John:       ....,,.........Don,,          Don_____
                    I gave, I gave up smoking cigarettes::.=
        Don:                                  .._____

2       Don:        =Yea:h,

3       John:       ..... Beth_____ ... Ann_____
                    1-uh: one-one week ago t'da:y. acshilly,
        Beth:
        Ann:                   . . . . .  Beth  , . . . .John

4       Ann:        Rilly? en y'quit fer good?
```

Goodwin shows that the subsequent development of the announcement cannot be properly understood without tracking the participants' gazes. Note that Don's response to the announcement (line 2) is rather minimal, as it does not take what is being announced as news. At line 3, John moves his gaze from Don to Beth, making her the addressed recipient. As his wife, however, Beth is a 'knowing' recipient. To compensate for the problem, John recasts the announcement of the event (giving up cigarettes) into an announcement of a one-week anniversary of the event. This is accomplished by replacing 'l-' (projecting something like 'last week') with 'one-one week ago t'da:y' (in line 3), as John's gaze reaches Beth. Beth, however, is otherwise preoccupied and does not reciprocate John's gaze. In search of an attending recipient, John shifts his gaze from Beth to Ann (line 3) while extending his turn further with 'actually' so that by the time the turn is possibly complete, the speaker is gazing at the gazing (and thus attentive) recipient. The addition of 'actually' again transforms the emergent meaning of the announcement: 'the discovery of the anniversary is transformed into a report about it' (C. Goodwin, 1979: 111) which can be appropriately received by an 'unknowing' recipient.

Goodwin (C. Goodwin, 1980) also showed that, during the course of a turn constructional unit, speakers can use phrasal breaks – such as restarts and pauses – to get a non-gazing recipient to bring her gaze to the speaker. For instance, at line 1 of Extract 7 (repeated below), John begins to turn his gaze towards Don (indicated by dots) and then, seeing a non-gazing recipient, quickly withdraws his gaze (see the commas) and restarts his utterance ('I gave, I gave up ...') while again shifting gaze to Don. This eventually succeeds in getting the recipient's (Don's) gaze:

```
1       John:   ....,,.........Don,,          Don_____
                I gave, I gave up smoking cigarettes::.=
        Don:                              .._____
```

A careful transcript of gaze movement, and its analysis by reference to talk, brings this aspect of conversational organization to light.

Speaker and recipient gazing behavior is important not only for how a turn at talk is constructed (as Goodwin's work discussed above demonstrates), but also for how courses of actions unfold. For instance, research by Rossano (2012) has shown that gaze plays an important role in how participants negotiate the closure of conversational activities and courses of action. Specifically, gaze withdrawal promotes sequence closure while interlocutors' failure to withdraw gaze leads to an expansion of the ongoing activity (Rossano, 2013). Furthermore, Stivers and Rossano (2010) suggest that a speaker may deploy gaze to pressure the gazed-at recipient to provide a response in situations where such a response might not be understood as conditionally relevant. Gaze may also be used to pursue a conditionally relevant but missing response (Rossano, 2013), as in the following extract. Extract 8 is taken from a dinner conversation between Kim and Mark, who are sitting at a table, at a 90-degree angle from each other. At line 1, Kim launches a new topic, asking Mark about plans for the weekend. While the question is being formulated, Mark picks up his glass (line 1) and starts drinking from it immediately upon the question's completion (line 2). This leads to the development of a long silence (line 2). About 2.2 seconds into the silence, Kim raises her gaze and turns from the plate in front of her to Mark on her right. She finds Mark drinking from his glass. As he is drinking, Mark looks straight ahead, not directly at Kim, but Kim is in his line of vision. Soon after Kim's gaze reaches Mark, he shrugs (while swallowing a mouthful of milk), which provides a non-verbal response to Kim's question, and she looks back down. Subsequently (lines 3–5), Mark elaborates on his answer. Note that Kim's gaze is transcribed here using Goodwin's conventions (see Box 7.2).

(8)
```
Sunday (Ravioli dinner 21:25)
01  Kim:      So [>wha'd'ya wanna do< on Sunday.
    Mark:        [((reaches for glass; raises glass))
02               [(2.0) (---------[x---------x[--)
    Kim:                      .._____,,
    Mark:        [((drinks))        [((shrugs)) [((puts glass down))
03  Mark:     It's up tuh you.
04            (0.5)
05  Mark:     tlk ich=yur weekend honey,
```

The transcript of participants' gaze – as well as of their other relevant embodied conduct – makes it possible for the reader to see that gaze is deployed in pursuit of a response.

Gaze also plays an important role in implementing a variety of social actions. In fact, Kidwell (2005, 2009) shows that gaze may implement different actions depending not only on its target (i.e. who is being looked at), but also on its duration and context of occurrence. Examining interactions between caregivers and very young children in a day-care setting, Kidwell (2005) demonstrates, for example, that both adults and children distinguish between 'a mere look' and 'the look': 'a mere look' is a quick glance by the caregiver towards the child produced concurrently with other activities; 'the look', on the other hand, is a relatively long, sustained gaze at the child produced as a discrete activity. Kidwell showed that these two different ways of looking are treated differently. When directed at a child engaged in some potentially sanctionable conduct (e.g., hitting another child), 'a mere look' prefigures no further action by the caregiver (and can, thus be 'ignored' by the child) while 'the look' projects intervention and may result in the child stopping the misbehavior. Kidwell (2005) provides detailed transcripts of gaze and other visible conduct (using a combination of Goodwin's notation symbols, transcriber comments and visual representations) in order to explicate the distinctive features of different looking practices and their interactional consequences.

Transcribing hand gestures

It is widely accepted that gestures are communicative and play an important role in the formation of social actions in interaction (e.g., Kendon, 1994; McNeill, 1992; Streeck, 2009). As with other visible conduct, gestures are not easy to represent on a printed page in ways that are both analytically useful and accessible (Kendon, 1994). A number of different approaches to transcribing gesture have been in use: some researchers rely on simple glosses (as discussed in the section on transcriber comments); some deploy more or less complex gesture codification schemes (e.g., McNeill, 1992) and specialized transcription symbols; some use visual representations (often in combination with other methods). The choice of a particular way to represent gesture is guided, first of all, by goals of the research project (e.g., is this a study of gesture or a study of some other aspects of interaction in which gestures are used?). Further, different notation systems embody different understandings of what aspects of gesture are analytically important. More complex systems take into account not only the gesture form (i.e. the shape of the gesturing hand(s)), but also how (and where) the hand is moving as a gesture is being produced. Transcription systems will vary depending on how precisely the hand shape and the movement are analyzed and codified (see, for example, Kendon, 2004; McNeill, 1992; Streeck, 2009). Here we only describe two relatively simple systems for transcribing gesture used by interaction researchers: Streeck's and Kendon's. Readers are also encouraged to look at Schegloff's (1984) conventions, which attempt to capture details of gesture production without reliance on visual representations, and Mondada's (2007b) conventions, which offer a relatively easy way to represent simultaneous gestures and other visible actions of multiple participants (see Expert Box 11).

········ **BOX 7.4** ··

Streeck's conventions for transcribing gesture (adapted from Streeck, 1993, 1994, 2009)

Streeck uses a relatively simple, but expandable notation system for representing gesture in relation to speech. In its simplest form, horizontal square brackets with a descriptive label are placed above the utterance to represent the duration of gesture and its shape. The label 'identifies either the type of motion or the assumed meaning-in-context of the gesture' (Streeck, 2009: 314). For example, in the following Annabelle uses her hands to show the size of her dog (a Chihuahua):

(9)

```
Chihuahua (GB07-7; 19:10)
1      A:      like he's a chihuahua

                            two palms
                  ┌─────────────────────────┐
2      A:      but he's- this (--------) like wi:de.
```

Streeck also uses visual representations of gestures instead of – or to supplement – the labels in some of the transcripts.

This basic notation can be further detailed to represent more granular information about hand movement. For instance, 'o' may be used to represent movement peaks or beats (Streeck, 1994). Here, Annabelle does two beats with her hands in time with 'this' and 'wi:de':

```
                      o   two palms         o
                  ┌─────────────────────────┐
2      A:      but he's- this (--------) like wi:de.
```

If a gesture is temporarily 'frozen', dots in the gesture bracket can be used to indicate that. For instance, in the following example, Brat initiates a 'fist bump' gesture with Chris (line 4). Brat quickly moves into position (while saying 'thank you,') and then holds his fist as he waits for Chris's responsive gesture. Here, 'x' is used to mark a place where the two fists touch. Chris's fist gesture is marked below the utterance:

(10)

```
Freaks and Geeks (MP 3Guys-1; 12:40)

1      B:      But noone remembers freaks an' geeks:.
2              (0.2)
3      C:      I: remember freaks an' geeks.

                            fist bump
                  ┌─────────── . . . . . . . . . . . . x ───────┐
4      B:      Thank you,=they had a marathon of it last weekend,
       C:                        └────────── x ──────┘
```

The notation can be further expanded to indicate participants' gaze at the gesture. This is done by adding a line of tildes (~~~) (Streeck, 1993), as in the following:

(11)

```
Chihuahua (GB07-7; 19:10)
```

(Continued)

(Continued)

```
                          o   two palms              o
                 ┌────────────────────────────────────────┐
                 │~~~~~~~~~~~~~~~~~~~~~~~~~~~~~~~~~~~~~~~~~  │
                 │                                         │
2      A:        but he's- this (--------) like wi:de.

       B:                          .~ A_____
```

The tilde line above the utterance represents the speaker's gaze at the gesture. A recipient's gaze may also be shown. In the above, Beth glances at Annabelle's gesture (represented by ~) and then shifts her gaze to Annabelle (represented by A).

....

······· **BOX 7.5** ··

Kendon's conventions for transcribing gesture (adapted from Kendon, 2004)

While it is possible to use Streeck's conventions for representing different aspects of gesture movement (e.g., gesture peaks and freezes), they do not embody a clear conceptualization of a pathway a gesture takes – which can be seen as either its strength (allowing the researcher maximal freedom) or a weakness (lack of systematicity). In contrast, Kendon's transcription system is much more focused on a step-by-step representation of the temporal unfolding of a gesture. Kendon conceptualizes the gesture trajectory as having several phases, each indicated separately on a transcript in relation to speech:

- the preparation phase (marked with ~~~), during which the hand (or hands) get into position ready to produce a gesture;
- the stroke (***), the main movement recognizable as the gesture; and
- the recovery (-.-.-.), during which the hand is returned to rest position.

Gesture may also be frozen after the stroke (the post-stroke hold, marked by ***) rather than returned to rest. Further, if the stroke has more than one action unit, a slash will be used to separate them (**/**). All of these phases, from the moment the hand begins to travel from a rest position and till it returns to rest, together constitute a gesture unit (its beginning and end are marked by l). Kendon supplements these transcription conventions with drawings (and detailed descriptions) that capture the shape and movement of the hand(s) during gesticulation, but – with a few exceptions – does not attempt to represent the shape of gesture on the transcript.

Here is a Kendon-style transcription of the 'Chihuahua' segment we saw before (as Extract 9):

(12)

```
Chihuahua (GB07-7; 19:10)
1      A:        like he's a chihuahua
                 |~~~~~~~~~~~~~~~~~
2      A:        but he's- this (--------) like wi:de. (--)
                 ~*********/******************/**-.-.-.|
```

As this transcript shows, Annabelle starts preparing for her gesture well ahead of its production. As she begins saying 'he's a chihuahua' (line 1), she raises her hands from her lap underneath the table (where they were resting) in position above the table where they are visible to others. The two beats of the gesture are indicated by the dashes (line 2). Immediately upon saying 'wi:de' (line 2), Annabelle lowers her hands back into her lap.

Student question: Why should we transcribe details of how people gesture?

Answer: Gestural transcription systems used by interaction researchers (such as those discussed above) highlight the fact that gestures are closely coordinated with talk and point to the processes of mutual elaboration involved in the formation of social actions. Close observations of timing of gestures vis-à-vis talk represented by these transcription systems have uncovered some interesting relationships between the two modalities. For example, the stroke (or the acme) of some types of gestures – specifically, iconic gestures that depict aspects of talk and pointing gestures that locate something in the environment – typically precedes their lexical affiliates (Kendon, 1980; Schegloff, 1984; Streeck, 1993). This can be seen in Extract 12: the speaker's hands are in position to show how wide her dog is well before the description 'this wide' is produced. The gesture here is a key component of the action: it complements what is being said, demonstrating for recipients how wide 'this wide' is (cf. C. Goodwin, 2003a). As Schegloff (1984) argues, the early gesture production 'prepares the scene' for the talk to come, while the subsequent talk retrospectively renders the gesture contextually coherent (p. 291). On the other hand, beat gestures (repetitive rhythmic hand movements) are timed to coincide with the stress in the stream of talk. For instance, as seen in Extract 12, the speaker doesn't hold her hands steady (in 'this wide' position) but rather thrusts them in time with the stress of 'this' and on 'wi:de' (line 2).

Streeck's conventions (Box 7.4) also highlight the relationships between gesture and participants' eye gaze. It has been shown that gestures can be used to coordinate mutual orientation and recipients' visual attention (C. Goodwin, 1986). For instance, while recipients may avert their eye gaze when the speaker is engaged in a self-groom (e.g., touching her face, hair, etc.) (M.H. Goodwin and Goodwin, 1986), they tend to shift their gaze to look at the speaker's gestures (Heath, 1992; Streeck, 1994). This is particularly true when speakers themselves turn to gaze at their own gestures, thereby highlighting their relevance to the interaction (Streeck, 1993). This can be seen in Extract 13, which combines Streeck's conventions for transcribing gesture and Goodwin's conventions for transcribing gaze. Annabelle, the speaker, looks at her own hands as she produces the gesture (line 2), directing the recipients' attention to them as well. One of the recipients, Beth, has been looking down at her plate (lines 1–2). However, in line 2, following disfluencies in Annabelle's talk (a cut-off of 'he's-' and the pause after 'this'), Beth raises her gaze to look at the gesture and then the speaker.

(13)

```
Chihuahua  (GB07-7;  19:10)

1    A:        C_____
               like he's a chihuahua
     B:
     C:        A_____


                        o   two palms          o
               ┌───────────────────────────────────┐
               │~~~~~~~~~~~~~~~~~~~~~~~~~~~~~~~~~~~~~ │
               │                                    │
2    A:        but he's- this (--------) like wi:de.

     B:                              .~ A_____
     C:        A_____
```

Research on gesture in interaction, facilitated by its detailed transcription, has demonstrated the importance of gesture in a range of conversational activities, including negotiation of speaking turns (Mondada, 2007b), the organization of word searches (M.H. Goodwin, 1983; M.H. Goodwin and Goodwin, 1986), and processes through which understandings are negotiated (e.g., C. Goodwin, 2000a; Jones and Zimmerman, 2003; Streeck, 1994). Recently, Lerner and Raymond (e.g., Raymond and Lerner, 2014) have described the underlying organization of embodied conduct (including – but not limited to – gestures and manual actions) by exploring how interlocutors adjust their actions (e.g., by accelerating or decelerating their movement) to deal with various sorts of 'trouble' or to manage their involvement in concurrent activities.

········ **EXPERT BOX 11** ···

Multimodal transcription and the challenges of representing time

Lorenza Mondada, University of Basel, Switzerland and
University of Helsinki, Finland

Transcribing video-recordings in a way that captures and documents the multimodal details (such as language, gesture, facial expressions, gaze, body positions, movements, and object manipulations) while preserving their relevant complexity is a challenge that raises conceptual, analytical and technical issues. These depend on the conception we have of time and sequentiality, as well as on how we treat the situated relevance of multimodal resources and their specific temporalities. They also concern the way we analyze and interpret the emergence, trajectory and projections of these resources. All this impinges upon the way we represent them within a coherent, robust and adequate system of conventions.

The conventions I have developed aim at making available for analysis the multiple relevant multimodal details mobilized and oriented to by participants in achieving their actions. Temporality is crucial in this respect, since it displays when a resource is mobilized in relation to others (most often earlier or later than them), when it progressively emerges (for example, the preparation of a gesture, the change of direction of the gaze, an incipient movement), when it is withdrawn, and how

```
1  FAC    &ou*i?& %*tout l`monde est+ d'a+cc#ord*? ça?Δ à* peu près +là &d`+ssus?+&#
          yes? everybody is agreeing? (about) that? roughly about that?
          &nods-&                                                    &nods-----&
              *.....*circular gesture w both hands*,,,,,,,*
              %looks on his right-->
   blo    >>looks at FAC----------------------------------Δlooks around--->
   nor                            +....+looks at FAC--------------+nods--+,,,,,+
                                  fig.1
```

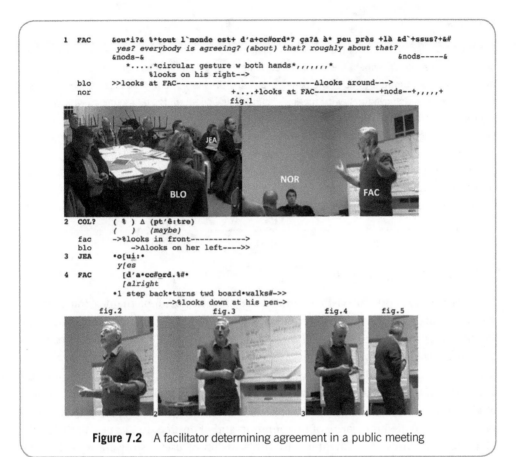

```
2  COL?   ( % ) Δ (pt'ê:tre)
          (   )   (maybe)
   fac    ->%looks in front------------>
   blo         ->Δlooks on her left---->>
3  JEA    •o[ui:•
          y[es
4  FAC    [d'a•cc#ord.%#•
          [alright
          •1 step back•turns twd board•walks#->>
                  -->%looks down at his pen->
       fig.2                 fig.3                fig.4        fig.5
```

Figure 7.2   A facilitator determining agreement in a public meeting

it is responded to in various ways. This grounds the annotation system: each embodied action is delimited left and right by symbols indicating its beginning and end (as well as its preparation and retraction) and is precisely coordinated with the others – inclusive of talk.

The conventions are illustrated in several papers (see Mondada, 2016) and explained in a tutorial available online (Mondada, 2001). To illustrate them and the issues they respond to, the fragment (Figure 7.2) shows how a facilitator in a public meeting checks the agreement of the participants with a previous idea, before turning to the board behind him, in order to write the agreed-upon proposal.

The facilitator responds to a participant, BLOndin, who made the proposal, with a nod and a *yes?* (line 1) and immediately checks the audience's agreement: his TCU (*everybody is agreeing?*) co-occurs with a circular gesture made with both hands (emerging shortly before – as indicated by .... – and retracting on the demonstrative – as indicated by ,,,,) and a gaze first on his right (line 1), then in front of him (line 2). This TCU is incrementally expanded, first with a demonstrative, then an extra increment: the gesture does not continue on them, but the gaze is maintained on the right, continuing to inspect the audience, until a participant (NORren) looks at him (fig. 1) and nods. At this point, the facilitator's turn is completed with a responding nod and he looks again frontally at the audience

(Continued)

(Continued)

(fig. 2). BLOndin – as author of the proposal – monitors the audience too, and turns to the area where two persons respond (JEAnnet, line 3, and COLay, line 2). This is treated as a good enough agreement by the facilitator, who now turns to the board, projecting the inscription of the agreed-upon proposal. This movement is achieved first with the lower part of his body turning and stepping away, while his gaze is still maintained on the audience (fig. 3) – orienting to possible late (dis)agreements – before he looks at the inscription tool (the pen, fig. 4) and definitively closes that sequence, walking away and projecting the inscription implementing the agreement (fig. 5).

The transcript shows how the intricate temporalities of various multimodal layers (turns at talk, gaze, gesture, walk ...) are methodically coordinated and responded to. The emerging, interactionally and reflexively organized multiple temporalities are at the core of the multimodal organization of sequentiality.

Using visual representations

Another way to represent visible conduct on paper is to supplement a transcript of vocal conduct with visual representations, such as digital video frames and drawings. When compared to the other methods we have discussed (i.e. transcriber comments and specialized notational systems), visual representations have the advantages of being easily interpretable and more holistic in representation, giving readers an easy access to multiple modalities involved in carrying out embodied actions (e.g., Streeck et al., 2011a). With the advent of digital video, video frame grabs can be quite easily produced and edited for clarity of presentation and, if desired, to disguise participants' identifiable features. (See Chapter 9 for a discussion of useful software tools for producing frame grabs from a digital video clip and for photo-editing stills.) Furthermore, digital stills from the video-recording can be selected to capture, with a high degree of precision, temporal unfolding of visible conduct in coordination with talk. In addition to – or in place of – frame grabs, hand drawings of gestures, material objects that are being used, or participants can also be integrated into a transcript.

Extract 14 illustrates the use of video frame grabs to supplement a transcript (see Figure 7.3). When incorporating video representations into a transcript, make sure to indicate how the representation relates to the transcript temporally. This can be done by, for example, embedding the pictures into the transcript of vocal conduct or by inserting references to the pictures (as in this example). Note that frames can be cropped to focus on particular aspects of the video.

(14)

```
Tickets - Transcript with frame grabs
((A is on the left; B on the right))
            ⇓1      ⇓2    ⇓3
01    A:    I tried yesterday: the who:le day, (.)
02             to get tickets for the Van[Gogh]
```

```
03      B:                                    [heh ] heh
04              .h[heh
05      A:        [°(exhibition)°

                ⇓4
06              (0.8)
07      A:      I am getting cra:zy.
                        ⇓5
08              (----------+---------+---------+-------)
```

Frame grabs can be edited and embedded into the transcript, as in Extract 15 (Figure 7.4) (from Bolden, 2003). Here, eye gaze is represented visually and in relation to the vocal conduct. Additionally, other visible aspects, such as body orientations, gestures, and the surrounding environment, can be seen and taken into an account.

When material objects become relevant to the interaction, the transcriber may need to represent them as well. Extract 16 (Figure 7.5) (from Bolden, 2003) attempts to capture Bob's manipulation of the machine he's talking about.

Note that Extracts 15 and 16 represent the same stretch of interaction but selectively highlight different aspects of the participants' visible conduct. This illustrates the fact that decisions about how to present visual data (at conferences and in publications) have

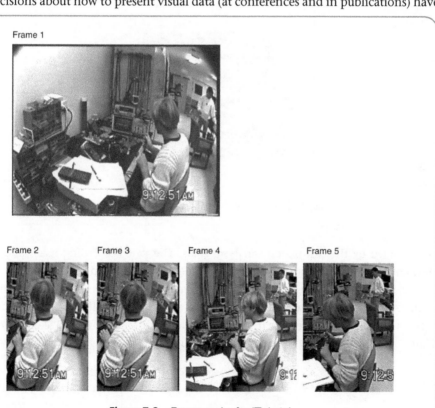

Figure 7.3 Frame grabs for 'Tickets'

(15)

Belt (WB17)
((Alex is on the left; Bob on the right))

```
1    Bob:          The problem with it like- (0.4)
2                  we had it (0.8) no:w      (0.6) i:s (0.2)
3                  we only ha:ve
```

(1.0)

```
4  →  Alex:   tangential.
```

```
5                   (0.5)
6     Alex:   (punch)=
```

Figure 7.4   Embedding frames into the transcript

to be guided by the researchers' analytic goals. The video-recording itself, and not its inevitably selective transcript, has to remain the object of the analysis.

It is possible to edit the video grabs (or, alternatively, to use hand drawings) to disguise the identities of the participants. For instance, the following is the transcript of the 'Chihuahua' segment that uses frame grabs edited with AKVIS Sketch[2] software (Figure 7.6) (see Chapter 9 for further discussion).

---

[2]Available here: http://akvis.com/en/sketch/index.php

(16)

```
Belt (WB17)
1     Bob:          The problem with it like- (0.4)

2                   we had it (0.8) no:w    (0.6) i:s (0.2)
```

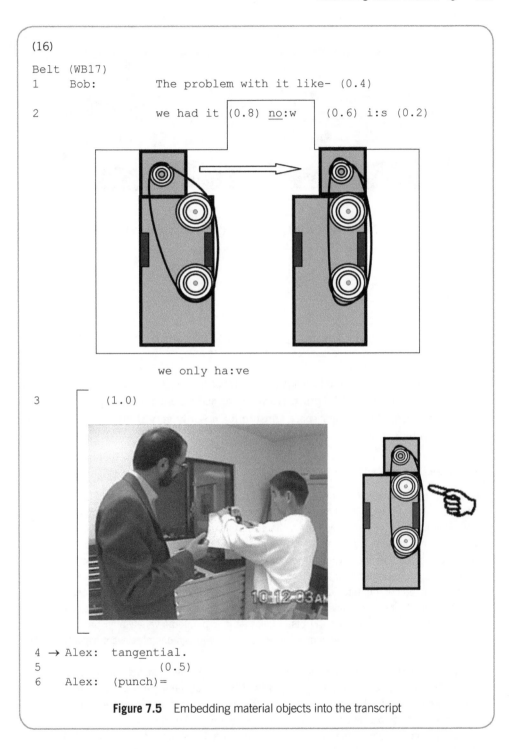

```
                    we only ha:ve

3                   (1.0)


4  → Alex:   tangential.
5                   (0.5)
6     Alex:   (punch)=
```

Figure 7.5 Embedding material objects into the transcript

Frame 1   Frame 2

Figure 7.6 Editing video grabs to disguise participant identities

(17)

```
Chihuahua
1       A:       like he's a chihuahua

2                but he's- this (0.8) like wi:de.
                 ⇑1                         ⇑2
```

Visual representations are sometimes the most accessible way of representing video data in public presentations and in print. However, as seen from the examples above, this way of representing data is very space consuming, so only very short transcripts can be included in publications.

> **Student question:** Why should we include visual representations in transcripts?
>
> **Answer:** In recent years, researchers concerned with embodied aspects of social interaction have used various types of visual representations (sometimes in combination with other approaches discussed in this chapter) to present their work at conferences and in writing (for a recent collection of such work, see Streeck et al., 2011b). Visual representations are particularly valuable when participants in interaction use material resources around them or when aspects of the environment become relevant to how the interaction unfolds. For instance, Goodwin (C. Goodwin, 2003a) examined multiple semiotic resources involved in producing and understanding pointing gestures. The analysis was enabled by transcripts of talk that incorporated a variety of visual representations (such as, edited video frame grabs and photographs of relevant aspects of the environment).
>
> Researchers concerned with interactional aspects of embodied conduct have also used visual representations. For instance, Schegloff's (1998a) work on the role of body torque in the organization of action sequences includes frame grabs that document participants' body movements across a sequence. (You can see the use of the body torque by tracking A's body positioning across the five frame grabs in Figure 7.3.) Seo and Koshik's (2010) research on gestural initiation of repair uses frame grabs to demonstrate how facial expressions and head movements can be deployed to display confusion.

CONCLUDING COMMENTS

Transcription of non-vocal conduct is constantly evolving. As researchers pose new questions about the organization of social interaction, they develop new ways of representing interaction – and their analysis of it – on paper. For example, in her work on collaborative turn construction, Iwasaki (2011) has developed a horizontal (musical score-type) transcription (vs. the usual vertical one) for representing different aspects of embodied conduct in order to better show the 'orchestration' of multiple modalities and 'the timing and sequencing of turns among conversational equals' (p. 108). Charles Goodwin nicely summarizes issues involved in transcribing visual data:

> To try to make the phenomena I'm analyzing independently accessible to the reader so that she or he can evaluate my analysis, I've experimented with using transcription symbols, frame grabs, diagrams, and movies embedded in electronic versions of papers. Multiple issues are involved and no method is entirely successful. On the one hand the analyst needs materials that maintain as much of the original structure of the events being analyzed as possible, and which can be easily and repetitively replayed. On the other hand, just as a raw tape recording does not display the analysis of segmental structure in the stream of speech provided by transcription with a phonetic or alphabetic writing system, in itself a video, even one that can be embedded within a paper, does not provide an analysis of how visible events are being parsed by participants. The complexity of the phenomena involved requires multiple methods for rendering relevant distinctions (e.g., accurate transcription of speech, gaze notation, frame grabs, diagrams, etc., see also Ochs, 1979). (C. Goodwin, 2000b: 161)

You'll need to figure out what works best for your project, following the guidelines and recommendations for best practices we have offered here.

RECOMMENDED READING

Many issues involved in using video for social science research are discussed in:
Heath, C., Hindmarsh, J. and Luff, P. (2010) *Video in qualitative research*. Thousand Oaks, CA: Sage.

A state-of-the-art collection of video-based interactional research that illustrates many different ways in which video-recorded data can be represented on paper is:
Streeck, J., Goodwin, C. and LeBaron, C. (Eds) (2011) *Embodied interaction: Language and body in the material world*. Cambridge: Cambridge University Press.

To find out more about the concepts discussed in this chapter, see examples of real transcriptions, and test your knowledge through exercises and quizzes, visit the supporting website at
https://study.sagepub.com/hepburnandbolden

EIGHT

Transcribing for Languages Other than English

Early conversation analytic studies were based on English conversation. Indeed, English is the medium of this book, and is the *lingua franca* for much interaction research. However, increasingly conversation analysts have been examining talk-in-interaction in a diverse range of communities around the word (e.g., Sidnell, 2009). This has necessarily raised questions about transcribing, analyzing and presenting data in languages other than English, often to audiences that are unfamiliar with the language(s) spoken in the community under investigation. Researchers working in languages other than English, and especially in languages that lack a rich tradition of conversation analytic research, face unique challenges. How does one produce a transcript that will accurately represent what was said, given the linguistic features of the particular language? How does one make a transcript accessible to audiences and readers unfamiliar with the language? Answers to these questions may be influenced not only by the linguistic properties of the language under study, but also by pragmatic constraints imposed by academic publishers and by existing disciplinary traditions.

In this chapter, we discuss some guidelines for dealing with issues involved in transcribing talk in languages other than English, when your audience is not familiar with your language. How to get started? How to decide on an orthographic representation of foreign-language speech? Can the standard English-language transcription conventions be used or should they be modified? How should multilingual interactions be represented? How should your data be presented to an English-speaking audience?

GETTING STARTED WITH TRANSCRIPTION

Before getting down to the task of transcribing data in a language that you haven't closely transcribed before, it is useful to seek out previous interactional work on this language to see how other researchers approached transcription. Some languages (including Finnish, French, German, Japanese and Korean) have a rich tradition of conversation analytic research and may have developed language-specific transcription conventions that can serve as at least initial guidelines. Even though most published studies give only a brief listing of employed transcription conventions (and some do not even do that), an examination of published transcripts in the language you are examining will provide a useful insight into the researchers' practices and can serve as a starting point in your own work.

Who is transcribing?

One of the first decisions the researcher needs to make is who will do the transcription. It is generally preferable that conversation analysts are native speakers of the language under analysis (or, at least, have a near-native proficiency in the language) and that they do the transcription of all or large portions of the data themselves since transcription is a vital part of the analytic process. However, conversation analysts also have worked on languages they are not native speakers of and, occasionally, on languages that they are not highly proficient in. While not ideal, it is sometimes unavoidable, especially for lesser-known languages. If you are not highly proficient in the language, you should consider working closely with native consultants throughout the transcription process and beyond (see Bilmes, 1996; Moerman, 1996).

Orthographic representation

If the language doesn't employ the Roman alphabet, but the language of your audience does, you need to make decisions about how the language is to be presented orthographically. Analysts have adopted several options, none of them ideal. (See Box 8.1 for an illustration.)

First, for languages that have a standard written form, the writing system of that language may be used in the transcript – modified, when necessary, to properly represent the spoken form of the language (similarly to English). While this initially seems like the easiest solution, it eventually brings up a host of problems, including difficulties in presenting data to English-speaking audiences who are unable to follow a non-Roman writing system when the data are presented (e.g., at conferences or data sessions) as well as problems involved in publishing the transcripts in English-language publications (which are often poorly equipped to deal with non-Roman characters). Further, some writing systems make it difficult, if not impossible, to represent variations in pronunciation and precise occurrence of overlapping speech (e.g., the logographic Chinese writing and Hebrew and Arabic consonantal alphabets; see Expert Box 12).

Second, transcribers may use a standard phonetic transcription system, such as the International Phonetic Alphabet (IPA). On the plus side, the use of the IPA makes it possible for linguistically trained audiences to follow the data when they are presented or to 'read' the data from a published transcript. However, there are a host of problems involved in using the IPA for transcription (see Chapter 10 for a full discussion). Both producing and reading an IPA-style transcript require specialized training. Further, from a pragmatic point of view, publishers (especially outside the linguistics journals) may not be adequately equipped to handle the specialized symbols of IPA transcripts. Some conversation analysts do use (simplified or modified) versions of the IPA, especially when working with languages that are phonetically very different from English, such as Thai (see, for example, Moerman, 1988) or Lao (Enfield, 2007).

Another choice, frequently adopted by researchers, is to use a standard Roman transliteration system for representing the language (known as Romanization). The advantages of this choice are that the researcher does not need specialized linguistic training in order to produce the transcript (as opposed to the IPA), the relative readability of the transcripts for English-speaking audiences, and the ease of publication in English-language venues.[1] Transcribers do, however, still have to make decisions about which transliteration system to use – as there are often several options – as well as whether any single system will adequately serve their purposes. Some transliteration systems are designed for representing written language in standard orthography (e.g., the Library of Congress Romanization system) and may be poorly equipped to represent spoken language. In some foreign language academic fields, there are traditionally accepted transliteration systems, such as the Yale system for some East Asian languages (e.g., for Korean, see Lee, 2006). However, if no single transliteration system adequately serves the goals of a conversation analytic transcript, the transcriber may need to develop his/her own way of representing the language by, for example, adapting one of the available standard Romanization systems (e.g., see Bolden, 2008).

------- **BOX** *8.1* --

Orthographic representations of talk

Here are three different orthographic representations of the Russian language equivalent of the question 'Did the repairs turn out well' (see Extract 4 for a full CA transcript). Written Russian uses the Cyrillic alphabet (the first line). The second line illustrates a simplified (or 'broad') IPA transcription. The third line uses a Romanization system developed by Bolden (2008). (Note that no prosodic information is indicated here.)

```
Cyrillic(modified spelling):   Ну а так харашо  ремонт сделали
IPA (simplified):              nʊ ə tak xɐrɐʃo rʲəmont sdʲelalʲi
Romanized (non-standard):      Nu a tak xarasho remont  sdelali
```

------- **BOX** *8.2* --

Tips on choosing an orthographic representation

The decision to adopt a particular orthographic representation is a very consequential one since changing from one system to another after a substantial amount of data has been transcribed is very time consuming. It is important to thoroughly investigate what other researchers working on your language (or a similar one) have done and assess whether the same approach would be beneficial for your goals and audiences. Using a standard approach makes it easier for researchers to understand

---

[1]Another possible advantage of transliteration is that, because it does not rely on the language's standard orthography, Roman transliteration avoids the issue of inadvertently presenting the speaker in a stigmatized way, which arguably occurs when the standard spellings are modified to represent pronunciation details (see Chapters 2 and 10 for further discussion of this issue).

each other's transcripts. In general, a Roman transliteration system would be accessible to the widest audiences and thus is, perhaps, the most versatile.

....

DEVELOPING LANGUAGE-SPECIFIC TRANSCRIPTION CONVENTIONS

Conversation analytic transcription has been developed on English materials and is, thus, fitted to the particularities of the English language. This may present challenges for researchers working in other languages, especially languages that are typologically distant from English. It is of course impossible to provide a full overview of transcription issues that might arise for analysts working with languages other than English (or to even predict what they might be). In the following, we focus on transcribing aspects of prosody to illustrate challenges a transcriber may face and to discuss possible ways of resolving them.

Tonal languages

According to a recent language survey (Maddieson, 2008), approximately 42 percent of world languages are tonal. In tonal languages (such as varieties of Chinese, Hmong, Lao, Navajo and Thai), pitch variations ('tones') are phonemic (or lexical) rather than pragmatic, as in English. This means that pitch contours in such languages change word meanings. For instance, in White Hmong, the sound combination /pɔ/ has several lexical meanings depending on the tone used: 'ball' when pronounced with 'high' tone, 'spleen' with 'mid' tone, 'thorn' with 'low' tone, 'female' with 'high-rising' tone, 'to throw' with 'mid-rising' tone, 'to see' with 'low-falling' tone, and 'grandmother' with 'mid-low' tone (Heimbach, 1979). Because conversation analytic transcription was developed for a non-tonal language (English), there are no standard ways of representing lexical tones in transcripts. Researchers have represented lexical tones using a number system (see, e.g., Enfield, 2007, for Lao) or (for languages with simpler tonal systems) diacritics (e.g., Hanks, 2007, for Yucatec Maya; Moerman, 1988, for Thai).

To illustrate, Extract 1 uses a numerical system (1–5 and ø) to represent tones. In this excerpt, 2 stands for 'high rising' tone, 5 for 'low falling', and ø for 'unstressed':

(1)

```
Lao (from Enfield, 2007: 102)
K     khòòj5 siø mùa2 nam2 phòø+luung2
      1sp_pol irr go with uncle
      I_polite will go with him_uncle
```

In Extract 2, the tones are represented with diacritics on vowels: <´> for 'high', <`> for 'low', and no marking for the 'mid' tone.

(2)

```
Yucatec Maya (from Hanks, 2007: 165, modified)

1       DC      le tz'àak a', máameh, (2.0) kulòok e há' o' kahoyik.
                This medicine Mama, (2.0) when the water boils you
                steep it

2       Wi      mhmm.
                Hmm.

3       DC      kintzikbatik tech tayík?
                I'm explaning it to you, got it?
```

Sometimes researchers omit tone information from transcripts, relying instead on interlinear gloss (the second line of the transcript) to provide the missing lexical information (for an example of Mandarin, see Wu, 2003). This is done to simplify the transcript for an audience unfamiliar with the language (see Expert Box 12).

······ **EXPERT BOX** *12* ··

Transcription in Mandarin Chinese

Kobin H. Kendrick, University of York, UK

The transcription system that Gail Jefferson invented may look foreign, but it adheres to the same basic principle as English orthography. The symbols it uses (e.g., the letters of the Roman alphabet) represent the sounds speakers produce, and each symbol corresponds to a single sound, with some exceptions (e.g., 'sh'). Jefferson pressed English orthography into new service, but this basic principle remains in force. The orthography of Mandarin Chinese, however, is fundamentally different. Chinese characters represent monosyllabic words or morphemes, with only vague associations to their sounds if any. The character 看, for example, corresponds to the word *kàn* 'to look', a syllable with three distinct sounds, none of which is represented by the character itself. For this reason, the orthography of Mandarin Chinese is fundamentally incompatible with the Jeffersonian transcription system. With Chinese characters it would be impossible to indicate prosodic stress on a specific sound (e.g., *kàn̠*), a sound stretch in the middle of a word (e.g., *kà:n*), aspiration or laughter (e.g., *k(h)àn*), overlap that begins before a word ends (e.g., *kà[n*), and many other details that one may wish to capture in a transcription. This means that conversation analytic transcripts of Mandarin Chinese conversation must employ a Romanization, an exogenous orthographic system that renders Chinese words in the Roman alphabet, as the examples above illustrate.

This Romanization, known as Pinyin, allows conversation analysts to access the full arsenal of Jeffersonian transcription conventions, but not without a cost. To appreciate what gets lost in translation, consider the Pinyin form *yì*. This single syllable corresponds to over 100 different Chinese characters, each with a different meaning. This is because Mandarin Chinese, for specific historical reasons, has a massive number of homophones, words with the same sounds but different meanings (e.g., *hot* in English). So whereas the standard orthography of Mandarin unambiguously indicates which of these 100 senses the author means by *yì*, a transcript in Pinyin alone requires the reader to infer based on the context which is the most plausible (indeed as one must do in conversation). To complicate matters further, words in Mandarin Chinese have what linguists call lexical tone: the pitch with which a syllable is produced determines what the syllable means. In Pinyin tones are represented by one of four diacritics above the vowel: *yī, yí, yǐ* or *yì*, for example. So if a transcription does not indicate lexical tones (e.g., *yi* without a diacritic), the problem of ambiguity increases by a factor of four.

In practical terms, this means that transcripts of Mandarin Chinese conversation in Pinyin can be difficult to read. The transcriber is faced with a dilemma: either transcribe a conversation in Chinese characters, with their full semantic richness, and forgo the precision of the Jeffersonian system, or employ a Romanization that represents the sounds of the language at the expense of its meaning. For conversation analytic research only the second option is viable. A practical compromise would be to include both Pinyin and Chinese characters on separate lines of the transcript, with interactional and productional details indicated only in the Pinyin, an option most appropriate for a Chinese readership (e.g., a data session in Taiwan or an article submitted to a Chinese linguistics journal). For the most part, conversation analysts who work on Mandarin have opted to present Pinyin transcripts without diacritics for lexical tones and without Chinese characters. Such transcripts, which include morpheme-by-morpheme glosses and translations in English, represent the precise meanings that Chinese characters would convey, just not in the form most familiar to speakers of the language.

....

Transcribing unit-final intonation contours

Unit-final prosody is an important aspect of the English language transcription system (as discussed in Chapter 4) because in English (and in many other languages), final intonation contour carries important pragmatic information about the action accomplished by the turn constructional unit (e.g., Auer, 1996; Ford and Thompson, 1996; Reed, 2004). For instance, in English (and many other languages), 'yes/no' (or 'polar') questions are quite often produced with a distinct rising final pitch contour (Enfield et al., 2010; Stivers, 2010), marked on the transcript with a question mark or, for lower rises, an inverse question mark (¿) or a comma (see Chapter 4). In English (and other languages), questions can take the shape of declarative assertions produced with rising intonation at the end of the TCU (turn constructional unit, see Box 3.1 for a definition), as in Extract 3 below (from a conversation between two teachers).

(3)

```
CH 4112 (0:05)
1  >  BEC:  An' the grou:p is getting ready to go to:: uh (Snu:)?
2             (1.5)
3       DAN:  No:. No they-they cancelled that-th-th- there was not
4             enough students.
```

While such 'declarative questions' do not exclusively rely on unit-final intonation to be understood as questions (Couper-Kuhlen, 2012; Geluykens, 1988; Heritage, 2012; Stivers, 2010), their prosodic realization – and especially unit-final intonation contour – is an intrinsic part of turn design and action formation.

Given the importance of unit-final intonation in English, the English transcription system is especially attuned to and designed for capturing pragmatically meaningful prosodic variations at unit endings. However, not all languages make use of unit-final prosody in the same way, which suggests that researchers may have to modify the standard notations to better reflect the intonational features of the language under study. Capturing unit-final prosody may not be particularly useful for some languages. For one, in tonal languages (see above), final pitch contours can be affected by the lexical tone of the final word (e.g., Tao, 1996). A transcriber working on a tonal language will need to decide whether (and how) unit-final intonation is to be marked. Note that the Yucatec Maya transcript (Extract 2 above) shows unit-final pitch contours in addition to lexical tones in ways that are similar to an English transcription, while the Lao transcript (Extract 1) leaves unit-final intonation unmarked (Moerman's, 1988, transcripts of Thai speech also lack information on unit-final intonation).

Further, prosodic patterns vary across languages, which may make it difficult (and undesirable) for a transcriber to rely on English-based transcription conventions. For example, in languages like Brazilian Portuguese, Bulgarian, Hungarian, Romanian, Russian (Hirst and Di Cristo, 1998), and some varieties of Italian (Rossano, 2010), unit-final prosody is heavily affected by the sentential stress pattern – i.e. the distribution of stressed and unstressed syllables and words across a turn-constructional unit. Specifically, 'yes/no' interrogatives in these languages are produced with the unit-*final* rising pitch contour only when the last stressed syllable of the unit occurs in the unit-final position (Hirst and Di Cristo, 1998). Otherwise, the unit-*medial* high pitch on the last stressed syllable is followed by a falling pitch on the following unstressed syllables, producing a final falling pitch contour (e.g., for Russian, see Svetozarova, 1998). In other words, in these languages, the characteristic prosodic shape of 'yes/no' interrogatives is not necessarily unit-final but can, rather, be unit-medial.

For one example, see Extract 4 taken from a Russian-language conversation. Here, Rima asks a 'yes/no' question about the repairs that were done in Ella's apartment. (Here, PRT stands for 'particle' – a difficult to translate word that conveys grammatical or discourse information.)

(4)

```
RP3, 5:35 [Russian]

1    RIMA:   .h Nu a   tak xara<u>sho</u>? remont sdelali/
                 PRT PRT PRT well        repair  made
                 Did the repairs turn out well?
                 ((or: The repairs turned out well?))

2    ELLA:   Da: tak xarasho/
                 yes PRT   well
                 Yes they did
```

In Russian, 'yes/no' interrogatives are very rarely marked morpho-syntactically,[2] and so Rima's question (line 1) can be translated into English as either 'Did the repairs turn out well?' or 'The repairs turned out well?' Russian 'yes/no' interrogatives are often produced with a distinct rising pitch contour. As Figure 8.1 shows, however, a sharp pitch rise characteristic of the 'questioning' intonation can occur in a unit-medial position (here on *xarasho* 'well') rather than the unit-final position. The turn constructional unit ends with a falling intonation.

Similarly, in Extract 5, Greg's question in line 1 is produced with a unit-medial pitch rise carried by the stressed syllable in the word *mnoga* 'many' (see Figure 8.2).

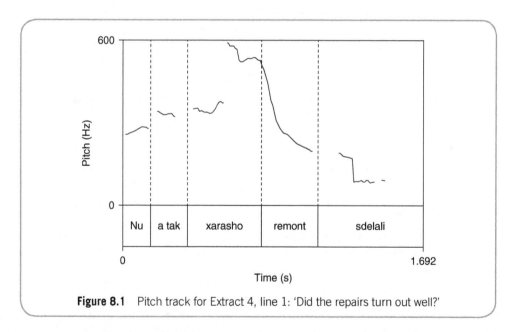

Figure 8.1   Pitch track for Extract 4, line 1: 'Did the repairs turn out well?'

[2]There is no subject–verb inversion in Russian. While a polar question particle does exist (*shto li*), it is used only under a narrow set of circumstances.

(5)

PF41 [Russian]

```
01    GREG:  <A russkix eh mno?ga krugom/ All/
              PRT Russians  many  around   NAME
              Are there many Russians around, Alla?
              ((or: There are many Russians around, Alla?))

02           (1.2)

03    ALLA:  Krugo?m/
              around
              Around?
```

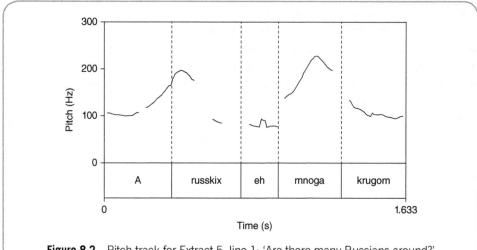

Figure 8.2 Pitch track for Extract 5, line 1: 'Are there many Russians around?'

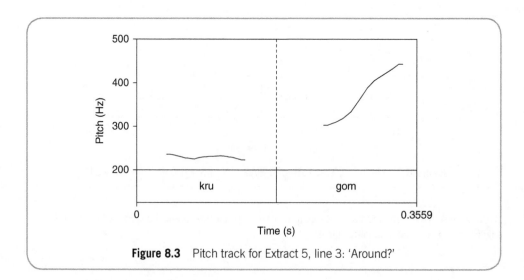

Figure 8.3 Pitch track for Extract 5, line 3: 'Around?'

After a gap (line 2), instead of answering, Alla initiates repair on Greg's turn by repeating *krugom* 'around' (line 3). In contrast to Greg's question, in Alla's repair initiation (also a 'yes/no' interrogative), the rising questioning intonation is unit-final, carried by the last stressed syllable of the unit (the second syllable in *krugom* 'around'), as seen in Figure 8.3.

This kind of intonation pattern cannot be adequately represented with English language transcription conventions (discussed in Chapter 4) for the following reasons. If we follow English language conventions and only mark unit-*final* prosody, Rima's and Greg's 'yes/no' interrogatives will appear on the transcript as assertions rather than as questions, even though both are produced as prosodic interrogatives in Russian. In other words, following ordinary English conventions would obscure our understanding of the action of the turn. Another solution would be to mark these turns with a unit-final question mark to indicate that some sort of questioning intonation *was* used. However, this would also be misleading since it is, in fact, possible to produce questions with unit-final rising intonation in Russian (as Alla's repair initiation in Extract 5 illustrates). In Russian, the understanding of what action a 'yes/no' interrogative accomplishes (e.g., what exactly is being asked) is influenced by which word is produced with the rising intonation. Leaving that information off the transcript will render the question itself open to different interpretations. As an illustration:

```
Dima uexal v Moskvu/          Dima left for Moscow.
```

Different intonational patterns:

```
Dima ue?xal v Moskvu/         Did Dima leave for Moscow?
Di?ma uexal of Moskvu/        Was it Dima who left for Moscow?
Dima uexal v Moskvu?/         Dima left for Moscow?! (surprise)
```

The transcripts in Extracts 4 and 5 use a different set of conventions to account for this feature of the intonation system in Russian. The syllable that carries the rising intonation is followed by the question mark, and a slash (/) is used to mark a prosodic unit boundary where the unit is prosodically complete (for a more complete description of the transcription conventions adopted for Russian, see Bolden, 2008).

> **Student question:** How do I decide if new transcription conventions might be needed for my language? There seems to be an incompatibility with the English system.
>
> **Answer:** The best way to figure out if any modifications to the English transcription system are needed is to start transcribing your data, paying careful attention to prosody. You should also familiarize yourself with what conventions other researchers working on the same language have used, and discuss your concerns with them. As you transcribe, ask yourself if the existing transcription conventions 'fit' your sense of the data or, importantly, if they deter you from accurately representing what you hear. If your sense of unease about the fit grows over time, you should consider whether modifications would solve the problem. This should be done in consultation with the community of interactional researchers working on the same language.

TRANSCRIBING MULTILINGUAL INTERACTION

In many speech communities and a variety of settings, more than one language (or dialect[3]) can be used in a single interaction. Research on multilingual interaction suggests that participants treat the choice of one or another language variety as interactionally significant (e.g., Auer, 1998; Clyne, 1994; Mondada, 2004; Nguyen and Kasper, 2009; Wei, 2002). In fact, it can be seen as a feature of turn design and an intrinsic part of action formation (Mondada, 2007a; Szymanski, 2003). In other words, how an action is understood can be informed by the speaker's language choices. For this reason, a transcript of a multilingual interaction should indicate what language varieties are used. In this section, we introduce some aspects of multilingual conversation and ways of representing them on a transcript.

A recording of an interaction involving multilingual speakers is likely to reveal a number of different 'language contact' phenomena.[4] First, participants may alternate between different language varieties (or 'codes') across or within turns at talk. This is typically referred to as *code switching* (e.g., Grosjean, 1982). Second, a speaker may *borrow* words (or phrases) from one language into another. Unlike code switching, borrowed words are grammatically incorporated into the turn in progress – i.e. they are phonetically and syntactically fitted into the language of the turn.

For an example of code switching (from English to Russian), see Extract 6 taken from a conversation in a bilingual Russian American immigrant family. In line 1, Lena uses English to ask a question about her grandfather's appointment with a cardiologist. When her grandmother initiates repair on it with a Russian 'open class' (Drew, 1997) repair initiator 'Shto?' ('What?', line 3), Lena provides a repair solution in the form of a Russian language translation of her original problematic turn (see line 5). Lena thereby treats her language choice (English in line 1) as the source of trouble for the grandmother (Bolden, 2012; Egbert, 2004).

(6)

```
I5a, 45:10 [English-Russian]

01      LENA:        Does he have flu̲id in his lu:ngs?

02                   (1.5)

03      GRM:         Shto̲?/
                     what
```

---

[3]A distinction between what might be considered a 'language' versus a 'dialect' is complex and often based on political factors (e.g., Trudgill, 1988). Linguists typically use the terms 'dialect', 'language variety' or 'code' in order to avoid making the distinction.

[4]Several alternative labels and typologies for characterizing language contact phenomena exist (e.g., Gafaranga, 2007; Johanson, 2002; Muysken, 2000). However, for the purposes of transcription, a generally accepted (if simplified) distinction between code switching and borrowing should be sufficient.

```
04                       (0.8)

05        LENA:          Zhidkast' v lëxkii?/
                         fluid      in lungs
                         Fluid in his lungs?

06                       (1.0)

07        GRP:           D[a/
                         yes

08        GRM:              [Eta: eta vada/
                            that that water
                            It's water
```

Similarly, in Extract 7 (from a face-to-face multiparty interaction), Maria, faced with no uptake from her recipients (see line 2), attempts to translate a Russian saying (in line 1) into English (at lines 3–5), and thus displays an orientation to the participants' asymmetrical language competencies.

(7)

M3-2, 14:45 [Russian-English]

```
01        MAR:           [A v-v Rashke gavarili:: kapejka rubl'  berezhët/
                         PRT in in Russia said    kopek   rouble saves
                         In Russia they'd say 'A kopek saves a rouble'

02                       (0.4)

03 >      MAR:           Eta ka:k eh::: one penny:: (0.4)
                         that how
                         It's like

04        IGO:           sa[ves the dollar.

05        MAR:             [make- saves you a dollar.
```

How should code switching be marked on the transcript? When one of the languages used by the participants in a bilingual conversation is known to those for whom the data are presented (e.g., English in Extracts 6 and 7 for the readers of this book), the transcriber may not need to identify the languages on the transcript since the change in code is transparent. However, when participants use language varieties unfamiliar to those reading the transcript, the transcriber will have to devise a method for distinguishing between the varieties: for example, use different fonts for representing different languages (such as regular vs. *italics* or **bold**) or make use of the languages' standard writing systems (Gardner-Chloros et al., 1999; Torras and Gafaranga, 2002).[5]

Lexical borrowing from one language into another may also become an oriented to feature of interaction and, thus, needs to be indicated on the transcript. In Extract 8, Tanya uses the English word 'pasta' (line 2) when explaining the kind of salad she is making to Faina, her elderly mother-in-law. In Russian, the word ordinarily means 'paste', but Russian immigrants in the US often use it as a borrowing from English to refer to pasta products. When Faina provides no uptake (line 3), Tanya goes on to give a Russian-language equivalent of the word ('makaronchiki'/'macaroni', line 4).

(8)

```
016, 21:00 [Russian]

01    FAI:      A eta shto vot ↑eta?/
                PRT this what PRT this
                And this, what is this?

02 >  TAN:      A- (i) eta: {pa:sta},/
                PRT    this  pasta/paste
                This is {pasta}

03              (.)

04    TAN:      eta makaronchiki takie,/
                this macaroni    such
                This is macaroni

05              (0.2)

06  FAI:        [Mm mm,
```

While Tanya may not have initially treated the word 'pasta' as a borrowing from English that Faina might not know, the subsequent Russian-language paraphrase (at line 4) shows that even commonly used words may become oriented to as imports from another language and, thus, potentially problematic. In order to make this datum more transparent to a reader, this transcript uses curly brackets for the English borrowing (at line 2). Other markings can also be used (e.g., italics) as long as they do not conflict with other transcription symbols.

---

[5]It may not always be possible to make a decision about which language variety is spoken at a particular moment; for example, various speech perturbations might not be identifiable as being of one or another language and some words could belong to any of the speaker's languages (Gardner-Chloros et al., 1999). This would make language differentiation on a transcript difficult if not impossible, and the transcriber would need to consider if, at that moment, the choice of a particular language variety is, in fact, a relevant feature of turn design. One may also devise a method for marking stretches of talk that do not identifiably belong to one or another language variety (e.g., Torras and Gafaranga, 2002).

Sometimes borrowed words and phrases are significantly altered to fit the grammar of the host utterance. In Extract 9, Rima incorporates the English phrase 'to take a nap' into her Russian turn, significantly changing its pronunciation and morphology (line 3). Rima is talking about her son and daughter-in-law's holiday with their small child.

(9)

```
NB1-2, 9:30 [Russian]

1    RIMA:     Schas ani eë palozhut spa:,t'/
               now   they her put       to-sleep
               Now they'll put her to sleep

               v   etu   deckaju kravatku¿/ [hh
               in this children's bed
               in a crib

2    ALLA:                                [Hm

3 >  RIMA:     .hhh i  sami (0.2) {tejkajut njap}/=heh
                   and themselves    take     nap
                   and they {take a nap} as well

4    ALLA:  A::/ Nu [panjatna/
               ah  PRT understood
               Ah, I see
```

Rima marks her language choice as unusual by adding a laugh token ('heh', line 3) following the incorporated English phrase as a 'post-completion stance marker' (Schegloff, 1996b). The phrasal borrowing is indicated on the transcript with the curly brackets (line 3), but the phrase is transcribed the same way the surrounding Russian is transcribed to capture the fact that Rima does not shift into English but rather adapts the English phrase to the Russian grammar.

······· **BOX** *8.3* ···

Tips on transcribing multilingual interaction

A transcript of a multilingual interaction should make it clear to a reader when a particular language variety is used. If you are working with two or more languages that won't be familiar to your audiences, decide on how you will represent each language (or dialect) on the transcript. Variations in font (e.g., regular vs. *italic*) are easy to implement, are readable, and should not create problems in publishing the materials. (Do not use different fonts for this purpose as publishers typically insist on using their own font(s) and may not allow font variations.) Decide, as well, if – and how – you will mark lexical borrowings from one language into another. Offsetting borrowed words with a symbol (e.g., curly brackets) is a simple solution. Make sure to adopt distinct conventions for these purposes.

···

PRESENTING DATA TO ENGLISH-SPEAKING AUDIENCES

Researchers working with languages other than English will often have to present their data to audiences that are not familiar with the language (or languages) used by the participants. In the following, we discuss best practices for making transcripts accessible to others and some difficulties involved in the process (see also Egbert et al., 2016).

How many lines?

When presenting transcripts of talk in languages other than English to English-speaking audiences, typically a multi-linear transcription is used (for a description and illustrations, see for example Sidnell, 2009). The most common practice is to provide a three-line transcription (as illustrated in the extracts above), where the first line represents the original talk (in the adopted orthography), the second line is a morpheme-by-morpheme English gloss of the original (a combination of word translations and grammatical information in an abbreviated way), and the third line is an idiomatic English translation that attempts to capture the local, interactional meaning of the original. The advantage of a three-line transcription (especially for languages that do not follow the English word order) is that the second line allows an English speaker some understanding of the talk as it unfolds, such as providing information about when (relative to what has been said) overlaps occur. (Though, as Bilmes (1996) observes, this might be of limited use since the reader unfamiliar with the language under study still won't be able to accurately assess the TCU's projectability, for example.) A two-line transcription – that would contain an orthographic representation of the original talk and an idiomatic English translation – is typically used for languages that closely follow the English word order. Finally, for some projects it might be possible to only provide an idiomatic English translation in the main text of a publication (Nikander, 2008), preferably supplemented by a full three-line transcript of the original talk in an appendix (some researchers working on interaction in institutional settings have done that – e.g., Lee, 2009; Peräkylä, 1998).

Whichever way of representation is used, the analyst then needs to decide whether details about how the talk is produced (such as emphasis, intonation, etc.) are going to be captured in the English idiomatic translation, and if so, how. The practices vary from providing no production details in the translation to an attempt to represent them fully. In the former, the reader is expected to access the information from the original transcription (the first line in the multi-linear transcript), which might be difficult to interpret, especially if the grammar of the language under investigation is drastically different from English. The latter option – providing all production details in the translation – can also be problematic as the transcriber is then put in the position of additionally 'translating' prosodic features of the original talk into English. However, this option would be preferable if the English translation is provided separately from the original language transcript.

Another issue that comes up in publishing work based on data in other languages is how to refer to talk in the analytic discussion of a transcript. Journals and publishers may have specific conventions for how such data should be quoted; however, the general rule is to include both the original talk and its idiomatic translation into English (or the language of the publication), offsetting both the original and the translation in some way (e.g., with quotation symbols and/or italics).

Student question: What sorts of information should be in the second line of a three-line transcript? I'm also unsure about how to best translate for the third line.

Answer: As you prepare a three-line transcript, keep in mind the goals of your project, the linguistic properties of the language you are studying, and the target audience for your work. When providing the interlinear gloss (the second line), you may choose to follow disciplinary conventions (such as, the Leipzig Glossing Rules for linguistics[6]). However, the level of linguistic detail you provide should reflect the linguistic properties of the language, the study's objectives (are you focusing on a linguistic phenomenon?) and audience (what level of linguistic knowledge do you expect?). If you only want your audience to be aware of the order in which the words were produced, very little linguistic detail may be required. On the other hand, if your focus is on a particular linguistic form, it should be clearly identified in the interlinear gloss.

It is hard to overemphasize the importance of providing a clear idiomatic translation (the third line in a three-line transcript). In fact, it is preferable to give a translation that is not completely faithful to the original language to one that is faithful but opaque to the audience. In the interests of clarity, you may want to add words that are only implied in the original speech (these can be specially marked – e.g., placed in double parentheses – in the idiomatic translation line), use different grammatical forms, idiomatic expressions, etc. Adding punctuation symbols (such as question marks) may sometimes be useful as well (but make sure that punctuation is not confused with prosodic transcription) as well as providing alternative translations of key lines (see for example line 1 of Extract 4). The clarity of the translation is especially important for conference presentations when audience members have only a limited time to examine the transcript. (See below for a discussion of translation issues.)

······· **EXPERT BOX 13** ···

The politics of transcribing and translating transcripts of languages other than English

Maria Egbert and Mamiko Yufu, University of Southern Denmark

It is for political reasons that English has become the *lingua franca* of international publication, thus requiring that data displays in more than 7,000 non-English languages be rendered accessible in English.

(Continued)

---

[6]See www.eva.mpg.de/lingua/resources/glossing-rules.php for an explanation.

(Continued)

An examination of 100 articles with transcripts of interactional data, drawn from a top journal, indicates that there is a tendency to treat results based on English data as generic, a lack of accessibility of the original non-English data, and problems with readability (Egbert et al., 2016). Thus, politics impacts scientific quality.

At the interface of politics and personal experience, there is a strong conflict between, on the one hand, striving for scientific accuracy in making as much as possible available of the original non-English data, and, on the other hand, the practicalities of preparing working transcripts, editing them for publication, following length restrictions, along with a bias towards Roman letters and scripts with left-to-right directionality. When working with languages for which other letters and scripts are used, this process can result in an alienation from one's own data.

The transcript below is prepared in order to provide for such an initial experience of alienation. For this purpose, we made the following English transcript accessible as if Japanese were the international language of publication.

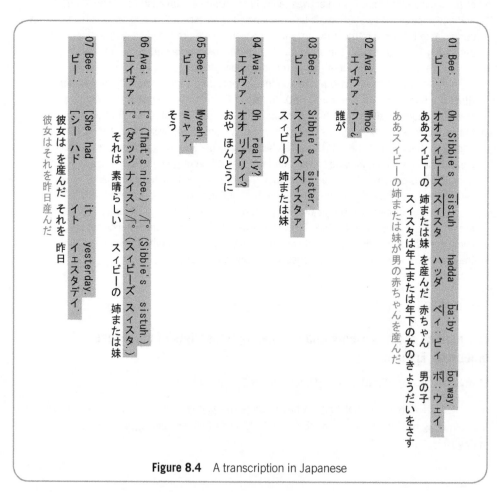

Figure 8.4 A transcription in Japanese

Two Girls, 19:01-19:08, Schegloff, 2007: 285 [American English
telephone data]
01 Bee: Oh Sibbie's sistuh hadda ba:by bo:way.
02 Ava: Who¿
03 Bee: Sibbie's sister.
04 Ava: Oh really?
05 Bee: Myeah,
06 Ava: [°(That's nice.)/(Sibbie's sistuh.)
07 Bee: [She had it yesterday.

The version made accessible in Japanese consists of a grid with sets of three to five lines, arranged from right to left, following a top-to-bottom directionality (Figure 8.4). The right-most, greyed line contains the original English. Moving to the left, the next line, also in a grey box, provides a transliteration into the Japanese phonetic syllabary. The third line from the right contains the gloss. If more detailed glossing is needed, a further line is added (see line 1 for an example). The idiomatic translation is provided in the left most line (lines 1 and 7), and may be omitted when glossing and translation are identical (lines 2–6).

English may 'feel normal' to scholars used to western alphabets and scripts. However, when we consider the linguistic and cultural variety across all languages, a quick look at only the ten most frequently learned first languages – Mandarin Chinese, Spanish, English, Arabic, Hindi, Portuguese, Bengali, Russian, Japanese and Lahnda (Lewis et al., 2016) – relativizes such a perspective of perceived normalcy.

Translation issues

Presenting data to an audience unfamiliar with the language under investigation involves translation of the original talk, which is difficult and fraught with problems (see, e.g., Bilmes, 1996; Moerman, 1988; Schegloff, 2002; Traverso, 2002). Difficulties involved in translation range from those researchers of talk-in-interaction share with translators of literary texts (e.g., translating idiomatic expressions, discourse markers and grammatical particles, word plays, representing regional or socio-dialects, etc.) to those that are unique to translating talk as it unfolds in real time, on a turn-by-turn basis (for an illustration, see Extract 10 below). Richards (1932: 7, as quoted in Moerman, 1988) calls translation an 'indirectly controlled guess', and Schegloff (2002), in a discussion of the role of translation in conversation analytic research, warns that translation inevitably suggests analysis. In fact, Schegloff (2002) points out an additional burden conversation analysts working on languages other than English have when presenting their data to English audiences:

> the translation needs to be rendered in a fashion sensitive not only to the detail and nuance of the material being studied in its language-of-occurrence, but also sensitive to the detail and nuance in comparable English language interactions as revealed in the already extant literature. (p. 263)

In other words, translation for a conversation analyst is not just a perfunctory step in the transcription process, but is part of the analysis of the original talk that has to be informed by what is known about English (or the language translated into). The best way to avoid conveying unwanted analytic hearings in the translation is, perhaps, to work on the data (in data sessions) with English-speaking conversation analysts unfamiliar with the language under study.

To illustrate some of the difficulties that are unique to translating turn-by-turn talk, let's consider Extract 10 from a conversation between Dina and Tanya. The two women are talking about a wedding Dina's sons have been invited to. At line 1, Tanya is responding to an earlier question about whether the groom ('on'/'he' at line 1) invited her daughters to the wedding (in fact, he did *not*).

(10)

RP4, 2:15 [Russian]

```
01    TAN:     Nu   vot<Nu=kuda:   kak on budet priglashat' devcho,nak/
               PRT  PRT  PRT  where how he will   invite        girls
               How can he possibly invite the girls

02             ty che[vo/
               you    what
               what are you ((saying))

03    DIN:          [Mm [mm:

04    TAN:              [esli emu glaza vycarap°(aet)°./
                        if    him  eyes  scratch-out [Future-3rd-Sing]
                        if ((she)) will scratch his eyes out

05             (.)

06    DIN:     Mm mm

07    TAN:     £Evo/£
               his
               His ((other half))

08             (.)

09    TAN:     £Madam/£
               Madam

10    TA?:     .h

11    DIN:     [Mm mm

12    TAN:     [Nu vot
               PRT   PRT
               Anyways,…
```

One aspect of this segment that neither the word-for-word gloss nor the idiomatic translation adequately capture is the fact that Tanya's turn in lines 4, 7 and 9 is built through a series of incremental extensions of the host TCU in line 4 (Bolden and Guimaraes, 2012; Ford et al., 2002; Schegloff, 2000a). Specifically, the utterance in line 4 is a possibly complete TCU that can be translated as '((she)) will scratch his eyes out' where who is being referred to (*she* or *the bride*) is not explicitly articulated but understood both from the sequential context and from the grammar of the utterance in line 4 (Bolden and Guimaraes, 2012). This tacit reference (she) is marked on the transcript in the translation line with double parentheses. In line 7, when the speaker adds 'evo' (translatable as 'his' or, in this context, 'his other half'), she extends her turn incrementally, so that the resulting turn is again a possibly complete TCU, now translatable as 'His other half will scratch his eyes out'. When Tanya goes on to add 'Madam' (at line 9), she extends her turn again with another increment, and the resulting TCU (from lines 7 and 9) is now translatable as 'His madam will scratch his eyes out'. Because of the disparities between Russian and English grammars, this analysis is obscured by the provided translation. The translation may suggest that 'evo' (in line 7) and 'Madam' (in line 9) together (i.e. 'his madam') replace the reference to the bride (in line 4) rather than each word being an incremental extension of what has come before. Unfortunately, there is no good way to overcome problems of this sort, and they are quite common when working with languages that are very distinct grammatically from English. An in-text analytic commentary will need to compensate for the unavoidable inadequacies of the translation.

CONCLUDING COMMENTS

In this chapter, we discussed some of the special issues that come up for researchers working with languages other than English. The expansion of conversation analytic research into other languages is a relatively recent phenomenon. This – and the tremendous diversity of the languages under investigation – makes offering a common set of transcription guidelines difficult. Inevitably, researchers will develop and adapt their ways of representing a wide variety of languages on paper so as to best capture the phenomena speakers of these languages treat as consequential. Ideally, this should be a collaborative process involving a number of researchers working on a particular language, so that a common set of best practices is gradually developed.

RECOMMENDED READING

For a good representation of conversation analytic research on a variety of languages (with a sampling of different transcription conventions employed), see:

(Continued)

(Continued)

Sidnell, J. (Ed.) (2009) *Conversation analysis: Comparative perspectives.* Cambridge: Cambridge University Press.

For a discussion of researcher practices for transcribing languages other than English, see:

Egbert, M., Yufu, M. and Hirataka, F. (2016) An investigation of how 100 articles in the *Journal of Pragmatics* treat transcripts of English and non-English languages. *Journal of Pragmatics, 94,* 98–111.

To find out more about the concepts discussed in this chapter, see examples of real transcriptions, and test your knowledge through exercises and quizzes, visit the supporting website at
https://study.sagepub.com/hepburnandbolden

NINE

Technological Resources for Transcription

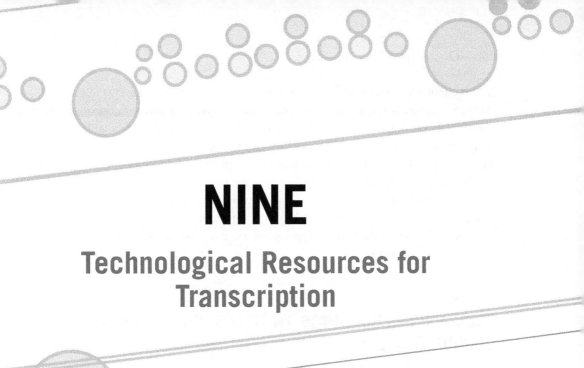

In this chapter we discuss technical tools that may be used in the process of transcribing, analyzing and presenting audio and video data. Given the rapid technological changes, this chapter is not meant to provide an exhaustive overview of the available technology (which will surely be outdated by the time of the book's publication), but only introduce a few useful tools and explore issues one may consider in selecting appropriate tools.

We start by discussing the process of creating transcription-ready digital recordings. Then we introduce a number of useful software programs for transcribing and analyzing recordings and discuss best practices for presenting data to audiences. Finally, we assess the possibility and implications of adopting an automated voice-to-text transcription solution.

FROM RAW RECORDINGS TO TRANSCRIPTION-READY COMPUTER FILES

Given the prevalence of digital technology, the current practice is to transcribe off digital audio or video files rather than tapes or other recording media. Using computer files has many obvious advantages for transcription, analysis and presentation of data, including easy editing, playback and zooming in on particular segments. This section describes steps involved in preparing transcription-ready digital files.

Non-digital audio- and video-recordings

If your data were recorded on old equipment – an old-fashioned analogue audio recorder or an analogue video camera – your first task would be to digitize the recordings. You will need some hardware to do this (minimally, a connection cable).

······· **BOX 9.1** ··

Tips on digitizing audio and video

File format: When digitizing recordings, it is best to use software that would create files in formats that are widely used across computer platforms. For audio-recordings, WAV, AIF and MP3 may be good choices. For video-recordings, MOV and MP4 are commonly used.

Ripping video files: If you have analogue video, you will need to use a hardware video converter to produce a digital video. One possibility: ADVC 110 by Grass Valley (www.grassvalley.com/products). To 'rip' the video to a digital file, you will need to use some software, such as iMovie (see below).

File size and compression: Be careful about the size of the files you create from the recordings. Most software packages will give you a variety of conversion settings. Consider different options before digitizing a large number of recordings. Your aim should be to preserve good quality of sound and video while keeping the file size under control. For example, a default audio setting may produce stereo (i.e. two-track) audio files from mono (one-track) recordings, which will double the file size without making a difference in the audio quality. Further, if you are working with video, you may want to compress the files – see some suggestions in Box 9.2.

Digital audio- and video-recordings

Most likely, you have recorded the data digitally, which simplifies the process of moving recordings to your computer. The first step is to import the recordings from the recorder's or camera's storage media. Some recording equipment is designed to be simply plugged into the computer and the files copied over to the computer hard drive (you should consider this feature if you are buying your recording equipment!). However, some recorders and cameras create proprietary file formats and require the use of proprietary software, which makes the transfer process significantly more elaborate and slow since your goal is to create a data file in a common file format that can be used by different programs.

······· BOX *9.2* ···

Tips on importing digital video-recordings

Importing video-recordings: The transfer from a digital camera can be accomplished with Apple's *iMovie* (www.apple.com/mac/imovie). However, the steps involved in the transfer will vary depending on the video camera and the computer you are using. If the camera records in a proprietary video format (as many popular Sony cameras, for example, do), you may first need to use the software provided with the camera. Once the video is imported into iMovie, you should export it (via the iMovie export function) into the versatile QuickTime movie format (MOV). However, no special importing may be needed with cameras that record in commonly used video formats, such as MP4, and allow you to simply copy the video file onto your computer. This significantly minimizes the time involved in preparing transcription-ready files.

    Video file compression: The original video files are usually very large, which makes them difficult to work with. It is much more convenient to work with compressed files, though you should keep the originals (on an external storage device) in case higher video/audio quality is needed for analysis. Compressing large video files can be done with *Squeeze* (by Sorenson Media: www.sorensonmedia. com). A much cheaper but significantly less effective option is *QuickTime 7 Pro* (see below). You will need to experiment with different compression settings; one general piece of advice is to keep the video sampling rate at 30 frames per second (a lower rate will create jumpy videos).

SOFTWARE FOR WORKING WITH AUDIO AND VIDEO FILES

Once you have your recordings in a workable digital format, there are a lot of useful software tools that can be used for different tasks involved in transcription, analysis and presentation of the data. In this section, we provide an overview of some useful programs for working with audio and video files during transcription and various stages of data analysis.

Working with video and audio: QuickTime Player 7 Pro

QuickTime Player is a basic, cross-platform video and audio player. The professional version is economical and extremely useful for working with video-/audio-recorded data. Because QuickTime is currently available for both PCs and Macs, it makes collaboration and moving between computers easy. Note that Apple currently offers QuickTime X as the basic movie player (free, pre-installed on Apple computers). However, it lacks many of the capabilities discussed below.

File formats: QuickTime natively plays MOV files. However, it is capable of playing (importing and exporting into) a number of different audio and video file formats. Format compatibility may be extended by installing additional components.

Basic uses of QuickTime Player 7 Pro

- To make clips of audio- and video-recordings for presentations and analysis.
- To control playback of audio-/video-recordings: you can change the speed of the playback (e.g., to slow it down), boost volume on quiet recordings, make low-quality (dark/blurry) video-recordings brighter and/or more contrastive (see Figure 9.1).
- To convert video-/audio-recordings into a number of different formats. You can also control the quality of the recording and thus the size of the data file (e.g., the size of the video frame, audio frequency, mono/stereo, etc.).
- To create video frame grabs from a video-recording for presentations and publications.

Figure 9.1   QuickTime 7 Pro playback control panel

Advanced uses of QuickTime Player 7 Pro

- Programming: Apple computer users can program QuickTime Pro operations via the Apple programming language AppleScript (included in OS X). For example, QuickTime Pro can be programmed to run in the background and be controlled via keyboard shortcuts (with Keyboard Maestro: www.keyboardmaestro.com). This allows one to transcribe in a word processing program while controlling QuickTime playback, without having to switch between windows or use the mouse. AppleScripts can be created for starting and stopping playback, starting playback at an earlier place in the recording (backtracking a couple of seconds), playing at a slower speed, fast-forwarding through the recording, etc.
- Subtitles: One can create subtitles with QuickTime 7 Pro. This is useful for presenting foreign language data or data that is difficult to hear/understand. (Subtitles can also be created in iMovie.)

Working with audio files: Amadeus and Adobe Audition

Amadeus and *Adobe Audition* are easy-to-use audio-editing programs that are quite similar in terms of their functionality. Amadeus is specific to Mac, and Adobe Audition can be used on both Mac and Windows computers.

Amadeus and Adobe Audition represent sound waves graphically as waveforms (see Figure 9.2), which can be useful for transcription. For example, visual representations can be used for measuring silences (see Figure 9.3; see Chapter 3 for further discussion) or for counting the number of laugh tokens (see Chapter 5).

Amadeus and Adobe Audition also offer a number of sound-editing functions that can, for example, be used to amplify a quiet recording, reduce noise (though this feature should be used sparingly as it can significantly change the recording), manipulate voice quality in order to anonymize individual speakers, and replace bits of sound (e.g., someone's name and address) with silence or other noise. They also offer basic editing functions for creating audio clips and many options for converting sound file formats, e.g., Adobe Audition can create a sound file from a video file.

Currently *Audacity* offers much of the functionality of both Amadeus and Adobe Audition, and is available as a free download: www.audacityteam.org/download

Prosodic and phonetic analysis: Praat

Freeware available at www.praat.org

Praat is a program designed for doing acoustic analysis of speech. The program can perform different sorts of analyses, but in conversation analytic research, it is primarily used to analyze and graphically represent intonation contours or, more precisely, changes in *fundamental frequency*, or f_0, which are perceived as changes in *pitch*. Praat works best for examining very short segments of talk (typically, a few seconds in length) that are produced in the clear, with no overlap.

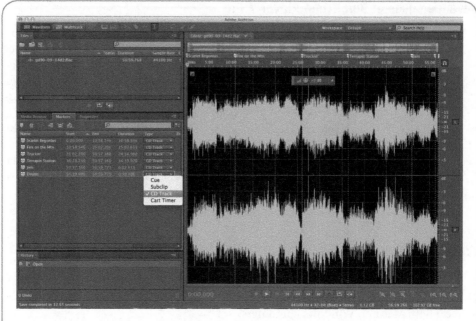

Figure 9.2 Sound wave representation in Adobe Audition © 2017 Adobe Systems Incorporated. All rights reserved. Adobe and Adobe Audition is/are either [a] registered trademark[s] or a trademark[s] of Adobe Systems Incorporated in the United States and/or other countries

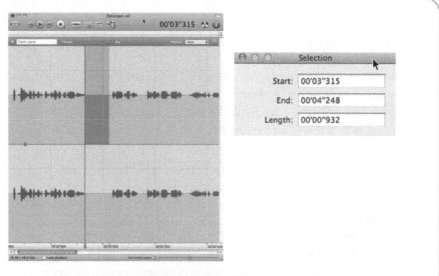

Figure 9.3 Measuring the length of silence with Amadeus

Praat is not a transcription program, but it may be used as a transcription aid since it allows the transcriber to check the hearing of pitch contours against a visualization. For example, in Figure 9.4, we can see the rising pitch contour at the end of the turn constructional unit (see Chapter 3), symbolized on the transcript by a question mark. Praat also produces representations of amplitude changes, as seen in Figures 9.5 and 9.6.

As an analytic tool, Praat is primarily used by researchers (such as interactional linguists) interested in aspects of prosody in interaction, who may supplement their (Jeffersonian) transcripts with visualizations of pitch tracks and other types of acoustic analyses (e.g., Barth-Weingarten et al., 2010; Couper-Kuhlen and Selting, 1996).

While Praat's visualizations of intonation might appear 'objective', these representations should be used with caution and not taken as having complete priority over hearing. For one, analytic claims should reflect what is auditorily available to participants in interaction, which is best assessed through close listening rather than acoustic measurements. The mapping between auditory perceptions and results of acoustic analyses is not straightforward, as there are documented discrepancies between acoustic representations and auditory perceptions (e.g., G. Walker, 2004). Further, pitch tracks produced by Praat can be greatly impacted by recorded ambient noise and other background sounds. (The program allows the analyst to 'clean up' the pitch tracks to correct for some interference.) Pitch tracks can also be manipulated in various ways to emphasize or deemphasize pitch movement, significantly changing the visual perception of the graphs. For a more

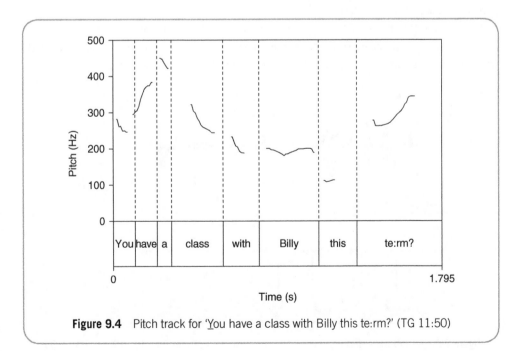

Figure 9.4   Pitch track for 'You have a class with Billy this te:rm?' (TG 11:50)

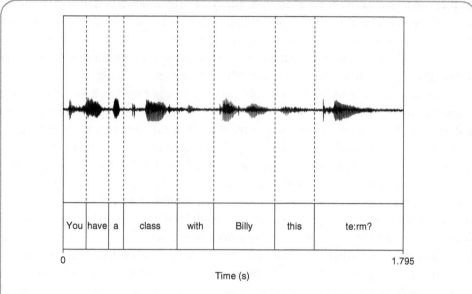

Figure 9.5 Sound wave for 'You have a class with Billy this te:rm?' (TG 11:50) showing amplitude changes (perceived as loudness)

detailed discussion of how to best represent pitch movements to account for pitch perception, see G. Walker (2004).

In a nutshell, Praat is useful for visualizing pitch movements in short bits of talk for transcription and analysis. You will need a relatively clean and loud recording with little background noise and no overlapping talk (during the analyzed segment).

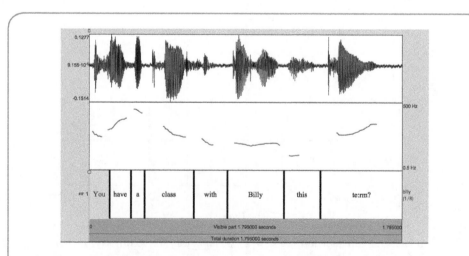

Figure 9.6 Sound wave and pitch track for 'You have a class with Billy this te:rm?' (TG 11:50)

COMPREHENSIVE TRANSCRIPTION PACKAGES

Many researchers create their transcripts using basic word processing programs. However, some prefer using specialized software packages for transcribing. Below we briefly introduce the two most popular ones: *Transana* (primarily on PC) and *ELAN* (cross platform). Both offer sophisticated tools for working with video-recordings, including transcription, analysis and collection building. Other useful packages include *CLAN* (http://talkbank.org/clan/) and *FOLKER* (http://agd.ids-mannheim.de/folker_en.shtml).

Before deciding to adopt one of the packages, however, you should carefully consider the balance of payoffs and (direct and indirect) costs of using this software. Adopting one of these packages is a significant commitment. For one, they may be quite difficult to learn. Additionally, because your transcripts are tied to a particular program, you may not be able to use previously created transcripts and may also have difficulty exporting newly created transcripts and other analytic products into other programs.

Transana

Website: https://www.transana.com/. PC and Mac versions are available (but it is currently more stable on PC).

Transana is used for transcribing and analyzing video- and audio-recorded data. It supports the standard Jeffersonian transcription system. Its major advantage is the ability to synchronize recordings with transcripts. It also has tools for coding data features and for creating and exporting data collections. The screen displays the video, the transcript and the waveform (see Figure 9.7).

ELAN

Website: https://tla.mpi.nl/tools/tla-tools/elan. Windows, Mac and Linux versions are available.

ELAN is a similar tool, developed by Max Planck Institute for Psycholinguistics in Nijmegen, the Netherlands. It is used for annotating and transcribing audio/video files in sheet-music (*partitur*) form. The ELAN screen (see Figure 9.8) shows waveforms and other audio characteristics (such as a pitch graph). ELAN synchronizes recordings with annotations and can create multiple annotation tiers for representing talk, non-vocal conduct, and various linguistic features. Additionally, it is designed to work with video from several cameras. Note, however, that it does not fully support the Jeffersonian transcription conventions, and so its usability for conversation analytic transcribing may be limited.

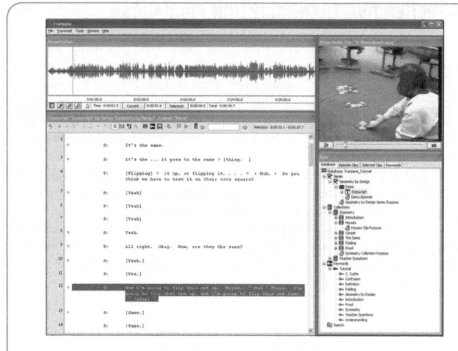

Figure 9.7   Transana user interface

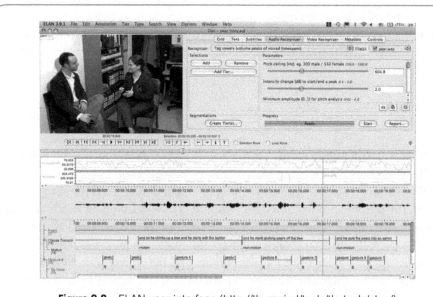

Figure 9.8   ELAN user interface (http://tla.mpi.nl/tools/tla-tools/elan/)

How to choose transcription software for conversation analysis

Saul Albert, Tufts University

Transcription software lets analysts synchronize media recordings with textual transcripts. This can be extremely useful for systematic transcription and analysis, but there are some important practical and methodological implications to bear in mind when choosing between and using these systems for conversation analysis (CA). One key choice is between two common approaches to representing transcripts for editing and viewing: either as 'tiers-of-timelines' (e.g., ELAN, EXMARaLDA and ANVIL) or as 'lists-of-turns' (e.g., CLAN, Transana and TranscriberAG). ELAN and CLAN are both good, free examples for a simple comparison of these approaches because both have very good documentation for further reference. There are also some excellent how-to videos for both CLAN and ELAN and other useful tools for CA transcription produced by the DIGIHUMLAB, available at http://beta.dighumlab.com/tools.

The advantages of tier-and-timeline software such as ELAN is that you can add as many tiers as necessary for any number of participants and phenomena along a horizontal timeline. This is particularly useful for bodily movements, facial expressions and other durational events that can be represented alongside talk as either independent or hierarchically structured tiers. ELAN's embedded media player is very sophisticated and enables analysts to align, review and transcribe multiple media files – shot from two or more angles, for example. The disadvantage of using ELAN for CA is that it can be hard to visually scan multiple tiers for precise moments of overlap and specific positions within units of talk. Also ELAN's ability to export files as a list-of-turns is basic and requires formatting to produce presentable transcripts. List-of-turns style transcription editors like CLAN, however, create transcripts that are easy to paste directly into a CA publication or presentation. CLAN may seem more intuitive for CA because the transcripts look Jeffersonian and the interface is more like a standard word processor. However, CLAN has a more basic media viewer, and relatively complex ways to create multiple tiers for bodily movements, images or for adding phonetic, grammatical and other annotation layers (Figure 9.9).

More generally, there are significant benefits and caveats for using either of these systems for CA. Synchronizing transcripts with recordings allows analysts to measure and review the precise timings of interaction, and analysts can also import and export transcripts in standardized machine-readable data formats. This can facilitate collaboration both within CA and in research groups that use various analytical approaches that combine, for example, video, sensor and motion capture data. Using these software tools and data formats also creates transcripts that are compatible with corpus databases and tools for searching, browsing and computational analysis. However, when researchers use software to combine primary data (recordings) and secondary data (transcripts), they should be careful to maintain these distinctions during analysis. For example, there is an important distinction between machine-measured clock-time and Jefferson's counting of 'beats' of interactional time, which typically include around 200 ms of latency in turn-transitions. If this

(Continued)

(Continued)

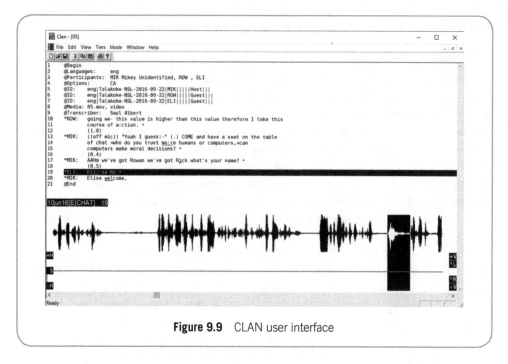

Figure 9.9 CLAN user interface

distinction is not accounted for, computational analysis might treat gaps as attributable silences[1]. The CA transcript is a descriptive representation of the course of social actions, whereas sensor readings or coded data show physiological or functional changes over time. Especially with corpus tools, researchers should be aware that it is impossible to 'search' for social actions which people may implement in various ways, and that key variations, 'deviant cases' and crucial CA points of interest may be effaced in this process.

INCORPORATING TRANSCRIPTS AND RECORDINGS IN PRESENTATIONS

Presenting results of your analysis in a clear and convincing way to audiences unfamiliar with your work may be quite a challenge, especially in a short public presentation. Some pitfalls could, however, be avoided by following a few relatively simple guidelines. In this section, we make recommendations about incorporating transcripts and recordings into oral presentations.

[1]See Hepburn and Bolden, 2013, and Chapter 3 of this book for further discussion of these issues.

Tips on using transcripts and recordings in presentations

If at all possible, prepare data handouts with transcripts to distribute to the audience. Make sure the text is large enough to be readable. Short transcripts can also be included in a slide (PowerPoint, Keynote, etc.) presentation. Make sure that the transcript font on the slides is at least 18 points and that you use easy-to-read, contrastive colors (for example, white background and dark text; avoid complex background designs). Longer transcripts are difficult to include on a slide in a large enough font. A longer transcript can be broken up into several slides. It is often better, however, to only include very short transcript extracts into the presentation and provide full transcripts on the handout. When you provide both a handout and presentation slides with the transcript, make sure that transcript line numbers match across different versions.

Using bright contrasting font colors (red, blue, etc.) may be helpful for drawing attention to a particular part of the transcript. Remember, however, that the colors on your computer screen may not correspond to the colors of the projector. For example, red and orange or brown may look the same when projected on a large screen. Instead of (or in addition to) contrasting colors, you may want to use boxes or arrows to highlight your analytic targets.

When you present your work, you will probably want to add audio and video data files to your slides. It is not uncommon to experience technical problems when attempting to play your clips in PowerPoint or another presentation program. For example, you may lose the links to the clips or the clips might not play. These problems are particularly common if you attempt to do a presentation on a computer provided by the venue rather than your own. The best solution may be to always use your own computer when presenting. In any case, it is important to have all your data clips in one place, together with the presentation file.

When you present your work, make sure that your clips are accurately cued to match the transcripts. When you include clips into your slides, you may want to set them up to begin playing automatically (on a click). Heath et al. (2010, chapter 7) offer a number of useful tips on presenting video data.

········ **EXPERT BOX *15*** ···

Presenting your transcript with the CARM technique

Elizabeth Stokoe, Loughborough University, UK

CARM is the Conversation Analytic Role-play Method (Stokoe, 2011; 2014; Stokoe and Sikveland, 2017). It is an evidence-based approach to communication training, grounded in conversation analytic (CA) research about what works and what is less effective in workplace and institutional interaction of all kinds. Traditional methods for training people in communication skills, and for

(Continued)

(Continued)

assessing those skills, are based on simulation or role-play. My research has shown that role-played interaction differs from the conversation it seeks to mimic (Stokoe, 2013). I have also observed that people are often assessed for 'skills' derived from normative assumptions about how talk works, rather than how it actually works. In turn, they may be trained to do the wrong thing, based on guidance founded on communication stereotypes that are not empirically grounded.

CARM takes findings about professional–client or service-provider–service-user interaction and turns the real-time, anonymized recordings into training workshops. Workshops have focused on scenarios such as how mediators can best explain mediation to prospective clients; how salespeople can best open a cold call; how neonatologists can most effectively initiate decision-making conversations with parents of premature babies; how GP (general practitioner) receptionists can keep patients satisfied when they phone the doctors; and how police hostage negotiators can talk to suicidal persons in ways that halt the progress towards suicide.

CARM works by, first, completing research about practices that work and practices that are less effective in a given setting (e.g., Shaw et al., 2016; Sikveland and Stokoe, 2016). Next, extracts that best represent effective/ineffective practice are anonymized and presented to workshop participants line-by-line in real time. Animation software (part of PowerPoint) is used to play the sound and technical CA transcript synchronously. This means that workshop participants live through conversations without knowing what is coming next, allowing them to 'role-play' what they might do next to handle the situation. If party A makes a particular comment, how might party B respond most appropriately? Participants discuss likely responses in small groups and report to the whole group. At that point party B's actual response is played. Participants evaluate what party B did, and report back to the whole group. Participants see and evaluate different responses, identifying effective practice on the basis of what actually happens in real interaction.

CARM provides participants with a unique (in terms of their training) opportunity to examine communicative practices in forensic detail, and to understand what works from a rigorous empirical basis. Examining the anonymized talk of people doing the work that participants do is instantly compelling; there is also a ready fit between CA research (in which analysts make explicit members' own analyses of each turn as an interaction unfolds), and showing conversational data to non-CA audiences, because the conceptual gap between research and practice is small.

Having run hundreds of workshops that have involved thousands of participants, and presented CARM and CA data to public audiences in many settings, it is clear that academic and non-academic people, untrained in CA and Jeffersonian transcription, find our work instantly accessible when it is presented this way. They learn quickly the power of the transcript. Many have an instinctive ethnomethodological sense of interaction and use the transcript to pin down their understanding of how practices are built and why some are more effective than others. I have found no need to present 'simplified' transcripts to the users of our research. The line-by-line presentation afforded by standard software – in contrast to using subtitles, which do not preserve the whole or sections of extracts on screen for discussion – gives CA researchers a tool for presenting magical findings about talk.

Links and references: www.carmtraining.org.

SOFTWARE TOOLS FOR PRESENTING VIDEO DATA

When presenting video data, it is often most useful to combine short bits of transcript with frame grabs (see Chapter 7 for a discussion of using video frame grabs in transcribing visible conduct). Video frame grabs can be easily created with, for example, QuickTime 7 Pro (see above). The images can then be edited using a graphics editing program.

One particularly useful program for editing frame grabs for publications and presentations is *AKVIS Sketch* (http://akvis.com/en/sketch/index.php). The program (which may be included as a plug-in in Adobe Photoshop) creates different types of drawing-style images from an original image (see Figure 9.10). This is useful for creating high-quality, contrastive images (for print and presentation) and images that mask participants' faces (for the purposes of anonymizing the interlocutors).

Figure 9.10   An original frame grab (left) and an AKVIS Sketch edited representation (right)

Subtitling video-recordings

If your video-recordings are in a language unfamiliar to the audience or if the recording is difficult to hear or understand, you should add subtitles to your video clips. Because the subtitles go by very fast, they should probably include only the words (or the idiomatic translation) of what is being said, without providing delivery details.

Subtitling videos may be quite time consuming, so it is important to choose a good tool. There are several programs that allow you to add subtitles. It is possible to create subtitles with *QuickTime 7 Pro* (Figure 9.11), though it is not a very straightforward process and it involves creating and importing a separate text file. Two other programs offer more user-friendly solutions. First, *iMovie* includes some options for adding subtitles (see Figure 9.12). Second, *InqScribe* (www.inqscribe.com) is an easy-to-use program specifically designed for creating subtitles (see Figure 9.13). It allows for quick editing and a number of basic formatting options, but is quite costly.

Figure 9.11   Subtitling in QuickTime Pro

Figure 9.12   Subtitling in iMovie

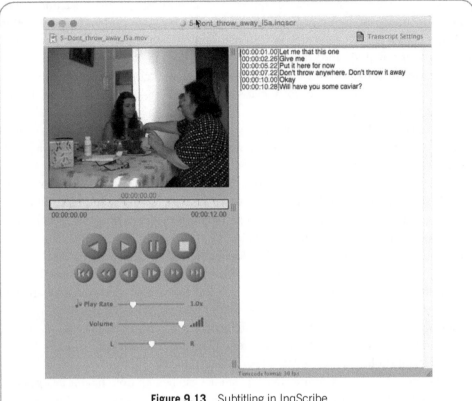

Figure 9.13   Subtitling in InqScribe

AUTOMATED TRANSCRIPTION

In recent years, there has been a growing interest in the possibility of using automated transcription technologies for conversation analytic research (Moore, 2015). Today's talk-to-text tools are not sophisticated enough to produce accurate detailed transcripts. However, as these technologies improve, they may become more attractive to interaction researchers – given their promise to alleviate the strain of the time-consuming transcription work and to enable access to much larger data corpora. We should, however, carefully consider the potential impact of these technologies on research. Here we offer a few words of caution to those who are thinking about adopting an automated transcription tool (for a longer discussion, see Bolden, 2015).

First, the process of transcribing has always been a key element of research and training in conversation analysis and aligned disciplines. Since interaction research necessitates intimate engagement with the recorded data, researchers have long emphasized the importance of the analyst's involvement in the transcribing process, and the integration of transcribing and analysis (e.g., Hepburn and Bolden, 2013; Hutchby and Wooffitt, 1998; Jefferson, 1985; Sidnell, 2010). In attempting to capture details of talk on paper, researchers become analysts rather than simple observers of interaction. Given the key role the transcription process plays in the analysis, development of transcription skills has been a fundamental step in research training. While transcribing is very time consuming, the analytic and educational payoffs are hard to overemphasize. We should therefore ensure that low-cost/low-labor approaches to transcription (which automating the process promises to be) do not replace good research practices and do not hinder training of new researchers.

Second, before choosing to adopt a new technology, we should be mindful of how technological affordances impact research agendas. A reliance on automated transcription may steer research and potentially negatively impact the kinds of data being studied and the kinds of analytic questions we ask. State-of-the-art automated transcription works best when used on high-quality recordings (such as, professional-quality broadcast recordings) in formal, less interactive contexts (where little overlapping talk occurs), and where all participants speak a standard dialect of a language (Moore, 2015). Researchers who adopt talk-to-text software may therefore be steered towards working on the kinds of data most suitable for this software and avoid collecting data in more interactive situations, with linguistically diverse populations, where high-quality recordings amendable to talk-to-text conversion are impossible to obtain. This might have a negative impact on three key areas of current interaction research: studies of ordinary conversation; studies into interactions between linguistically diverse people and interactions in lesser-known languages; and studies into complex interactional contexts.

Furthermore, only a very limited range of studies can benefit from having a large bank of (low-quality) transcripts to search through automatically. A majority of interactional phenomena a conversation analyst might study – from turn-taking practices to sequence organization, repair and action design (Sidnell and Stivers, 2013) – are not based on specific lexical practices and will be inaccessible to automated searches. Even the interactional phenomena that are based on lexical practices – such as, repetition (Bolden, 2009; Robinson and Kevoe-Feldman, 2010; Schegloff, 1996a; Stivers, 2005) or word selection (Kitzinger and Mandelbaum, 2013) – are not typically amendable to automated searches for specific word strings (for a discussion of collection building in an analysis of social actions, see, for example, Schegloff, 1996a). Additionally, a reliance on automated searches prevents discoveries of new actions and practices, which are only possible through direct and careful engagement with the data (Schegloff, 1996a). Thus, a decision to rely on a large bank of (computer-generated) transcripts may well influence research directions, prompting analysts to opt for word-hunting techniques, to the detriment of a vast number of analytic topics not permeable to this kind of investigation.

Third, automated transcription appears to encourage researchers to work on unfamiliar data corpora because it makes it possible for researchers to easily access vast banks of machine-transcribed data. The question is whether this is something to strive towards. It is often analytically important to be able to build a substantial collection of cases, and it is, in fact, a common practice to extend one's collection of an interactional phenomenon by examining other widely available data corpora. However, when interaction researchers search through 'classic' data corpora, they ordinarily have a good familiarity with the data, since these corpora are often examined in data sessions and heavily represented in the literature. This process is quite different from running an automated search through a bank of transcripts of unfamiliar recordings, locating and briefly examining potential cases, and then adding them to the collection. Without a familiarity with the data – i.e. without a good understanding of the larger course of action a segment contributes to or of the activities that comprise the interaction – researchers may well lose key aspects of the phenomenon they are trying to investigate.

Finally, from a practical standpoint, several aspects of the current talk-to-text technologies make their usage very labor intensive and rather off-putting (see Moore, 2015). Currently, these technologies produce transcripts with missing speaker identifications, arbitrary line segmentation, word identification errors, etc. Going from an automatically produced transcript of this sort to even a simple orthographic transcript where these shortcomings are corrected appears to be a very time-consuming task, without the analytic payoffs of the careful listening required for producing a Jeffersonian transcript. It is, of course, possible that future versions of this technology will address some of these problems and make automated transcription more cost effective. Even then, however, we may want to carefully consider the intended and unintended consequences of adopting this technology.

CONCLUDING COMMENTS

In this chapter we introduced some technological solutions for data transcription, analysis and presentation that can facilitate – but not replace – the work of transcribers. We have outlined specific ways in which different tools can contribute to transcription and data presentation.

RECOMMENDED READING

For a useful discussion of a number of technical tools for working with video, see:
Heath, C., Hindmarsh, J. and Luff, P. (2010) *Video in qualitative research*. Thousand Oaks, CA: Sage.

To find out more about the concepts discussed in this chapter, see examples of real transcriptions, and test your knowledge through exercises and quizzes, visit the supporting website at
https://study.sagepub.com/hepburnandbolden

TEN

Comparisons, Concerns and Conclusions

In the course of this book we have detailed the system and practice of transcribing inter-action for social science. As we have gone along, we have highlighted the virtues of a Jeffersonian system in capturing features of interaction that are consequential for action. The fundamental argument is that a system and method of transcription that can sup-port a social science approach to human life will benefit immeasurably from capturing these features of social interaction. The Jeffersonian system is not the only one. This final chapter will consider some of the more important alternatives and how, if our goal is to understand social interaction, a Jeffersonian transcription rectifies some of their limitations. It also investigates and responds to some of the concerns that have been raised about the Jeffersonian system. Finally, it will look toward the future as social life, research, technology and social science develop.

ALTERNATIVE SYSTEMS OF TRANSCRIPTION

In this section, we briefly discuss three well-known approaches to transcribing talk – the International Phonetic Alphabet (IPA), the Gesprächsanalytisches Transkriptionssystem (GAT) and the Discourse Transcription (DT) system – and consider their suitability for research into social interaction. See also Expert Box 16 on transcribing computer-mediated text-based interaction.

The International Phonetic Alphabet

The International Phonetic Alphabet (IPA) is designed to represent speech sounds across all human languages in a standardized way. The notation system is based on how the sounds are articulated (what speech organs are involved in producing sounds and how). Unlike many orthographic writing systems (e.g., English, French, etc.), there is a one-to-one cor-respondence between a sound and a symbol in the IPA: i.e. each sound is represented by one symbol, and a symbol always stands for the same sound. The IPA is not the only pho-netic transcription system; the American Phonetic Alphabet (APA) is another commonly used variation of the phonetic alphabet. The APA is based on the same principles as the IPA but some of the symbols used are different.

The IPA is the most commonly used phonetic transcription system in the field of lin-guistics. It is regulated by the International Phonetic Association (International Phonetic Association, 1999). However, there is a lot of variation in how the IPA is used in practice: both in what symbols are used (this often depends on the language under study) and in how detailed the transcripts are in describing the speech sounds.

Linguists distinguish between phonemic and phonetic representations of speech sounds. *Phonemes* are sounds that mark meaningful contrasts in a language. For instance, word-initially 't' and 'd' are different phonemes in English because replacing one with the other will change the word's meaning ('tale' vs. 'dale'). In the IPA, the most basic transcript is *phonemic*. A phonemic transcript of the English word 'top' would be /top/ (note the use of the slashes). This kind of transcript doesn't say much about how the word is produced in a particular context. Linguists also use the IPA to transcribe *phonetically* – that is, to provide a description of a string of speech sounds without making a claim about meaningful sound distinctions within a language. Phonetic transcripts can be produced at varying levels of detail, from a relatively *broad* transcription that only shows most prominent features of pronunciation (for example, the aspiration on 't' in 'top' [tʰɔp] in a standard American English dialect) to a relatively *narrow* one, which attempts to represent some particulars of the speaker's articulation. For instance, a more narrow phonetic transcript might indicate whether – in producing the word 'top' – 't' is dentalized (t̪), 'o' is voiced or unvoiced (o̥) and 'p' is released ([t̪ʰɔ̥p̚][1]). Linguists often use phonemic and broad phonetic transcripts to represent how a speaker of the standard language variety may pronounce a word in an idealized situation (Kelly and Local, 1989). According to Peter Ladefoged, a prominent linguist and phonetician, they rarely create 'impressionistic' transcripts that attempt to represent sounds as they are heard, but are instead guided by their 'hunches and preconceptions' about which sound distinctions should be represented and which should not (1993: 279).

Issues in using the IPA for transcribing talk-in-interaction

The IPA and other phonetic transcription systems are designed for transcribing very short speech segments (usually isolated words or phrases), often produced in an experimental setting, for the purposes of a linguistic analysis (e.g., Luebs, 1996). It is not intended for representing long stretches of multiparty interaction and especially data recorded outside of a sound booth in less than ideal situations.

More significantly, the IPA aims to facilitate a linguistic analysis that segments speech into discrete sounds and categorizes speech sounds on the basis of their articulation. An IPA transcript pays no attention to issues of sequencing and little attention to timing and prosody.[2] For example, there are no symbols for indicating overlapping talk. In fact, the IPA is best suited for 'spoken prose' produced by a single speaker rather than conversation (Kelly and Local, 1989). Silences are typically not marked; however, the extensions to the basic IPA have ways of indicating 'short', 'medium' and 'long' pauses, as well as timed pauses. The extensions to the IPA also have a number of symbols for representing some aspects of prosody (tempo, stress, loudness, pitch movements) and some symbols for non-speech sounds (e.g., lip-smacking), but their adequacy for representing spontaneous talk has been questioned (e.g., Ball and Local, 1996). Overall, the IPA focuses on aspects of speech sound articulations that are seen as important in linguistics and downplays other features of talk.

---

[1]The symbol underneath 't' is dental; superscript 'h' is aspirated; the symbol with 'p' means 'no audible release'); [ɔ] is open [o]; the circle underneath is for voiceless.

[2]In linguistics, these are called 'suprasegmentals' – i.e. features of speech that operate above individual speech sounds or 'segments'.

When it might be useful to use the IPA

Conversation analysts have used the IPA in a limited way for transcribing aspects of phonetic production. This is usually done to supplement a standard Jeffersonian transcript that captures aspects of timing, sequencing and prosodic realization. The inclusion of the IPA might be particularly useful when dealing with speech that is difficult to represent using modified orthography; e.g., disordered speech and speech pathology, talk by very young children (Wells and Corrin, 2004) and novice language learners, as well as dialectal pronunciation differences. Some of these usages of the IPA for interactional research are discussed in Chapters 4 and 8.

For more information on the IPA, see www.internationalphoneticassociation.org

Gesprächsanalytisches Transkriptionssystem

Gesprächsanalytisches Transkriptionssystem (GAT) (the current version is GAT 2) is a transcription system developed by a group of German conversation analysts and interactional linguists (Couper-Kuhlen and Barth-Weingarten, 2011). GAT is quite similar to the Jeffersonian transcription, but it emphasizes the representation of prosodic aspects of talk. Like the DT (discussed below), lines are segmented according to 'intonation phrases' and a special attention is paid to intonation within the intonation phrases and at the intonation phrase boundaries. Transcripts can be presented at different levels of detail. GAT 2 distinguishes three levels: minimal, basic and fine. While a 'basic' transcript is similar to a CA transcript in the amount of detail about timing and delivery aspects of speech it provides, a 'fine' transcript attempts to capture and represent more information, especially with regards to prosody. So far, GAT has been used primarily for German language, though some interactional linguists working in other languages also use the system. Empirical work will attest to the suitability of this system for conducting interaction analysis across social science disciplines.

For more information on GAT, see http://agd.ids-mannheim.de/gat_en.shtml

Discourse Transcription system

The Discourse Transcription (DT) system was developed by John W. Du Bois and his colleagues in the department of linguistics at the University of California, Santa Barbara (Du Bois et al., 1992, 1993). The system is designed for transcribing various forms of spoken interaction. Like Jeffersonian transcription, the DT has conventions for capturing many aspects of timing and sequencing of talk (silences, overlap, etc.) and details of speech delivery (prosody, volume, etc.). One distinctive feature of this transcription system is its reliance on the notion of 'intonation units' – 'a stretch of speech uttered under a single coherent intonation contour' (Du Bois et al., 1992: 17). In contrast to the

Jeffersonian transcription, transcript lines are segmented according to intonation units, so that a single speaker's turn-at-talk may be represented on several short lines.

There are quite a few differences in the kinds of notations used by the DT in comparison to the CA transcription. While many of these differences may be seen as simply different ways of representing the same interactional phenomena, some aspects of interaction are captured quite differently and in ways that may be insufficiently precise. For example, in representing laughter, while a Jeffersonian transcript captures many aspects of laughter delivery (see Chapter 5), a DT transcript only indicates the number of laugh particles (with @) and where they occur sequentially.

For more information on DT, see www.linguistics.ucsb.edu/projects/transcription/index.html

········ **EXPERT BOX** *16* ··

Transcription of online interactions using screen-capture software

Joanne Meredith, University of Salford, UK

Recently, there has been an increase in researchers interested in studying the interactional properties of online data collected using screen-capture software (Bhatt and de Roock, 2013; Meredith and Stokoe, 2014). Screen-capture software may be used to record text-based online interaction, thereby providing researchers with a video of the interaction occurring as 'live'. There are various ways to represent these kinds of data; for example, by simply using screenshots to represent the actions appearing on-screen (e.g., Keating and Sunakawa, 2011) or by using a written transcript which uses the text of the interaction and also includes descriptions of some of the participants' multi-modal actions (e.g., Beisswenger, 2008; Garcia and Jacobs, 1999). As new data are collected using screen-capture across a variety of interactional platforms, new transcription systems may need to be developed.

Multi-modal text-based data pose a number of challenges for transcription. Firstly, since the interaction is text-based, some symbols used in a Jeffersonian transcript to represent, say emotional expression, cannot be used, as these symbols may be typed as part of the interaction (e.g., by using LOL or various emoticons). Secondly, when data are recorded using screen-capture of one of the interactants, there will be information available to the transcriber that the online recipient can't see, such as what the participant is writing then deleting, or what other behavior/conversations they are engaged in at the same time as their interaction. So it is necessary to distinguish between what data are available to the researcher (and the participant being recorded), and what data are visible, and therefore interactionally available to both participants. Thirdly, the data collected may well involve moving text as well as other actions (such as opening web pages, searching for information, talking to different people online, and so on). Depending on the focus of the analysis, this information may not need to be transcribed in detail. However, it will be important to find ways of easily representing these other actions, such as through using icons or images.

For more detail on the transcription system I used for my Facebook chat data, see Meredith (2015).

JEFFERSONIAN TRANSCRIPTION: CRITICISMS AND COUNTERS

In this section we examine some of the criticisms that have been levelled at Jeffersonian transcription. Some researchers have raised objections to transcription on the grounds that it embodies researchers' theoretical orientations, and that its complexity and lack of reflexivity about its own product is a hindrance to research, and creates pretense at scientific rigor. Many criticisms of transcription practices relate to a broader dissatisfaction with the project of conversation analysis, for example many question the status of transcripts as unproblematic representations of 'participants' orientations' in the talk. We will take claims that seem to embody different forms of criticism, explore them in turn and develop some counter points. We then consider more broadly the versions of empiricism that seems to underpin different types of criticism.

Transcription as theory

Some researchers have endorsed the value of transcribing the specifics of interaction but argued that transcribers should be more reflexive about what they produce. For example, Ochs (1979) suggests that there are assumptions about the world wired into transcription, and that we should consider the way they work and be cautious about them. She developed the notion of 'transcription as theory' precisely to illustrate these concerns. Similarly, Bucholtz (2000) advocates a reflexive transcription practice that highlights the assumptions made in the process. Bucholtz spells out what such a reflexive practice would involve: 'we must seek reactions from colleagues, from lay people and from the voices we record' (2000: 1462) and through this process we can avoid simply validating our own perspective.

A response

Most conversation analysts would accept the notion that issues of interpretation and reflexivity are fundamental to a robust analysis of practices. One unique feature of CA practice is that everyone involved in doing it has the opportunity to highlight the limitations of the transcription system and to produce a better one. CA works with sound and video alongside transcript, unlike common alternative approaches. Future publishing will increasingly allow readers and the broader community to work with both together. Our argument in this book is that as a community of researchers, interaction analysts need to agree on the best way of representing interactional elements of talk. Jefferson's system does not depend on any realist justification of what is simply there in talk, rather (and unlike approaches that simply try to 'capture the words') it is *explicitly* theorized, in that it evolved through the tradition of work in CA, and through the focus on talk as performing actions. One way of reading this book has been as a way of explicating the theoretical assumptions and practices that go into Jeffersonian transcription. Far from hiding theory, it has developed in concert with it. This has proved to be an analytically powerful approach; critics have the opportunity to enter the fray *analytically* and show how analyses are limited or misguided, or how transcription could be more interactionally sensitive. Ochs (1979) has done the community a good service by highlighting the importance of theoretical considerations in transcription. We have pushed this argument further on in our current book.

Bucholtz's advice, that we should more readily seek reactions from lay people and from the people we record is an interesting one, and has been taken on board by some CA researchers, especially where institutional environments are concerned. It is now fairly common practice that research projects include advisory boards peopled by various stakeholders who have the opportunity to engage with, and help to refine, the findings. This can be good practice. However, as Potter and Hepburn (2005a, 2012) have shown with their analysis of interview practices, talking to participants post hoc about what they intended or thought when they engaged in particular types of practice is fraught with reflexive trouble. One useful way around these problems is by engaging institutions with transcripts and recordings of their own practices. This has been done by Hepburn and colleagues with helplines (Hepburn, 2006; Hepburn and Potter, 2004; Hepburn et al., 2014) where we have found that our analysis and transcript precisely support a sophisticated engagement with professionals' own practices. Stokoe has also elevated this practice to a fine art by her development (with professional mediators) of the 'conversation analytic role-play method' (CARM – Stokoe, 2011, and see Expert Box 15 in Chapter 9). The CARM rolling transcript technique allows participants to work with the interaction alongside its more technical representation.

Varying practices of transcription

Some researchers have argued that the style of transcription used should relate to the specific research questions being asked. In other words, the analytic object of study may not necessarily be social interaction, in which case why bother with an interactionally sensitive transcript? (For example, Kvale, 1983; Du Bois, 1980, and also Ochs, 1979, develop this argument.) To take an example, if the researcher were focused on identifying narratives in talk, then she would not need the level of detail that CA has developed. Blommaert (2007) provides an example of this – he suggests that although conversation looks primary, instead narrative 'could well be seen as an *a priori* genre for the organisation of interaction' so we need to 'do justice to variation in talk by means of variation in transcription procedures' (Blommaert, 2007: 828).

A response

Conversation analysis is a program that is empirically progressive. Its studies and their cumulative success provide a robust demonstration of the adequacy of the form of

Jeffersonian transcription. If Blommaert and others could empirically demonstrate how 'variations in talk', for example, CA's lack of focus on narratives, were causing problems for analysis, then that might push interaction researchers towards incorporating them into analysis. If they were able to build an empirically cumulative field working with a transcription that captures narrative, that would be more powerful. The next step would be competing studies working with the same kinds of material.

There is an important point to be made here. As we have shown throughout this book, the Jeffersonian system of transcription has evolved in response to studies that highlight the importance of features of the delivery of talk. It is essential to avoid developing a rigid system that only encodes some features of talk, risking a failure to capture the analytic consequentiality of features of talk that have not been so encoded. Interaction analysts are typically open to the possibility that different features of talk may need to be encoded in some way, and the system of transcription modified. The point is that such features should be *demonstrably* relevant to interaction. That is, they should be shown to be features that the participants find consequential.

We have argued in this book that interaction analysis is not coextensive with the nature of transcription. It is possible to highlight two kinds of evolution. First, as we highlighted throughout the book, there is the development of CA into new domains: studies of young children and disability (Chapter 4), and of embodied action (Chapter 7). Second, there have been various refinements to the system. In Chapter 6 we noted the importance of representing interactionally relevant elements of upset that were not captured in the original system. In Chapter 7 we have also seen that CA has been grappling with how to represent various non-vocal features and increasingly seeing details of visible conduct as crucial to face-to-face interaction. In other words, CA modes of representation are not static. It is also the case that CA transcripts do get adapted to analytic goals, to some extent. This is particularly true of transcripts of visible behavior, which are always extremely selective (Chapter 7).

Transcription as rhetoric

Critics such as Elliot Mischler (1991) and David Bogen (1992) claimed that there is a display of professionalism and technicality in transcription symbols and their use, and this can interfere with analysis and suggest access to a mythic realm of description that is free of theory and interpretation. The suspicion is that there is a persuasive role in the way transcription is deployed, suggesting some kind of deception may be underway. This may even involve a separation between the researcher's chosen form of research (e.g., ethnomethodology, narrative or phenomenological analysis) and CA, where the former is presented as sophisticated and subtle, while CA is mechanical and positivistic, taking practitioners away from any interest in what their participants are thinking or feeling, or their cultural or political context. The conclusion is that most researchers would be better off doing different styles of research, and ignoring the specifics of their participants' interactions.

A response

We can develop a similar counter to our previous one – there is an onus on those developing criticisms of conversation analysts' current practices to show the relevance of their arguments to the practice of analysis. It may be that there are important things related to subtlety and complexity of interaction that are missed by the practice of transcription. However, there is a difference between highlighting a possibility in principle and showing its relevance in an analytic study.

It is certainly the case that a good, precise transcript is a display of quality, of taking the words and actions seriously. This might be rhetorical – a good architects' plan, with measurements and the right number of rooms and floors, might persuade us to hire that architect over a plan that has no measurements and just an impression of room numbers. Likewise, we can be enormously pleased with the achievement of a high-quality transcript that captures, say, the evolution of extreme upset in a child protection call. It is a serious practice that puts much time and effort into its precision in capturing talk; as such it deserves to be taken seriously.

Transcripts as epistemological grounding

Ashmore and Reed (2005) develop a critique of CA through the notion of 'professional hearing' – the fact that transcribers are trained to hear certain things in certain ways. Like Mischler (1991), they suggest that this makes CA work look objective, and they also claim that it obscures what can be revealed analytically. However, they develop a more sophisticated epistemological argument along the lines that all hearings are mediated and so reports of those hearings are interpretative. Ashmore et al. (2004) also argue that this 'professional hearing' suggests the ability to transcend epistemic doubt. Their overall point is that we should have a more skeptical and finessed view of the status of the transcript as evidence.

A response

Ashmore and colleagues are undoubtedly right in their argument that all representations are open to radical epistemic doubt, and that transcription is an empirical practice and involves assumptions and hearings. However, this book is designed to make those assumptions explicit, and it is designed to assist researchers in their hearings and the translation of those hearings into a form that supports shared communication. A Jeffersonian transcript doesn't have to have a guarantee of epistemic uniqueness to make it more powerful than other alternatives. The key point in analysis – and again this is cumulative – is that what is captured is shown, repeatedly, to be relevant to the ongoing interaction. That is the profound importance of being able to work with participants' orientations. The training and hearing of the transcriber is informed by that focus on what is hearable and oriented to.

······· **EXPERT BOX** *17* ···

Cross-transcriber reliability

Jeffrey D. Robinson, Portland State University, USA

While being an unapologetically qualitative approach, conversation analysis (CA) was intended (by Harvey Sacks, among many others) to be a replicable social science. Replicability relies on assessment tools being reliable, and the most important of these tools in CA is its method of transcription (of verbal, vocal and non-vocal conduct). Transcription supplies the primary source of evidence for and against CA claims in published research. When a transcript indicates that a word is pronounced in a non-standard fashion, or that overlap begins in a particular place, or that someone pauses for a particular amount of time, there needs to be a social-scientifically acceptable level of confidence that any given trained conversation analyst would have produced the same transcript, and thus that they would have heard or viewed the same behavior in the same manner (i.e. that the transcript is reliable).

Roberts and Robinson (2004) tested the reliability of a 2.5-minute stretch of transcript (of a previously unknown, naturally occurring, mundane telephone call) produced by four trained conversation analysts (who were not also trained phoneticians). Each transcriber spent an average of three hours on the task. Very importantly, acceptable levels of reliability were found for the existence, sequencing, semantics and orthography of silences, words and sound units (including breathing and laughing). Additionally, transcribers exhibited acceptable levels of reliability for speaker designation, overlap (at the lexical level), silence length using the perceptual/counting method, sound stretch (at the lexical level), sound cut-offs, pitch and smile voice. In contrast, transcribers were not acceptably reliable with regard to unit-final intonation shifts (e.g., none, period for fall, question mark for rise), stress/amplitude (i.e. underlining), pace/duration (e.g., carats for fast or slow), or silence length when relying on machine timing (e.g., computer software that displays sound waves); the reliability of these phenomena may be increased by reading this book and practicing with the accompanying online materials, and by collaborating with trained phoneticians. Future research needs to test the reliability of the transcription of non-vocal phenomena involving, for example, gaze and body orientation, and the utilization of artifacts.

···

Reflections on transcription and empiricism

Many concerns about transcriptions seem to revolve around the status of the transcript as a piece of 'empiricism' in conversation analysis, so it is worth stopping to consider this more closely.

Sociologists of scientific knowledge have highlighted the diversity of scientific practices. Knorr Cetina (1999), for example, has argued against the notion of sciences being characterized by a limited set of methods used in a standard fashion across astronomy, biochemistry or sociology. Instead she showed that detailed research studies of the operation of different scientific practices have highlighted the existence of a disparate set of *'epistemic cultures'*. At the center of these cultures is their construction of the empirical – while molecular biologists may be looking for change in bacteria growth in petri dishes, high-energy physicists may compare hypothetical events in a particle collider, reconstructed with the aid of several concurrently available theoretical systems.

If we build on Knorr Cetina's findings, then for interaction analysts, Jeffersonian transcript is the agar in the petri dish of the 'epistemic culture' that supports conversation analysis.

EXPERT BOX *18*

Transcription as culture

John Heritage, UCLA, USA

During the 1970s Gail Jefferson began circulating her transcripts among a growing group of interested researchers. More importantly, she also circulated the recordings on which the transcripts were based. The consequences of this latter decision were remarkable. First, we were all presented with a transcription equivalent of the Rosetta Stone. The tape allowed us to see the decisions she had made in creating the transcripts – what kind of thing warranted an underline, or an arrow indicating a pitch reset, and so on – and allowed us to emulate those decisions in our own transcripts. At the same time, the transcripts highlighted features of the recordings that we might have otherwise overlooked, and pointed up practices in the talk which turned out to be highly relevant to our analyses. Because the tapes and transcripts were quite widely circulated, they contributed to a 'culture of transcribing', to the development of a set of common standards that we learned to share, and tried to live up to. The standards allowed us to recognize failure – our own and other people's – as well as success. The consequence of all this was the rapid creation of a conversation analytic culture which has remained coherent up to the present day.

A broader consequence, however, was that we bypassed a deeply problematic feature of qualitative and ethnographic research which I think of as the 'my island' problem. The problem looks like this: an ethnographer visits an island community (it could just as easily be an inner city gang), and reports that 'They do A and B here'. Subsequently a second ethnographer goes to a second island, and reports that 'They don't do A and B here, but they sometimes do C'. The 'my island' problem stems from the fact that, while both ethnographers could be right and there are clear differences in how the islanders do things, one (or both of them) could be wrong either by misunderstanding something that happened, or by missing it altogether, so that the islands might be a lot more similar than either of them thought.

From the very beginning of CA, the circulation of tapes and transcripts side-stepped that problem. As a result, CA could be informative in the sense that as Sacks (1984: 26) put it 'others could look at what I had studied and make of it what they could, if, for example, they wanted to be able to disagree with me'. Gail Jefferson's transcription system, and her circulation of recordings and transcripts had a remarkable impact in bootstrapping the common culture of CA, and in making sure that it was founded in commonly witnessed and verifiable fact.

Jeffersonian transcription has developed in concert with the evolution of conversation analytic studies of interaction and provides a shared, standard system for rendering talk-in-interaction in a form that can be readily reproduced in textual form. However, the ubiquity of this method of transcription should not be confused with assigning it a special epistemic privilege. It is not a form of naïve positivism as some critics assert. CA researchers pervasively work in data sessions with other experienced analysts. A typical data session will involve multiple playing of the recordings and often a period of checking hearings and refining transcript. Analytic observations will refer back to the transcript or the recording, and often both. Even well-used transcripts by expert transcribers can be subject to improvement, as new hearings, perhaps with better equipment, or with refined conventions, allow for minor changes. There is often a particular focus in data sessions on the transcription of those sections of recordings that will have a role in supporting research claims.

Many of the critics of current practices of transcription would like it to be more reflective and more critical and consider alongside this the way in which meaning is constructed through discourses, repertoires, narrative and other underspecified interactional objects. It is hard to escape the conclusion that a number of critics of the use of Jeffersonian transcription would prefer something easier to replace it. There is a sense of resentment against the injunction to take the delivery of talk as consequential and therefore the injunction to produce a form of transcription that is adequate to that delivery. It would, indeed, be easier to work with a simple orthographic typescript produced by a fast-typing PhD student or internet transcription service. But that would lose many of the features that have repeatedly been shown to be fundamental to people living their lives. Ultimately, it would involve deliberately bypassing the subtlety and sophistication of those very people that we are interested in studying.

CONCLUDING COMMENTS

> From close looking at the world we can find things that we could not, by imagination, assert were there. We would not know that they were 'typical' ... Indeed, we might not have noticed that they happen. Therefore, the kind of phenomena I deal with are always transcriptions of actual occurrences in their actual sequences. (Sacks, 1984: 25)

For much of this book we have focused on Jeffersonian transcription for its role in conversation analysis. Let us now stand back a bit. If human life is fundamentally transacted through talk and texts in interaction, whether mediated or face-to-face, then this approach to transcription that best captures the features of talk that are interactionally live ought to have a broader significance. For all social scientists who want to put down their clipboards and step outside the laboratory door to study the world as it happens, Jeffersonian transcript is a fundamental tool. For decades, psychologists, sociologists, geographers and other social scientists have, with few exceptions, been reluctant to move away from the settings where they have irresistible control over what they are studying.

Structured surveys and questionnaires, so-called open-ended interviews, and experimental protocols have defined much of the last century of social science. Whatever their virtues, such methods flood the research interaction with the terms and assumptions of the researcher; they are designed to answer questions and address theory developed in the internal traditions of social science. As Potter and Shaw (forthcoming) have argued, part of what held back earlier moves towards field work was the absence of a scheme that could capture human life in a rigorous and reproducible way. Jeffersonian transcription combined with high-quality digital audio and video can help social scientists of all persuasions better engage with the world, share their findings, develop new questions and challenge their own assumptions.

One role of this book is to show how reflective and critical Jefferson was in her development of transcription, and how the practice of transcription will be improved by continued critical engagement with other developments. However, it can only do this if we work as a community, with accepted conventions, which require strong interactional evidence to change or discard.

The central aim of Jeffersonian transcription has always been 'to get as much of the actual sound as possible into [the] transcripts, while still making them accessible to linguistically unsophisticated readers' (Sacks et al., 1974: 734). CA transcripts are compact, transportable and reproducible, and provide for easy random access, unlike audio or video records. They are a fundamental resource for data sessions, presentations and journal articles, and, as such, are often the medium through which analysts encounter and evaluate each other's' work. They effectively *decelerate* the interaction, so that key features that might prove difficult to hear on a one-off hearing are *visible*, to both the analyst and to those who are reading or assessing the analysis. Perhaps most crucially, a good transcript provides a legacy for future researchers – Gail Jefferson's transcripts from many years ago are still being used, due to their accurate representation of details relevant to analysis.

Jeffersonian transcription has evolved, and will continue to evolve, with the gradual progression of conversation analytic studies of interaction. It sits at the center of the epistemic culture of conversation analysis.

References

Antaki, C. and Wilkinson, R. (2012) Conversation analysis and the study of atypical populations. In J. Sidnell and T. Stivers (Eds) *Handbook of conversation analysis* (pp. 533–50). Oxford: Blackwell-Wiley.

Aoki, H. (2011) Some functions of speaker head nods. In J. Streeck, C. Goodwin and C. LeBaron (Eds) *Embodied interaction: Language and body in the material world* (pp. 93–105). Cambridge: Cambridge University Press.

Ashmore, M. and Reed, D. (2005) Innocence and nostalgia in conversation analysis: The dynamic relations of tape and transcript. *Historical Social Research, 30*(1), 73–94.

Ashmore, M., MacMillan, K. and Brown, S.D. (2004) It's a scream: Professional hearing and tape fetishism. *Journal of Pragmatics, 36*(2), 349–74.

Auburn, T.C. and Pollock, C. (2012) Laughter and competence: Children with severe autism using laughter to joke and tease. In P. Glenn and E. Holt *Studies of Laughter in Interaction* (pp. 135–160). London: Continuum Books.

Auer, P. (1996) On the prosody and syntax of turn-continuations. In E. Couper-Kuhlen and M. Selting (Eds) *Prosody in conversation: Interactional studies* (pp. 57–101). Cambridge: Cambridge University Press.

Auer, P. (Ed.) (1998) *Code-switching in conversation: Language, interaction and identity*. New York: Routledge.

Auer, P., Couper-Kuhlen, E. and Müller, F. (1999) *Language in time: The rhythm and tempo of spoken interaction*. New York: Oxford University Press.

Ball, M.J. and Local, J. (1996) Current developments in transcription. In M.J. Ball and M. Duckworth (Eds) *Advances in clinical phonetics* (pp. 51–89). Amsterdam: John Benjamins.

Barth-Weingarten, D., Reber, E. and Selting, M. (2010) *Prosody in interaction*. Amsterdam: John Benjamins.

Beisswenger, M. (2008) Situated chat analysis as a window to the user's perspective: Aspects of temporal and sequential organization. *Language@Internet, 5* (Article 6).

Bhatt, I. and de Roock, R. (2013) Capturing the sociomateriality of digital literacy events. *Research in Learning Technology, 21*.

Bilmes, J. (1996) Problems and resources in analyzing Northern Thai conversation for English language readers. *Journal of Pragmatics, 26*(2), 171–88.

Blommaert, J. (2007) Narrative, interaction, or both. *Discourse Studies, 9*(6), 828–30.

Bogen, D. (1992) The organization of talk. *Qualitative Sociology, 15,* 273–96.

Bolden, G.B. (2003) Multiple modalities in collaborative turn sequences. *Gesture, 3*(2), 187–212.

Bolden, G.B. (2008) Reopening Russian conversations: The discourse particle -*to* and the negotiation of interpersonal accountability in closings. *Human Communication Research, 34,* 99–136.

Bolden, G.B. (2009) Beyond answering: Repeat-prefaced responses in conversation. *Communication Monographs, 76*(2), 121–43.

Bolden, G.B. (2010) 'Articulating the unsaid' via *and*-prefaced formulations of others' talk. *Discourse Studies, 12*(1), 5–32.

Bolden, G.B. (2011) On the organization of repair in multiperson conversation: The case of 'other'-selection in other-initiated repair sequences. *Research on Language and Social Interaction, 44*(3), 237–62.

Bolden, G.B. (2012) Across languages and cultures: Brokering problems of understanding in conversational repair. *Language in Society, 41*(1), 97–121.

Bolden, G.B. (2015) Transcribing *as* research: 'Manual' transcription and conversation analysis. *Research on Language and Social Interaction, 48*(3), 276–80.

Bolden, G.B. and Guimaraes, E. (2012) Grammatical flexibility as a resource in explicating referents. *Research on Language and Social Interaction, 45*(2), 156–74.

Bucholtz, M. (2000) The politics of transcription. *Journal of Pragmatics, 32,* 1439–65.

Clayman, S.E. (2001) Answers and evasions. *Language in Society, 30*(3), 403–42.

Clemente, I. (2009) Progressivity and participation: Children's management of parental assistance in paediatric chronic pain encounters. *Sociology of Health & Illness, 31*(6), 872–88.

Clemente, I. (2015) *Uncertain futures: Communication and culture in childhood cancer treatment.* Chichester: John Wiley & Sons.

Clyne, M. (1994) *Inter-cultural communication at work: Cultural values in discourse.* Cambridge: Cambridge University Press.

Couper-Kuhlen, E. (2001) Interactional prosody: High onsets in reason-for-the-call turns. *Language in Society, 30,* 29–53.

Couper-Kuhlen, E. (2012) Some truths and untruths about prosody in English question and answer sequences. In J.P. De Ruiter (Ed.) *Questions: Formal, functional and interactional perspectives.* Cambridge: Cambridge University Press.

Couper-Kuhlen, E. and Barth-Weingarten, D. (2011) A system for transcribing talk-in-interaction: GAT 2. *Gesprächsforschung, 12,* 1–51.

Couper-Kuhlen, E. and Ford, C.E. (Eds) (2004) *Sound patterns in interaction: Cross-linguistic studies from conversation.* Amsterdam: John Benjamins.

Couper-Kuhlen, E. and Selting, M. (Eds) (1996) *Prosody in conversation: Interactional studies* (Vol. 12). New York: Cambridge University Press.

Drew, P. (1997) 'Open' class repair initiators in response to sequential sources of troubles in conversation. *Journal of Pragmatics, 28,* 69–101.

Du Bois, J.W. (1980) Beyond definiteness: The trace of identity in discourse. *The pear stories: Cognitive, cultural, and linguistic aspects of narrative production, 3,* 203–274.

Du Bois, J.W., Cumming, S., Schuetze-Coburn, S. and Paolino, D. (1992) Discourse transcription. *Santa Barbara Papers in Linguistics, 4*(1), 1–225.

Du Bois, J.W., Schuetze-Coburn, S., Cumming, S. and Paolino, D. (1993) Outline of discourse transcription. In J.A. Edwards and M.D. Lampert (Eds) *Talking data: Transcription and coding in discourse research* (pp. 45–89). Hillsdale, NJ: Erlbaum.

Egbert, M. (2004) Other-initiated repair and membership categorization – some conversational events that trigger linguistic and regional membership categorization. *Journal of Pragmatics, 36*(8), 1467–98.

Egbert, M., Yufu, M. and Hirataka, F. (2016) An investigation of how 100 articles in the *Journal of Pragmatics* treat transcripts of English and non-English languages. *Journal of Pragmatics, 94,* 98–111.

Enfield, N.J. (2007) Meaning of the unmarked: How 'default' person reference does more than just refer. In N.J. Enfield and T. Stivers (Eds) *Person reference in interaction* (pp. 97–120). Cambridge: Cambridge University Press.

Enfield, N.J., Stivers, T. and Levinson, S.C. (2010) Question–response sequences in conversation across ten languages: An introduction. *Journal of Pragmatics, 42*(10), 2615–19.

Firth, A. and Wagner, J. (1997) On discourse, communication, and (some) fundamental concepts in SLA research. *The Modern Language Journal, 81*(iii), 285–300.

Ford, C.E. and Thompson, S.A. (1996) Interactional units in conversation: Syntactic, intonational, and pragmatic resources for the management of turns. In E. Ochs, E.A. Schegloff and S.A. Thompson (Eds) *Interaction and grammar* (pp. 134–84). Cambridge: Cambridge University Press.

Ford, C.E., Fox, B.A. and Thompson, S.A. (2002) Constituency and the grammar of turn increments. In C.E. Ford, B.A. Fox and S.A. Thompson (Eds) *The language of turn and sequence* (pp. 14–38). Oxford: Oxford University Press.

Fox, B.A. (2001) An exploration of prosody and turn projection in English conversation. In M. Selting and E. Couper-Kuhlen (Eds) *Studies in interactional linguistics* (pp. 286–315). Philadelphia: John Benjamins.

Freese, J. and Maynard, D.W. (1998) Prosodic features of bad news and good news in conversation. *Language in Society, 27*(2), 195–219.

Gafaranga, J. (2007) *Talk in two languages.* New York: Palgrave Macmillan.

Garcia, A.C. and Jacobs, J.B. (1999) The eyes of the beholder: Understanding the turn-taking system in quasi-synchronous computer-mediated communication. *Research on Language and Social Interaction, 32*(4), 337–67.

Gardner-Chloros, P., Moyer, M., Sebba, M. and van Hout, R. (1999) Towards standardizing and sharing bilingual data. *International Journal of Bilingualism, 3*(4), 395–424.

Gaskill, W.H. (1980) Correction in native speaker–nonnative speaker conversation. In D. Larsen-Freeman (Ed.) *Discourse analysis in second language research* (pp. 125–37). Rowley, MA: Newbury.

Geluykens, R. (1988) The myth of rising intonation in polar questions. *Journal of Pragmatics, 12*(4), 467–85.

Glenn, P. (2003) *Laughter in interaction.* Cambridge University Press.

Glenn, P.J. and Holt, E. (2013) *Studies of laughter in interaction.* London: Bloomsbury Publishing.

Goffman, E. (1978) Response cries. *Language,* 787–815.

Goodwin, C. (1979) The interactive construction of a sentence in natural conversation. In G. Psathas (Ed.) *Everyday language: Studies in ethnomethodology* (pp. 97–121). New York: Irvington Publishers.

Goodwin, C. (1980) Restarts, pauses, and the achievement of a state of mutual gaze at turn-beginning. *Sociological Inquiry, 50*(3–4), 272–302.

Goodwin, C. (1981) *Conversational organization: Interaction between speakers and hearers.* New York: Academic Press.

Goodwin, C. (1986) Gestures as a resource for the organization of mutual orientation. *Semiotica, 62*(1–2), 29–49.

Goodwin, C. (2000a) Gesture, aphasia, and interaction. In D. McNeill (Ed.) *Language and gesture.* Cambridge: Cambridge University Press.

Goodwin, C. (2000b) Practices of seeing: Visual analysis: An ethnomethodological approach. In T. van Leeuwen and C. Jewitt (Eds) *Handbook of visual analysis* (pp. 157–82). London: Sage.

Goodwin, C. (2000c) Action and embodiment within situated human interaction. *Journal of Pragmatics, 32*(10), 1489–522.

Goodwin, C. (2003a) Pointing as situated practice. In S. Kita (Ed.) *Pointing: Where language, culture and cognition meet.* NJ: Lawrence Erlbaum.

Goodwin, C. (2003b) Conversational frameworks for the accomplishment of meaning. In C. Goodwin (Ed.) *Conversation and brain damage* (pp. 90–116). New York: Oxford University Press.

Goodwin, M.H. (1980) Processes of mutual monitoring implicated in the production of description sequences. *Sociological Inquiry, 50,* 303–17.

Goodwin, M.H. (1983) Searching for a word as an interactive activity. In J.N. Deely and M.D. Lenhart (Eds) *Semiotics* (pp. 129–38). New York: Plenum.

Goodwin, M.H. and Goodwin, C. (1986) Gesture and coparticipation in the activity of searching for a word. *Semiotica, 62*(1–2), 51–75.

Griffin, C. (2007a) Being dead and being there: Research interviews, sharing hand cream and the preference for analysing 'naturally occurring data', *Discourse Studies, 9,* 246–69.

Griffin, C. (2007b) Different visions: A rejoinder to Henwood, Potter and Hepburn, *Discourse Studies, 9,* 283–7.

Grivicic, T. and Nilep, C. (2004) When phonation matters: The use and function of yeah and creaky voice. *Colorado Research in Linguistics, 17,* 1–11.

Grosjean, F. (1982) *Life with two languages: An introduction to bilingualism.* Cambridge, MA: Harvard University Press.

Haakana, M. (2010) Laughter and smiling: Notes on co-occurrences. *Journal of Pragmatics*, 42(6), 1499–1512.

Hanks, W.F. (2007) Person reference in Yucatec Maya conversation. In N.J. Enfield and T. Stivers (Eds) *Person reference in interaction* (pp. 149–71). Cambridge: Cambridge University Press.

Heath, C. (1989) Pain talk: The expression of suffering in the medical consultation. *Social Psychology Quarterly*, 52(2), 113–25.

Heath, C. (1992) Gesture's discrete tasks: Multiple relevancies in visual conduct and in the contextualisation of language. In P. Auer and A.D. Luzio (Eds) *The contextualization of language* (pp. 101–27). Amsterdam: John Benjamins.

Heath, C., Hindmarsh, J. and Luff, P. (2010) *Video in qualitative research*. Thousand Oaks, CA: Sage.

Heimbach, E.E. (1979) *White Hmong–English dictionary*. Ithaca, NY: Southeast Asia Program, Cornell University.

Henwood, K. (2007) Beyond hypercriticality: Taking forward methodological inquiry and debate in discursive and qualitative social psychology, *Discourse Studies*, 9, 270–5.

Hepburn, A. (2004) Crying: Notes on description, transcription, and interaction. *Research on Language and Social Interaction*, 37(3), 251–90.

Hepburn, A. (2006) Getting closer at a distance: Theory and the contingencies of practice, *Theory & Psychology*, 16(3), 325–42.

Hepburn, A. and Bolden, G.B. (2013) The conversation analytic approach to transcription. In J. Sidnell and T. Stivers (Eds) *The handbook of conversation analysis* (pp. 57–76). Oxford: Blackwell.

Hepburn, A. and Brown, S.J. (2001) Teacher stress and the management of accountability, *Human Relations*, 54(6), 531–55.

Hepburn, A. and Potter, J. (2004) Discourse analytic practice. In C. Seale, D. Silverman, J. Gubrium and G. Gobo (Eds) *Qualitative research practice* (pp. 180–96). London: Sage.

Hepburn, A. and Potter, J. (2007) Crying receipts: Time, empathy, and institutional practice. *Research on Language and Social Interaction*, 40(1), 89–116.

Hepburn, A. and Potter, J. (2011) Threats: Power, family mealtimes and social influence. *British Journal of Social Psychology*, 50, 99–120.

Hepburn, A. and Potter, J. (2012) Crying and crying responses. In A. Peräkylä and M.L. Sorjonen (Eds) *Emotion in interaction* (pp. 194–210). Oxford: Oxford University Press.

Hepburn, A. and Varney, S. (2013) Beyond ((laughter)): Some notes on transcription. In P.J. Glenn and E. Holt (Eds) *Studies in laughter in interaction* (pp. 25–38). London: Bloomsbury.

Hepburn, A., Wilkinson, S. and Butler, C.W. (2014) Intervening with conversation analysis in telephone helpline services: Strategies to improve effectiveness. *Research on Language and Social Interaction*, 47(3), 239–54.

Heritage, J. (1984) *Garfinkel and ethnomethodology*. New York: Polity Press.

Heritage, J. (2012) Epistemics in action: Action formation and territories of knowledge. *Research on Language and Social Interaction*, 45(1), 1–29.

Heritage, J. (2013a) Action formation and its epistemic (and other) backgrounds. *Discourse Studies, 15*(5), 551–78.

Heritage, J. (2013b) Epistemics in conversation. In J. Sidnell and T. Stivers (Eds) *Handbook of conversation analysis* (pp. 370–94). Boston: Wiley-Blackwell.

Heritage, J. and Raymond, C.W. (2016) Are explicit apologies proportional to the offenses they address? *Discourse Processes, 53*(1–2), 5–25.

Higginbotham, D.J. and Engelke, C.R. (2013) A primer for doing talk-in-interaction research in augmentative and alternative communication. *Augmentative and Alternative Communication, 29*(1), 3–19.

Hirst, D. and Di Cristo, A. (1998) A survey of intonation systems. In D. Hirst and A. Di Cristo (Eds) *Intonation systems: A survey of twenty languages* (pp. 1–44). Cambridge: Cambridge University Press.

Hoey, E.M. (2014) Sighing in interaction: Somatic, semiotic, and social. *Research on Language and Social Interaction, 47*(2), 175–200.

Hollway, W. (2005) Commentary on 'Qualitative interviews in psychology', *Qualitative Research in Psychology, 2*, 312–14.

Holt, E. (2010) The last laugh: Shared laughter and topic termination. *Journal of Pragmatics, 42*(6), 1513–1525.

Hutchby, I. and Wooffitt, R. (1998) *Conversation analysis: Principles, practices and applications*. Malden, MA: Polity Press.

International Phonetic Association (1999) *Handbook of the International Phonetic Association: A guide to the use of the International Phonetic Alphabet*. Cambridge: Cambridge University Press.

Iwasaki, S. (2011) The multimodal mechanics of collaborative unit construction in Japanese conversation. In J. Streeck, C. Goodwin and C. LeBaron (Eds) *Embodied interaction: Language and body in the material world*. Cambridge: Cambridge University Press.

Jefferson, G. (1973) A case of precision timing in ordinary conversation: Overlapped tag-positioned address terms in closing sequences. *Semiotica, 9*(1), 47–96.

Jefferson, G. (1979) A technique for inviting laughter and its subsequent acceptance/declination. *Everyday language: Studies in ethnomethodology, 79*, 96.

Jefferson, G. (1983) Issues in the transcription of naturally occurring talk: Caricature versus capturing pronunciational particulars. *Tilburg Papers in Language and Literature, 34.*

Jefferson, G. (1984a) Notes on some orderlinesses of overlap onset. In V. D'Urso and P. Leonardi (Eds) *Discourse analysis and natural rhetorics*. Padua: Cleup Editore.

Jefferson, G. (1984b) On the organization of laughter in talk about troubles. In J.M. Atkinson and J. Heritage (Eds) *Structures of social action* (pp. 346–69). Cambridge: Cambridge University Press.

Jefferson, G. (1985) An exercise in the transcription and analysis of laughter. In T.A. v. Dijk (Ed.) *Handbook of discourse analysis* (Vol. 3, pp. 25–34). New York: Academic Press.

Jefferson, G. (1986) Notes on 'latency' in overlap onset. *Human Studies, 9*(2/3), 153–183.

Jefferson, G. (1989) Preliminary notes on a possible metric which provides for a 'standard maximum' silences of approximately one second in conversation. In D. Roger and P. Bull

(Eds) *Conversation: An interdisciplinary perspective* (pp. 166–96). Clevedon: Multilingual Matters.

Jefferson, G. (1993) Caveat speaker: Preliminary notes on recipient topic-shift implicature. *Research on Language and Social Interaction, 26*(1), 1–30.

Jefferson, G. (2004a) Glossary of transcript symbols with an introduction. In G.H. Lerner (Ed.) *Conversation analysis: Studies from the first generation* (pp. 13–31). Philadelphia: John Benjamins.

Jefferson, G. (2004b) A sketch of some orderly aspects of overlap in natural conversation. In G.H. Lerner (Ed.) *Conversation analysis: Studies from the first generation* (pp. 43–59). Philadelphia: John Benjamins.

Jefferson, G. (2010) Sometimes a frog in your throat is just a frog in your throat: Gutturals as (sometimes) laughter implicative. *Journal of Pragmatics, 42*(6), 1476–84.

Jefferson, G., Sacks, H. and Schegloff, E.A. (1987) Notes on laughter in the pursuit of intimacy. In G. Button and J.R.E. Lee (Eds) *Talk and social organization* (pp. 152–205). Philadelphia: Multilingual Matters.

Jenkins, L. and Hepburn, A. (2015) Children's sensations as interactional phenomena: A conversation analysis of expressions of pain and discomfort. *Qualitative Research in Psychology, 12*(4), 472–91.

Johanson, L. (2002) Contact-induced change in a code-copying framework. In M.C. Jones and E. Esch (Eds) *Language change: The interplay of internal, external and extra-linguistic factors* (pp. 285–314). Berlin: Mouton de Gruyter.

Jones, S.E. and Zimmerman, D.H. (2003) A child's point and the achievement of intentionality. *Gesture, 3*(2), 155–85.

Keating, E. and Sunakawa, C. (2011) 'A full inspiration tray': Multimodality across real and virtual spaces. In J. Streeck, C. Goodwin and C. LeBaron (Eds) *Embodied interaction: Language and body in the material world* (pp. 194–204). Cambridge: Cambridge University Press.

Kelly, J. and Local, J.K. (1989) On the use of general phonetic techniques in handling conversational material. In P. Bull and D. Roger (Eds) *Conversation: An interdisciplinary perspective* (pp. 197–212). Philadelphia: Multilingual Matters.

Kendon, A. (1972) Some relationships between body motion and speech: An analysis of an example. In A. Siegman and B. Pope (Eds) *Studies in dyadic communication* (pp. 177–210). Elmsford, NY: Pergamon.

Kendon, A. (1980) Gesture and speech: Two aspects of the process of utterance. In M.R. Key (Ed.) *Nonverbal communication and language* (pp. 207–27). The Hague: Mouton.

Kendon, A. (1994) Do gestures communicate? A review. *Research on Language and Social Interaction, 27*(3), 175–200.

Kendon, A. (2004) *Gesture: Visible action as utterance.* New York: Cambridge University Press.

Kidwell, M. (2005) Gaze as social control: How very young children differentiate 'the look' from a 'mere look' by their adult caregivers. *Research on Language and Social Interaction, 38*(4), 417–49.

Kidwell, M. (2006) 'Calm down!': The role of gaze in the interactional management of hysteria by the police. *Discourse Studies, 8*(6), 745–70.

Kidwell, M. (2009) Gaze shift as an interactional resource for very young children. *Discourse Processes, 46*(2), 145–60.

Kitzinger, C. and Mandelbaum, J.S. (2013) Word selection and social identities in talk. *Communication Monographs, 80*(2), 176–98.

Knorr Cetina, K.K. (1999) *Epistemic cultures: How the sciences make knowledge.* Cambridge, MA: Harvard University Press.

Koshik, I. (2005) *Beyond rhetorical questions: Assertive questions in everyday interaction.* Philadelphia: John Benjamins.

Kurhila, S. (2001) Correction in talk between native and non-native speaker. *Journal of Pragmatics, 33*(7), 1083–110.

Kvale, S. (1983) The qualitative research interview: A phenomenological and a hermeneutical mode of understanding. *Journal of Phenomenological Psychology, 14*(2), 171.

Ladefoged, P. (1993) *A course in phonetics* (3rd ed.). New York: Harcourt Brace Jovanovich.

Lee, S.-H. (2006) Second summonings in Korean telephone conversation openings. *Language in Society, 35*, 261–83.

Lee, S.-H. (2009) Extended requesting: Interaction and collaboration in the production and specification of requests. *Journal of Pragmatics, 41*(6), 1248–71.

Lerner, G.H. (2002) *Practice does not make perfect: Intervening actions in the selection of next speaker.* Paper presented at the Plenary address to the Conference on Language, Interaction, and Culture, University of California, Los Angeles.

Lerner, G.H. (2003) Selecting next speaker: The context-sensitive operation of a context-free organization. *Language in Society, 32*(2), 177–201.

Lerner, G.H. (2004) Collaborative turn sequences. *Pragmatics and Beyond New Series, 125*, 225–256.

Lerner, G.H. and Linton, L. (2004) *Before beginning: Breath taking in conversation* (unpublished manuscript). University of California, Santa Barbara.

Lewis, M.P., Simons, G.F. and Fennig, C.D. (Eds) (2016) *Ethnologue: Languages of the world* (19th ed.). Dallas, Texas: SIL International. Available online at: www.ethnologue.com (accessed 28 August 2016).

Local, J.K. (2004) Getting back to prior talk: And-uh(m) as a back-connecting device in British and American English. In E. Couper-Kuhlen (Ed.) *Sound patterns in interaction: Cross-linguistic studies of phonetics and prosody for conversation* (pp. 377–400). Amsterdam: John Benjamins.

Local, J.K. and Walker, G. (2004) Abrupt-joins as a resource for the production of multi-unit, multi-action turns. *Journal of Pragmatics, 36*(8), 1375–403.

Luebs, M.A. (1996) *Frozen speech: The rhetoric of transcription.* Unpublished PhD Dissertation, University of Michigan.

Maddieson, I. (2008) Tone. In M. Haspelmath, M.S. Dryer, D. Gil and B. Comrie (Eds) *The world atlas of language structures online* (chapter 13). Munich: Max Planck Digital Library. Available online at: http://wals.info/feature/13

McCleary, L. and de Arantes Leite, T. (2013) Turn-taking in Brazilian sign language: Evidence from overlap. *Journal of Interactional Research in Communication Disorders, 4*(1), 123–54.

McNeill, D. (1992) *Hand and mind: What gestures reveal about thought.* Chicago: University of Chicago Press.

Meredith, J. (2015) Transcribing screen-capture data. The process of developing a transcription system for multi-modal text-based data. *International Journal of Social Research Methodology.* http://dx.doi.org/10.1080/13645579.2015.1082291.

Meredith, J. and Stokoe, E. (2014) Repair: Comparing Facebook 'chat' with spoken interaction. *Discourse and Communication, 8*(2), 181–207.

Mischler, E.G. (1991) Representing discourse: The rhetoric of transcription. *Journal of Narrative & Life History, 1*(4), 255–80.

Mischler, E. (2005) Commentary on 'Qualitative interviews in psychology', *Qualitative Research in Psychology, 2*, 315–18.

Moerman, M. (1988) *Talking culture: Ethnography and conversation analysis.* Philadelphia: University of Pennsylvania Press.

Moerman, M. (1996) The field of analyzing foreign language conversations. *Journal of Pragmatics, 26*(2), 147–58.

Mondada, L. (2001) Conventions for multimodal transcription. Tutorial available online: https://franz.unibas.ch/fileadmin/franz/user_upload/redaktion/Mondada_conv_multimodality.pdf.

Mondada, L. (2004) Ways of 'doing being plurilingual' in international work meetings. In R. Gardner and J. Wagner (Eds) *Second language conversations* (pp. 18–39). London: Continuum.

Mondada, L. (2007a) Bilingualism and the analysis of talk at work: Code-switching as a resource for the organization of action and interaction. In M. Heller (Ed.) *Bilingualism: A social approach* (pp. 297–318). New York: Palgrave.

Mondada, L. (2007b) Multimodal resources for turn-taking: Pointing and the emergence of possible next speakers. *Discourse Studies, 9*(2), 194–225.

Mondada, L. (2016) Challenges of multimodality: Language and the body in social interaction. *Journal of Sociolinguistics, 20*(2), 2–32.

Moore, R.J. (2015) Automated transcription and conversation analysis. *Research on Language & Social Interaction, 48*(3), 253–70.

Muysken, P. (2000) *Bilingual speech: A typology of code-mixing.* Cambridge: Cambridge University Press.

Nguyen, H.t. and Kasper, G. (2009) *Talk-in-interaction: Multilingual perspectives.* Honolulu, Hawaii: National Foreign Language Resource Center – University of Hawaii.

Nikander, P. (2008) Working with transcripts and translated data. *Qualitative Research in Psychology, 5*(3), 225–31.

Ochs, E. (1979) Transcription as theory. In E. Ochs and B.B. Schieffelin (Eds) *Developmental pragmatics* (pp. 43–72). New York: Academic Press.

Ogden, R. (2001) Turn transition, creak and glottal stop in Finnish talk-in-interaction. *Journal of the International Phonetic Association, 31*(01), 139–152.

Olsher, D.A. (2003) *Collaborative group work in second and foreign language classrooms: Talk, embodiment, and sequential organization.* Unpublished PhD Dissertation, University of California, Los Angeles.

Osvaldsson, K. (2004) On laughter and disagreement in multiparty assessment talk. *Text-Interdisciplinary Journal for the Study of Discourse, 24*(4), 517–545.

Patterson, A. and Potter, J. (2009) Caring: Building a psychological disposition in pre-closing sequences in phone calls with a young adult with a learning disability. *British Journal of Social Psychology*, 48(3), 447–465.

Peräkylä, A. (1998) Authority and accountability: The delivery of diagnosis in primary health care. *Social Psychology Quarterly, 61*(4), 301–20.

Pillet-Shore, D. (2012) Greetings: Displaying stance through prosodic recipient design. *Research on Language and Social Interaction, 45*(4), 375–98.

Pittam, J. (1987) Listeners' evaluations of voice quality in Australian English speakers. *Language and Speech, 30*(2), 99–113.

Pomerantz, A. (1984) Agreeing and disagreeing with assessments: Some features of preferred/dispreferred turn shapes. In J.M. Atkinson and J. Heritage (Eds) *Structures of social action: Studies in conversation analysis* (pp. 57–101). New York: Cambridge University Press.

Pomerantz, A. and Heritage, J. (2013) Preference. In J. Sidnell and T. Stivers (Eds) *The handbook of conversation analysis* (pp. 210–28). Oxford: Blackwell.

Potter, J. (1998) Fragments in the realization of relativism. In I. Parker (Ed.) *Social constructionism, discourse and realism* (pp. 27–45). London: Sage.

Potter, J. (2003) Discourse analysis and discursive psychology. In P.M. Camic, J.E. Rhodes and L. Yardley (Eds) *Qualitative research in psychology: Expanding perspectives in methodology and design* (pp. 73–94). Washington DC: American Psychological Association.

Potter, J. and Hepburn, A. (2015) Somewhere between evil and normal: Traces of morality in a child protection helpline. Journal of Applied Linguistics and Professional Practice, 9, 245–262.

Potter, J. and Hepburn, A. (2005a) Qualitative interviews in psychology: Problems and possibilities. *Qualitative Research in Psychology, 2*, 38–55.

Potter, J. and Hepburn, A. (2005b) Action, interaction and interviews – Some responses to Hollway, Mischler and Smith, *Qualitative Research in Psychology, 2*, 319–325.

Potter, J. and Hepburn, A. (2010) Putting aspiration into words: 'Laugh particles', managing descriptive trouble and modulating action. *Journal of Pragmatics, 42*, 1543–55.

Potter, J. and Hepburn, A. (2012) Eight challenges for interview researchers. In J.F. Gubrium and J.A. Holstein (Eds) *Handbook of interview research* (2nd ed.) (pp. 555–70). London: Sage.

Potter, J. and Shaw, A. (forthcoming) The virtues of naturalistic data. In U. Flick (Ed.) *The SAGE handbook of qualitative data collection*. London: Sage.

Potter, J. and Wetherell, M. (1987) *Discourse and social psychology: Beyond attitudes and behaviour*. London: Sage.

Raymond, G. (2010) Grammar and social relations: Alternative forms of yes/no type initiating actions in health visitor interactions. In A.F. Freed and S. Ehrlich (Eds) *Why do you ask? The function of questions in institutional discourse* (pp. 69–107). Oxford: Oxford University Press.

Raymond, G. (2013) At the intersection of turn and sequence organization: On the relevance of 'slots' in type-conforming responses to polar interrogatives. In B. Szczepek and G. Raymond (Eds) *Units of talk – Units of action* (pp. 169–206). Amsterdam: John Benjamins.

Raymond, G. and Heritage, J. (2006) The epistemics of social relations: Owning grandchildren. *Language in Society, 35*(05), 677–705.

Raymond, G. and Lerner, G.H. (2014) A body and its involvements: Adjusting action for dual involvements. In P. Haddington, L. Mondada and M. Nevile (Eds) *Multiactivity in social interaction: Beyond multitasking* (pp. 227–46). Amsterdam: John Benjamins.

Reed, B.S. (2004) Turn-final intonation in English. In E. Couper-Kuhlen and C.E. Ford (Eds) *Sound patterns in interaction: Cross-linguistic studies from conversation* (pp. 97–117). Amsterdam: John Benjamins.

Richards, I.A. (1932) *Mencius on the mind*. New York: Routledge and Kegan Paul.

Roberts, F. and Robinson, J.D. (2004) Interobserver agreement on first-stage conversation analytic transcription. *Human Communication Research, 30*(3), 376–410.

Robinson, J.D. and Kevoe-Feldman, H. (2010) Using full repeats to initiate repair on others' questions. *Research on Language and Social Interaction, 43*(3), 232–59.

Rossano, F. (2010) Questioning and responding in Italian. *Journal of Pragmatics, 42*(10), 2756–71.

Rossano, F. (2012) *Gaze behavior in face-to-face interaction*. Unpublished PhD Dissertation, Radboud University Nijmegen, Nijmegen.

Rossano, F. (2013) Gaze in conversation. In J. Sidnell and T. Stivers (Eds) *The handbook of conversation analysis* (pp. 308–29). Oxford: Blackwell.

Rossano, F., Brown, P. and Levinson, S.C. (2009) Gaze, questioning, and culture. In J. Sidnell (Ed.) *Conversation analysis: Comparative perspectives* (pp. 357–406). Cambridge: Cambridge University Press.

Sacks, H. (1984) Notes on Methodology. In J.M. Atkinson and J. Heritage (Eds) *Structures of social action* (pp. 21–27). Cambridge: Cambridge University Press.

Sacks, H., Schegloff, E.A. and Jefferson, G. (1974) A simplest systematics for the organization of turn-taking for conversation. *Language, 50*, 696–735.

Schegloff, E.A. (1982) Discourse as an interactional achievement: Some uses of 'uh huh' and other things that come between sentences. In D. Tannen (Ed.) *Analyzing discourse: Text and talk* (pp. 71–93). Washington DC: Georgetown University Press.

Schegloff, E.A. (1984) On some gestures' relation to talk. In J.M. Atkinson and J. Heritage (Eds) *Structures of social action: Studies in conversation analysis* (pp. 266–96). New York: Cambridge University Press.

Schegloff, E.A. (1987a) Between macro and micro: Contexts and other connections. In J. Alexander, B. Giessen, R. Munch and N. Smelser (Eds) *The macro–micro link* (pp. 207–34). Berkeley and Los Angeles: University of California Press.

Schegloff, E.A. (1987b) Recycled turn beginnings: A precise repair mechanism in conversation's turn-taking organization. In G. Button and J.R.E. Lee (Eds) *Talk and social organization* (pp. 70–85). Philadelphia: Multilingual Matters.

Schegloff, E.A. (1996a) Confirming allusions: Toward an empirical account of action. *American Journal of Sociology, 104*(1), 161–216.

Schegloff, E.A. (1996b) Turn organization: One intersection of grammar and interaction. In E. Ochs, E.A. Schegloff and S.A. Thompson (Eds) *Interaction and grammar* (pp. 52–133). Cambridge: Cambridge University Press.

Schegloff, E.A. (1998a) Body torque. *Social Research, 65*(3), 535–96.

Schegloff, E.A. (1998b) Reflections on studying prosody in talk-in-interaction. *Language and Speech, 41*(3–4), 235–63.

Schegloff, E.A. (2000a) *On turns' possible completion, more or less: Increments and trail-offs.* Paper presented at the 2000 Annual Conference of the National Communication Association, Seattle, Washington.

Schegloff, E.A. (2000b) Overlapping talk and the organization of turn-taking for conversation. *Language in Society, 29*(1), 1–63.

Schegloff, E.A. (2002) Reflections on research on telephone conversation: Issues of cross-cultural scope and scholarly exchange, interactional import and consequences. In K.K. Luke and T.-S. Pavlidou (Eds) *Telephone calls: Unity and diversity in conversational structure across languages and cultures* (pp. 249–81). Amsterdam: John Benjamins.

Schegloff, E.A. (2003) Conversation analysis and communication disorders. In C. Goodwin (Ed.) *Conversation and brain damage* (pp. 21–55). New York: Oxford University Press.

Schegloff, E.A. (2005) On integrity in inquiry ... of the investigated, not the investigator. *Discourse Studies, 7*(4–5), 455–80.

Schegloff, E.A. (2007) *Sequence organization in interaction: A primer in conversation analysis.* Cambridge: Cambridge University Press.

Schegloff, E.A., Jefferson, G. and Sacks, H. (1977) The preference for self-correction in the organization of repair in conversation. *Language, 53*, 361–82.

Selting, M. (1996) Prosody as an activity-type distinctive cue in conversation: The case of so-called 'astonished' questions in repair initiation. In E. Couper-Kuhlen and M. Selting (Eds) *Prosody in conversation: Interactional studies* (Vol. 12, pp. 231–70). Cambridge: Cambridge University Press.

Seo, M.-S. and Koshik, I. (2010) A conversation analytic study of gestures that engender repair in ESL conversational tutoring. *Journal of Pragmatics, 42*(8), 2219–39.

Shaw, C., Hepburn, A. and Potter, J. (2013) Having the last laugh: On post-completion laughter particles. In Glenn, P. and Holt, E. (Eds) *Studies of laughter in interaction* (pp. 91–106). London: Bloomsbury.

Shaw, C., Stokoe, E., Gallagher, K., Aladangady, N. and Marlow, N. (2016) Parental involvement in neonatal critical care decision-making. *Sociology of Health and Illness.*

Sidnell, J. (Ed.) (2009) *Conversation analysis: Comparative perspectives.* Cambridge: Cambridge University Press.

Sidnell, J. (2010) *Conversation analysis: An introduction.* Malden, MA: Wiley-Blackwell.

Sidnell, J. (2013) Basic conversation analytic methods. *The handbook of conversation analysis*, 77–99.

Sidnell, J. and Stivers, T. (Eds) (2013) *The handbook of conversation analysis*. Oxford: Blackwell.

Sikveland, R.O. and Stokoe, E. (2016) Dealing with resistance in initial intake and inquiry calls to mediation: The power of 'willing'. *Conflict Resolution Quarterly, 33*(3), 235–253.

Smith, J. (2005) Advocating pluralism. *Qualitative Research in Psychology, 2*, 309–11.

Stivers, T. (2005) Modified repeats: One method for asserting primary rights from second position. *Research on Language and Social Interaction, 38*(2), 131–58.

Stivers, T. (2008) Stance, alignment, and affiliation during storytelling: When nodding is a token of affiliation. *Research on Language and Social Interaction, 41*(1), 31–57.

Stivers, T. (2010) An overview of the question–response system in American English conversation. *Journal of Pragmatics, 42*(10), 2772–81.

Stivers, T. and Heritage, J. (2001) Breaking the sequential mold: Answering 'more than the question' during comprehensive history taking. *Text – Interdisciplinary Journal for the Study of Discourse, 21*(1–2), 151–85.

Stivers, T. and Rossano, F. (2010) Mobilizing response. *Research on Language and Social Interaction, 43*(1), 3–31.

Stivers, T., Enfield, N.J., Brown, P., Englert, C., Hayashi, M., Heinemann, T. et al. (2009) Universals and cultural variation in turn-taking in conversation. *PNAS, 106*(26), 10587–92.

Stokoe, E. (2011) Simulated interaction and communication skills training: The 'Conversation Analytic Role-play Method'. In C. Antaki (Ed.) *Applied conversation analysis: Changing institutional practices* (pp. 119–39). Basingstoke: Palgrave Macmillan.

Stokoe, E. (2013) The (in)authenticity of simulated talk: Comparing role-played and actual conversation and the implications for communication training. *Research on Language and Social Interaction, 46*(2), 1–21.

Stokoe, E. (2014) The Conversation Analytic Role-play Method (CARM): A method for training communication skills as an alternative to simulated role-play. *Research on Language and Social Interaction, 47*(3), 255–65.

Stokoe, E. and Sikveland, R.O. (2017) The Conversation Analytic Role-play Method: Simulation, endogenous impact and interactional nudges. In V. Fors, T. O'Dell and S. Pink (Eds) *Theoretical scholarship and applied practice*. Oxford: Berghahn Books.

Streeck, J. (1993) Gesture as communication I: Its coordination with gaze and speech. *Communication Monographs, 60*(4), 275–99.

Streeck, J. (1994) Gesture as communication II: The audience as co-author. *Research on Language and Social Interaction, 27*(3), 239–67.

Streeck, J. (2009) *Gesturecraft: The manu-facture of meaning*. Philadelphia: John Benjamins.

Streeck, J., Goodwin, C. and LeBaron, C. (2011a) Embodied interaction in the material world: An introduction. In J. Streeck, C. Goodwin and C. LeBaron (Eds) *Embodied interaction: Language and body in the material world* (pp. 1–26). Cambridge: Cambridge University Press.

Streeck, J., Goodwin, C. and LeBaron, C. (Eds) (2011b) *Embodied interaction: Language and body in the material world*. Cambridge: Cambridge University Press.

Svetozarova, N. (1998) Intonation in Russian. In D. Hirst and A. Di Cristo (Eds) *Intonation systems: A survey of twenty languages* (pp. 261–74). Cambridge: Cambridge University Press.

Szymanski, M.H. (2003) Producing text through talk: Question-answering activity in classroom peer groups. *Linguistics and Education, 13*(4), 533–63.

Tao, H. (1996) *Units in Mandarin conversation: Prosody, discourse, and grammar*. Amsterdam: John Benjamins.

Tarplee, C. and Barrow, E. (1999) Delayed echoing as an interactional resource: A case study of a three year old child on the autistic spectrum. *Clinical Linguistics & Phonetics, 13*(6), 449–82.

Torras, M.-C. and Gafaranga, J. (2002) Social identities and language alternation in non-formal institutional bilingual talk: Trilingual service encounters in Barcelona. *Language in Society, 31*(4), 527–48.

Traverso, V. (2002) Transcription et traduction des interactions en langue étrangère. *Cahiers de Praxématique, 39*, 77–99.

Trudgill, P. (1988) *Sociolinguistics: An introduction to language and society*. New York: Penguin Books.

Tufte, E.R. (2006) *Beautiful evidence*. New York: Graphics Press.

Walker, G. (2004) *The phonetic design of turn endings, beginnings, and continuations in conversation*. Unpublished PhD Dissertation, University of York, UK.

Walker, G. (2012) Phonetics and the management of talk-in-interaction. *Pragmatics of Society, 5*, 153.

Walker, T. (2014) Form ≠ function: The independence of prosody and action. *Research on Language and Social Interaction, 47*(1), 1–16.

Wei, L. (2002) 'What do you want me to say?': On the conversation analysis approach to bilingual interaction. *Language in Society, 31*, 159–80.

Weiste, E. and Peräkylä, A. (2014) Prosody and empathic communication in psychotherapy interaction. *Psychotherapy Research, 24*(6), 687–701.

Wells, B. (2010) Tonal repetition and tonal contrast in English carer–child interactions. In D. Barth-Weingarten, E. Reber and M. Selting (Eds) *Prosody in interaction* (pp. 243–62). Amsterdam: John Benjamins.

Wells, B. and Corrin, J. (2004) Prosodic resources, turn-taking and overlap in children's talk-in-interaction. In E. Couper-Kuhlen and C.E. Ford (Eds) *Sound patterns in interaction: Cross-linguistic studies from conversation* (pp. 119–44). Philadelphia: John Benjamins.

Whalen, J. and Zimmerman, D.H. (1998) Observations on the expression and management of emotion in naturally occurring activities: The case of 'hysteria' in calls to 911. *Social Psychology Quarterly, 61*(2), 141–59.

Wilkinson, R. (2007) Managing linguistic incompetence as a delicate issue in aphasic talk-in-interaction: On the use of laughter in prolonged repair sequences. *Journal of Pragmatics, 37*(3), 542–69.

Wilkinson, R., Bloch, S. and Clarke, M. (2011) On the use of graphic resources in interaction by people with communication disorders. In J. Streeck, C. Goodwin and C. LeBaron (Eds) *Embodied interaction: Language and body in the material world* (pp. 152–68). Cambridge: Cambridge University Press.

Wilkinson, S. and Kitzinger, C. (2006) Surprise as an interactional achievement: Reaction tokens in conversation. *Social Psychology Quarterly, 69*(2), 150–82.

Wilson, M. and Wilson, T.P. (2005) An oscillator model of the timing of turn-taking. *Psychonomic Bulletin and Review, 12*(6), 957–68.

Wilson, T.P. and Zimmerman, D. (1986) The structure of silence between turns in two-party conversation. *Discourse Processes, 9*, 375–90.

Wu, R.-J.R. (2003) *Stance in talk: A conversation analysis of Mandarin final particles.* Philadelphia: John Benjamins.

Index